ENDORSEMENTS

I highly recommend this author, Pamela Keyser, as I know her to be a remarkable person who has overcome abuse as a child that most could not have grown to be the normal, productive, and giving person that I know and am proud to call friend.

Mary Ann Kinsey
~ Author of For the Love of a Child

Anyone having gone through abuse should read this and *The Red Glass,* her first book. Anyone working with children at risk or foster children should read it. Also, it is a must-read for DCF workers and "relative placements." The author masterfully tells how the aftermath of abuse goes on long after the abuser is no longer around. It took courage to work her way free from the aftermath; and it will give courage to anyone needing to do the same.

Barbara Meister Vitale
~ Author of Free Flight and *Unicorns are Real*

CRACKS
IN THE
RED GLASS

Growing Through the Aftermath of Abuse

PAMELA K. KEYSER

ISBN 978-1-0980-9010-4 (paperback)
ISBN 978-1-0980-9011-1 (digital)

Christian Faith Publishing, Inc.
832 Park Avenue
Meadville, PA 16335
www.christianfaithpublishing.com

Printed in the United States of America

To my husband, who is steadfast in his love; and for my children, who have taught me many lessons.

It is also for anyone going through abuse now, in the past, and is dealing with the aftermath of abuse; it casts a long shadow.

Other Books by Pamela K. Keyser:

The Red Glass; From Abuse Hell to Living Well

CONTENTS

INTRODUCTION

MY IMAGINATION HELPED me build comforting presences, and it has continued to do so throughout my life. It particularly helped in childhood, as you'll read, when no one had my back. I still have imaginary places I can go to whenever I need to find peace and quiet.

Today, I'm a joy-filled woman with a quirky sense of humor who is not afraid to be different. Remember that as you read what follows, the person tapping on the computer keys, telling you this story, would not change one thing—not one!

Even though I use the name Sadie, instead of my own, it's my life. My mind stalled anytime I tried to say what happened to Pam. I separated myself from the pain, a common defense mechanism for abused kids. One day I drafted a short story of one particularly horrible incident using the name Sadie, and it became easy to get the words on paper. Sadie became the way I could tell it. Sadie is me.

I was a hurt, wounded, scared child; but I came through, got therapy, surrounded myself with honorable people and healed. I've been married for forty-seven years to a wonderful man who has helped me when I've asked. Otherwise, he would know it was my work to do. As a child, if anybody had told me that I would be married long-term and filled with joy, I would have laughed at them or perhaps cursed at them. During my childhood, I built walls around my heart.

I trusted few, and I was not always an easy kid to be around. Why would I have been?

Today, I have a variety of wonderful friends, talented kids who I'd like even if they were not mine, and awesome grandkids. You can come out the other side better than okay! Believe it. I lived it, and I did.

In this book, I will go into the thoughts and emotions of what happened to me and how I came out of those experiences to achieve wholeness. From the age of five years old, I started shutting off my emotions, and so until age eighteen, when I started therapy, I had few feelings. Recovery is never a straight line. I could go along fine for a while, trusting as far as I was capable, and something would trigger me, forcing me to retreat into a past survival behavior. The behaviors that helped me in childhood became an enormous hindrance in adulthood.

I have reconstructed the dialogue to the best of my memory. In *The Red Glass*, I told the story from *A* to *Z*. This time I will include my emotions and feelings (something harder to access). I will be brutally honest and include some things I left out of *The Red Glass*, either because someone begged me not to put it in or because I was hesitant. No longer will I censor myself. What happened, happened. And the truth isn't always pretty, but it is always the truth.

Remember, I did more than survive, and now, I thrive!

WARNING

THIS IS A true story. I have chosen to tell graphically what happened to me when I was raped as a child. I did this because rape has become just a four-letter word—a word no one wants to talk about because it is an ugly word. It's not, it's reality. It was my reality, and also of millions of other women. The word rape is not ugly; the act of rape is.

I'll also put a warning at the beginning of the two sections that tell about my rape incident; so if you just cannot read it, you'll be able to skip it.

IMAGINARY FRIENDS

THEN

MY HORSE HERD kept up with our car as my father maneuvered it down the highway. We headed toward California Napa State Mental Institution where my mother resided as a patient.

"What are you doing? Why so quiet?" my father asked.

"Watching my horse herd run beside the car."

"You understand horses can't keep up with automobiles, don't you?"

I nodded. *But my horses can!*

"You want to know their names?" I asked.

He glanced at me and shook his head. "They are make-believe, right?"

I nodded again.

My herd may have been imaginary, but they existed to me. They kept me company whenever my parents argued or left me alone in the house. They ran with me through the streets of the Presidio and the woods. Although I knew my herd wasn't real, they were alive to me.

We arrived at Napa State Mental Institution to find my mother sitting in the courtyard. I ran over to her and gave her an enormous hug before my parents inelegantly embraced. When their conversation died, I asked my mother if she wanted to meet my herd. When my father objected, she gave him a hard look and he quietly sat back in his chair.

First, I introduced my big black stallion, Debbie, who led the other six. When I named him, I didn't realize stallion meant a male horse. With his neck arched and his mane trailing in the wake of his speed, Debbie could run for miles without panting. He towered over the other six horses and had chiseled features in his face. When galloping, his tail curved high before cascading behind like vapor from a jet engine. I described how he bent one of his front legs and bowed to my mother, who laughed and clapped her hands. She greeted him. "Thanks for keeping my daughter company."

Next came Candy. Brown covered the front of her body with tan spots sprinkled over her white back. Her hooves had white stripes in them, which was why I had named her Candy. She loved to joke and liked to charge at the others. A book informed me that she was an Appaloosa. She didn't bow but pranced her front legs around until Debbie snorted for her to stop. My mother smiled as I explained her characteristics.

Gracie had a solid golden-brown face. That color ran halfway down her front feet. She was an American paint. The rest of her body gleamed white with splotches of gilded brown. I had just finished describing Gracie's tail as white when one of the aides interrupted me to ask if my mother wanted a drink.

My mother shushed her and said, "My daughter is introducing me to some very important friends."

The assistant looked around and could only see the three of us. My father belted out of his chair, saying he was going for a walk. The aide excused herself and walked away. I continued telling my mom about Gracie's white tail and how she and her best friend, Candy, always cantered together.

Next, we had Betsy. She looked exactly like Buttermilk, Dale Evans's horse, on an old TV show. She ran alongside Fee-Fee, a big beautiful red horse and Debbie's best friend.

Bringing up the rear was Anne and Heaven. Anne was a palomino, dark yellow with a white diamond on her face and a light straw-colored mane and tail. Heaven was a light cream color with a very dark mane and tail.

My mother graciously met my entire herd and said a kind word to each of them.

My father returned and angrily said, "Crystal, you're in the loony bin. You shouldn't encourage your daughter to be crazy too."

It was not the first time I had noticed how whenever he was mad at me, I became "her" daughter and not "his" or "theirs." My mother laughed and told him to relax, that she was encouraging my imagination.

I interrupted to say, "We're gonna go run around now," and my herd and I took off galloping around the grounds. I didn't want to hear my father's angry voice or the argument that ensued. They seldom talked and always argued. I stayed in the field with my friends until my father called me, saying we were leaving. I hurried over to my mother, telling her I was sorry I'd spent so little time with her. She said it was okay, that we'd talk longer next time. She said to take care of me and, looking at my father, added, "And your horses too."

On the way home, my father said we would celebrate by stopping and getting two T-bone steaks. I didn't know what we were celebrating. He unwrapped one, and I found the steaks disappointing; they merely looked like meat. He showed me how the bone looked like the letter *T*.

"Oh goody," I exclaimed. "Can you go back and get an *H*-bone? *H* is my favorite letter."

He called on Jesus to help him, and he hastily rewrapped the steak. As he drove out of the parking place, he said, "Steaks don't come in all the shapes of the alphabet. T is the only one. Don't forget that."

But he was wrong. I've seen *Y*-bones, *J*-bones, and *I*-bones steak. I'm still looking for the *H*-bone steak, and I know it'll show up someday.

EARLIEST MEMORY

My first pre-speech memory illustrates how I survived abuse. My family and I (eighteen months old) were living in San Diego. I slept in a crib, and my parents could attach a wire top to keep me inside. I woke up early and went into their bedroom. I could reach my father the easiest. My mother slept on the other side against the wall. I shook my father, and he awoke my mother.

My parents got up; and both walked into my bedroom, placed me back in the crib, and secured the top on it. I pushed against the wire cover. But found it impossible to push off. Next, I placed my feet opposite each other on the wide wooden slats of the crib and walked my way up the sides. Then I pulled my mattress up, which allowed me to pull up the wire bottom panel and escape.

Again, I woke my father. They wondered how I got out. My mother asked my father if he'd secured the top tightly. He said he had. He picked me up, and we went into my bedroom. The spring-wire bottom and my mattress had all fallen back in place. The crib remained locked. *How did she get out?* they wondered. Finally, they unlatched the top, placed me in the crib, secured it again, and walked out of the room. But they peeked around the corner. The second time I did it faster. And they walked in just as I crawled out from under my crib.

They picked me up again and wondered aloud how I'd learned to do that and how would they ever keep me in the crib now. Then they took me to the kitchen and sat me in my high chair for some cereal. Maybe I'd wanted breakfast all along.

The whole incident demonstrates an inner fortitude to not accept boundaries. To push the envelope and to challenge circumstances. I'm glad I had that inner fire. It helped me later.

PIVOTAL POINT IN TRUST

I might have given the impression (in my first book, *The Red Glass*) that life with my family before divorce consisted of cotton candy and rainbows. But like all families, we had our own dysfunctions. The first time I remember distrusting my parents, at five years old, involved a knife.

I was singing as I headed around our house in Ila Palms, South Carolina, to scoop up pine needles for the floor of my pretend fort. As I approached the middle of the sidewalk to our front door, my father called to me.

"Sadie, come here."

His voice sounded funny, and my head whipped around to see him standing at the half-opened picket gate. He stood in his Navy uniform, and his eyes weren't looking at me. I turned my head to see where he was looking.

My mother stood at the half-opened door to our two-story house with a large carving knife in her hand. "Tia, come here." She also did not look at me.

My father gave me my first name, Sadie. My mother gave me Tierra as my middle name. They had called me different names since birth.

"No, Sadie, come here. Your mother is acting crazy again."

"Tia, honey, come here. I'm not crazy, and your father is drunk. You know what he's like when he gets like that." Fear made me pull my hands up in fists to my stomach. *Quit! Quit! Please stop.*

My mother's voice told me she'd been drinking too. I remembered how they both got when they drank. But usually arguments happened late at night, and I could go back to sleep. Often, their arguments made me throw up. Afraid to anger them, I'd bend over my trash can. Their raised voices made my body quake. Again, I'd silently beg them to stop.

"Sadie, come here."

"No, Tia, come here."

They continued to call me, hissing the words.

Fear seeped into my limbs. Who should I go to? My mother held the knife. Did she hold the knife in her hand to protect me and her? My father stood at the gate. He didn't look dangerous, but I'd heard him roar and say nasty things during their late-night arguments. My stomach clenched as if hit by something outside my body. I bent over and clutched my middle. Still, they called me. My heartbeat echoed in my head, and my mouth dried up. A deep ocean of sadness radiated out of my heart. In those moments, I was orphaned. I sat down, cross-legged, in the middle of the sidewalk and cried.

Both parents dashed to my side (my mother minus the knife), each telling me it was okay, that they were merely playing a pretend game. They didn't mean it. Kneeling beside me, they said, "It's okay, baby. We were just pretending. We didn't mean it."

They're lying! The thought shocked me. They hadn't been pretending. If they'd said, "Honey, our anger got out of control," I would have felt better. They lied, and from that moment forward, distrust seeped into my head because they might lie to me. I sobbed harder. *Mommy! Daddy! I just want you to hug me and tell me it will be okay.*

DIVORCE

The fighting became too much, and my parents divorced. I was glad because it meant I could resign as the peacekeeper. *Who did I want to live with?* they asked. The decision seemed loaded and fraught with danger. Who? I didn't know and didn't want to decide.

They had given me decision-making power way too early in life. They let me decide if I wanted to repeat first grade or not. The Department of Defense school worried about how many days I had missed (I'd had pneumonia three times). I wasn't being held back. With a lot of work, I would catch up. But it might be easier if I repeated the grade. My parents said going back wouldn't change a thing.

I visited the first-grade class. During art, I got a gold star on my picture and the teacher complimented my artistic ability. Based on that star, I chose to go back a grade, and it changed a lot. I was teased about being stupid at recess. And I never received another gold star in that class. The teacher conned me. It made me furious at myself. The kids didn't have to call me stupid. I agreed with them. It was another reason not to trust adults. Why didn't my parents make the choice for me? It made me afraid of deciding.

So now, who I lived with rested on my decision? My father promised to take me by Disneyland and buy me a horse when we got to where he was going, Florida. He said it would be dangerous for me to live with my mom. My mother didn't promise me anything. She said I should live with the parent I loved best, and she cried while saying it. *Mommy. She needed me.*

My job to save the marriage might have been ending, but my role as the rescuer was already ingrained. I stayed with my mother. I didn't want her to assume I loved my father more, and she might need me. I told my father repeatedly that I loved him. I didn't want him to imagine I loved him less than I loved my mother. Desperately, I'd paint him picture after picture, hoping to heal his heart, even if mine was breaking. I stayed awake nights devising plans to make my parents happy. I hoped this wasn't like my choice to go back to the first grade, one I'd regret later.

The day my father left, I pretended to be watching Saturday morning TV. He called me over, gave me a stiff hug, and said he might not see me for a while. Then he whispered that my mother wasn't stable and living with her would be dangerous for me. I twisted the tag off his suitcase, hugged him, and went back to the TV. My mother told him I didn't understand. I sang the theme song to the next program to drown them out. I hated others assuming they knew my emotions. I furiously bit my fingernails and breathed deeply to keep my stomach from revolting.

I sat in front of the small black-and-white TV pretending I was watching. But I heard my father shut the door and walk down the stairs. My mother said, "Good riddance." I kept wondering why he'd go so far away if it was dangerous for me to stay with Mommy. I was finding out that most of my inner questions didn't have answers or at least not ones I could find.

AFTER THE DIVORCE

I thought my mother would be happier without my father. She wasn't. We moved to a second-floor apartment in the Richmond section of San Francisco. I finished second grade there. Moving meant a new school. Before, I had gone to Department of Defense (DOD) schools. In DOD schools, kids moved in and out all the time. Every student had been the "new kid," so friendships formed quickly. But in this neighborhood school, many of the friendships had already formed, some since kindergarten. Still, in third grade, I had a friend, a new girl who lived with her grandmother. Sadly, in midyear she left to live with her mom.

My mother trekked to bars and drank every night. Sometimes my half brother, Tom, stayed home with me. But frequently, both traveled out. The first time my mother and brother left me alone in the house, I had gotten terrified. But

I remembered when I attended a Catholic kindergarten. They told us everyone had a guardian angel. I got down on my knees, put my hands together, shut my eyes hard, and prayed for my angel to help me. My stomach knotted, and I cried, "Help. Please, I'm scared." When a sense of peace rolled over me. I took my hands down and sat back, awed that it worked! Then I put my hands back in the prayer position and said, "Thanks." I was okay, and the rest of the night passed without incident.

I remained calm until the night my mother's recent friends left me with their two-month-old baby girl. They handed me two bottles full of milk and some diapers. She slept most of the night, but my fear kept me from closing my eyes. This little bundle didn't at all feel like the baby dolls I used to have. The baby squeaked, mewed, and moved her tiny arms. It was up to me to make sure she stayed alive until her parents returned. I rocked her and prayed to my mother and guardian angels. Panic filled my body. *Please, please help me. I have this baby. Please, Mommy, come home.* As the sun shone in the front windows, they finally did. They took the baby and thanked me. My mother said hello on her way to bed. I grabbed my empty rock-filled lunch paper bag and left for school.

She began staying out more and more at night, and many of her friends ended up sleeping at our house. Multitudes slept on the floor in the living and dining room; they never noticed me. They slept with my mother, in her room, my room, and on the couch. Our house became filled with drug addicts and little food and fleas. Small black crawlies infested our house. They colored my socks and bit me, and I scratched myself raw. One day in school my desk mate pointed to my hair and shrieked, "Oh, she's got bugs in her hair!" I slapped my hand to where she pointed, scratched, and hoped the flea traveled to a less visible part of my head.

I had taken to sleeping in the corner that our curved sectional couch made in the living room. I saw people shoot up a whitish liquid. I saw them make love, although many times it looked like fighting. I didn't enjoy seeing all this, and if it were warm enough, I'd go to Golden Gate Park. There I would sleep in a hollow under the roots of a tree, one of many that formed a circle.

I got pneumonia four more times during this period and many other illnesses. I couldn't understand why I was still getting sick. Now it served no purpose. Where before it had called for a peace truce between my parents; now it was inconvenient. My mother tried curing me without taking me to the doctor, which only prolonged my illnesses. I hated missing so much school. *What if they ask me to go back a grade or I fail?*

Many men flocked around my mother. They shared her bed and gave her drugs. They put her in tight dresses or nightgowns and took pictures of her. They would use cooking oil to slick up the private parts of her body so they would draw attention. I hated them touching her, and I'd cry. It made me sick to my stomach. The photographer would tell her to get me to shut up. Later she took me aside and told me that the pictures were important to her and to not cry. So anytime anyone showed up with a camera, I dove behind the couch to my sleeping place. And in that tight little space, I'd curl up into a ball and softly cry, *"Mommy, Mommy, make them stop."*

"What's happened to you?" my mother asked me one day. "You used to have a sense of humor and fun."

For a moment, my heart leapt to my throat. She saw me!

"Mommy?" I said. But she shooed me away.

"Come back when you can make me laugh."

Then her eyes went to half-mast, and she was out of communication range. I spent the night roaming Golden Gate Park. I knew it was dangerous, and I didn't care. I chewed the inside of my mouth until it bled. *Mommy*, I cried inside. Then I scratched the inside of my arms. Angry that I wanted her when I knew she wasn't able to care, but

I couldn't tell her. She needed the money. Finally, my trembling outsides would subside and go inward. Toward morning, I was a walking zombie. Still I would go home to make sure my mom still breathed before putting on my dress and going to school.

WORSE UNTIL RESCUE

SICKER

IT CONFUSED ME. I had really thought the divorce would make things better. I wanted to please my mother. I felt honored when she told me *why* the men were taking pictures of her for others to view and that having sex with them would bring in much needed money. She said she saw me as a grownup so she could tell me these things. I valued her seeing me as a grownup, but that meant I couldn't reveal the scared, screaming child I was inside. I ached for her to take me in her arms and tell me everything would be all right. I longed for the words, "*It's gonna be all okay.*" Instead, I hugged her and told her comforting words whenever she erupted into a crying jag.

At about nine years old, my mother asked me to give her the heroin.

"You've the steadiest hands in the house."

The first time she mixed the white power and water in a spoon and heated it with her lighter. She told me to place the rubber at the top of her arm.

"Pull tight," she instructed. "Tighter."

I did.

"Now put the needle tip in the spoon and draw the plunger out."

Slowly, I did so. I watched the white liquid entering the glass tube.

"Good. Now always let a dribble or two out. To let air bubbles out. Air can kill me."

The bubbles can kill her! I stopped.

She urged me on, and I tapped the plunger and let some liquid dribble out.

"Good. Good. Never let too much out because it is expensive."

I nodded.

"Now put your fingers around the vein in the crook of my arm. If the vein isn't sticking out much, smack it with your fingers. Try it."

I gently tapped her arm.

"No, bang it like this." She demonstrated. "See the vein raise up? Try it."

"It's already raised up. I don't have to." I really didn't want to strike her.

"Oh, don't be a baby. Hit my arm."

So I did.

"Now place a finger on each side of my vein and guide the needle in, not deep but sideways and into the vein. Your fingers will keep the vein from rolling."

I bit the inside of my mouth as I poked the needle through her skin. She minutely jumped, and I stopped.

"No, no, don't quit. I need this stuff. You know that."

I knew that. I'd seen her go into convulsions when she needed it. I thought she would die and threw my body on hers to keep it from quaking. I'd also gone with a friend to a movie a year ago that was about a guy putting something in his arm like that. He said he had a "monkey on his back." Afterwards, I asked what that meant and was told that he had an addiction to heroin.

"Is that bad?" I asked.

"Yes, it will eventually kill him."

My mother's voice insisting that I "push the plunger" broke into my recollection.

"Come on, honey. Push it!"

So I did, hoping that this wouldn't be the time that killed her, that this would be the time that helped her.

I hated, absolutely hated shooting her up. Others in the house wanted me to help them. But I refused. At first, I had vomited in the bathroom afterwards, but now I didn't have enough in my stomach to throw up. My stomach bunched itself up into a dense wad when it came time to give her a hit. I had nightmares about my mother dying. Yet I hurried home from school in case she needed me. And each time she asked, I "helped."

RETROSPECT

Yes, at nine and ten years old, I possessed a steady hand, but just five years later that would change. At age fourteen. I first noticed my hand shook or spazzed when I wanted to draw or paint some fine line. I tried hiding it, but by age twenty-one, the trembling prevented me from signing my name if I got nervous.

The shaking embarrassed me, but I resigned myself to God's public punishment. Twenty years later I learned I had benign essential tremor. A neurological disconnect in my wiring. Causes for it included genetic inheritances or blows to the head. It didn't run in my family.

FOURTH GRADE

Every day I went to school, I would put on my one remaining dress. And every night I'd throw it in the dirty clothes, only to take it out and wear it the next day—day after day. I never took a bath, never even thought of it. Twice, I can remember drawing a tub of water to get rid of the fleas. I'd get in, and black dots would float to the surface. As soon as I pulled the plug, the ebony dots swirled in a water tornado to their death. But they covered my socks and ankles the moment I put my feet on the floor.

By fourth grade, no one chose me for their team. When captains stood to choose team members, I wanted to disappear. I would fill a paper bag with rocks so it wouldn't blow away. At lunchtime, I'd go into the bathroom where I'd remain for the hour. I started acting as if I enjoyed being by myself. Not only did I not want the class to see I had no lunch, I also didn't want to see them eating theirs. I became prickly. If anyone bumped into me, I'd push them away and yell something like, "Watch out! Moron." I developed a smart mouth with an arsenal of verbal weapons.

I wandered the city at all hours of the clock, trying to avoid home. When everyone had gone out, I'd get scared and imagine someone trying to get in the locked door. At first, I'd jump into my sleeping place behind the couch, but fright made it impossible to lie still. The bogeyman's presence horrified me, but there was no one to tell, no one to call. So I trained myself to go to the door, put my ear against it, and listen. If I heard nothing, I'd slowly look around, then close and relock the door. The bogeyman terrified me. If a bad man hid behind the door, I didn't have the luxury of not knowing. I had to know. I had to find out.

Fear ruled me. I felt it when I awoke, got out behind the couch, and tiptoed past the bodies passed out on the floor. I learned the art of tiptoeing, putting my heel down first worked better than starting with my toes. Heels meant I wouldn't wobble into someone by mistake. Fear doubled me over when my teacher asked for homework, a permission slip, or a signed report card.

After school, I'd wander the streets until 11:00 p.m. or later, not wanting to go home. If I scored a quarter in someone's pants, I'd ride the bus in circles all over the city. Often, I fell asleep to the gentle rocking of the tires passing over the pavement. Many times, the bus driver would wake me in the wee hours of the morning, saying, "Hon, this is my last loop. You gotta get off."

WHAT DID PEOPLE SEE?

My first and second grade teachers knew my homelife wasn't stable. I remember crying during second grade and my teacher taking me out into the hallway to ask me what was wrong. I told her my mother had thrown clothes from her closet onto the floor and then into a suitcase that morning. She had said she was leaving. My teacher led me to the office where the secretary finally tracked down my father. He talked to me on the phone and told me he'd take care of it. It relieved me to find her sleeping when I got home.

However, in subsequent grades, I was in much worse shape. I was dirty and painfully thin. My mother's boyfriends tried not to hit me where it would show. But one day I went to school with black eyes and a swollen nose. That was why I always looked people in the eye so I could turn my head when they hit me and avoid getting my nose involved. I'm sure I had other bruises. I was told to lie, and I did. If my second grade teacher could tell my homelife was bad, how did my following teachers go blind?

In third grade, I missed a lot of school due to pneumonia and injuries, like having a goose-egg knot on my forehead from being knocked into a wall.

Didn't anyone wonder why I was so ill? So absent? So secretive?

In fourth grade, I wore the same dirty dress every day, had fleas in my hair, and my teeth were green. I'd lost almost all my eyebrows and eyelashes, and my hair fell out and became thin and brittle. I had little appetite, even though I was starving. I frequently had diarrhea and fever, and my bones hurt. My muscles and joints throbbed. Along with my thinning hair, I had tiny red spots where the blood gathered around my hair follicles. My gums bled easily, puffy and swollen beneath my green teeth. My skin was yellowish, like old newspaper. I had no energy to play at recess, and I'd sit on the sideline and watch kids my age run and tumble. My teacher saw me every day, as did neighbors. Were they near-sighted or indifferent?

I'd show up at a birthday party wearing filthy clothes, matted hair, and holding up a jar with a goldfish in it. I'd stolen it from a neighbor's pond. It was common knowledge that I stole from this man's pond. Later, I'd hear that they returned the goldfish to its rightful owner. How did that seem normal? Was it a case of "not our business?"

When the state of California took me away from my mother, I was ten years old and weighed thirty-nine pounds. The doctor at the intake visit said I had anemia and scurvy. He instructed them to start me eating on soft foods and that I'd need vitamin C injections for a while. After the first shot (even though I hated shots) the pain in my bones improved. Then within two weeks the red blood dots on my scalp went away and my gums no longer bled. After a couple of months, I felt good, could eat proper food, and had tons of energy at the playground.

How did no one notice? Report? Or do something about a child with green teeth and yellowing skin? I had to have looked sick. Why didn't anyone see me?

FEAR

Fear became my copilot, my Tonto, my shadow. It was my headache, my stomachache, my sore bones. I pushed it down as far as possible. I made myself confront danger, like bogeymen at the window, but it didn't lessen the fear, not even temporarily. So I shoved it down further and acted tough. Being terrified became my normal, but since there was no one to help me, I vowed not to let anyone see it. I was alone, lonely, and scared.

Fear followed me to the juvenile home and to the farm where my father placed me with his twin brother and wife. My aunt perfected my fear. Being backhanded or hit every other day concerned me but did not panic me, neither did the belt buckle nor the board. The unpredictability of the violence, anger, and punishments kept me on edge. I never knew what privilege they would take away. I'd already become a kid who showed nothing on her face and tried to vanquish ever wanting anything. But some adults still managed to fool me.

FATHER-DAUGHTER REUNION

Eventually, my father's child support check came back to him. Stamped with "Addressee Unknown," he thought we'd moved. He tried to find out where we'd gone, to no avail. Finally, he asked a Navy buddy to run by our old place and find out. He discovered I lived in a juvenile home and my brother was an army private and my mother resided in a mental institution because of a suicide attempt. He called the juvenile home to find out how to get me out. The answer? He had to prove his fatherhood via a birth certificate and provide me a stable home.

One evening, the matron in charge told me to leave the recreation hall and go to the school classroom. No one would tell me why. They told me to wait. I didn't wait well. I didn't like not knowing. This one-room school taught two groups. The little kids, kindergarten to sixth grade, and seventh to twelve. I'd been in the third grade the first time I'd been in juvie. Now I had passed fourth grade and would be in the fifth in the fall. I wandered around the desks, touching and naming everyone who sat in the seats. On my third pass, my father walked in the door. Shocked, I ran to him and jumped into his arms. A silly voice in my head noticed that my legs didn't fit around him in the same way. I'd grown.

He put me down. "It may take a couple of days, but you are coming with me."

"Where?" I asked.

"To where I live, or the town I live in. You'll stay with my brother, Uncle Hess, and Aunt Essie. Do you remember them?"

I ignored his question. "Why can't I live with you?"

"Oh, a woman needs to raise you. You'll like Essie."

No matter what I said, it was decided. I would be staying with my aunt and uncle. He wouldn't allow me to see my mother before we left. "She doesn't give a crap about you! She left you!"

I said nothing. But my right hand clawed my left forearm. But *he's leaving me too.*

"You understand that, don't you, Sadie? She never loved you."

I bit down on the inside of my lip so hard that it started bleeding, and I spit blood into my hand.

"Whoa, what happened?" He found me some tissue, and I wiped my mouth. "Are you okay?"

I nodded. "I had a blister in my mouth, and it busted."

"Oh, okay. Hold that tissue there."

I nodded.

Awkwardly, he said, "Well, it'll be a couple of days until I get you out. And we'll drive part way to St. Louis, then we'll take a plane the rest of the way."

I nodded again.

"Okay," he gave me a one-armed hug and walked out of the door. A matron escorted me to my dormitory bed, where everyone was asleep.

I crawled into bed and watched her walk away. When she was out of sight. I sat up, doubled over with stomach pain. My heart beat loudly; I hoped it didn't wake up the other kids. My mouth was dry. I hit myself in the face hard. When the sting abated, I did it again. It felt better to hurt on the outside than on the inside.

RETROSPECT

The other kids in juvie patted me on the back, happy for me. My father was taking me home. We always celebrated when someone got out. But as I snuggled under my sheets that night, I wondered why he couldn't afford a horse *now*. And I pondered why he'd moved so far away if he thought living with my mother remained dangerous? Why didn't he stick around to protect me? My daddy, back then, wanted me to live with him. He talked about finding a little house for the two of us. Now we would live in separate places. My daddy's arms felt so strong and solid when I jumped into them in that schoolroom. But when I walked away from the classroom, I walked away from my father. I never called him Daddy again. Had my mother been right? He wasn't safe either…

3

FARM RULES

CALIFORNIA TO GEORGIA VIA ST. LOUIS

I FELT APPREHENSIVE about living with my father's twin and his wife, Aunt Essie. My mother had not liked her at all. It still confused me about why I'd be living with them and not with him. I twisted myself into knots trying to find the words and the right time to ask him again why we couldn't live together. He stopped to visit and drink with Navy friends along our drive to St. Louis. I found no appropriate time to broach the subject.

But after the plane took off from the St. Louis Airport on its way to Georgia, and I still hadn't asked him. He answered, "I know nothing about raising a girl. You need a woman." I contemplated that. Did he only grasp how to raise me, a girl, when my mother was around? Then why did he divorce her? It was true; I didn't see many fathers raising their daughter's alone. I'd watched TV shows that had clever fathers alone raising their kids. Penny's dad, on *Sky King*, raised her alone. And on my very favorite TV show, *Fury*, there was no Mom on that show. He raised a boy, but boy-girl. What's the difference?

My father interrupted my thoughts. "What do you remember of Uncle Hess and Aunt Essie?"

I turned from the airplane's window. "Umm, I remember I got Uncle Hess mixed up for you once when he was playing the piano. Aunt Essie…"

"You'll like her a lot. Your mother has said some awful things about her, but she's a real sweetheart. Really."

I shook my head. "No, Mommy never told me anything about them."

He looked doubtful.

"But I remember what she looks like. She's real tall and got long black hair and a crooked nose with a bump on it."

"Sadie!" he snarled. "You just described a witch! That's your mother's influence. Essie's petite, blond, and attractive."

I nodded and settled back in my seat, upset that I'd made him angry.

During that flight, I fell asleep and sleepwalked to the bathroom at the front of the plane. Instead of returning to the seat beside my father, I sat on an aisle seat beside a stranger.

When I awoke, it disoriented me. *Where am I?* I peered back down the aisle. Where's my father? My stomach tightened, and I grabbed my middle.

The man beside me asked, "Are you all right, honey?"

I shook my head. *Oh no. My father got angry at me and got off the plane and left me here.* "I can't…can't… Where's my father?"

He smiled, a nice smile that showed the light behind his light-brown eyes, and said, "No problem." Then he waved to the lady who was collecting pillows from people.

She was tall and pretty. "Yes, can I help you?"

The man indicated me. "She can't find her seat."

"Come on, hon, I'll take you there. Follow me."

I smiled at the nice man and followed the pretty lady to the back third of the plane where my father sat. "She got a little lost, it seems."

My father stood to let me in by the window. "Yeah, she went to the bathroom and then sat up front. I don't know why she did that? Sadie, what's wrong with you."

The flight attendant asked if we wanted anything. My father said no, sighed, folded his arms, and closed his eyes.

I sat, confused. I didn't remember getting up to go to the bathroom. How'd I get there? If my father watched me sit in the wrong seat, why didn't he come get me? Why'd he let me sit so far away from him with a stranger? I could not figure it out.

RETROSPECT

In hindsight, it foreshadows our relationship. My father remained distant and not accountable for anything that happened to me. It was also the first incident I remember of sleepwalking. I'd been told I did it but had never woken up in the middle of an episode. Today, I still walk in my sleep when stressed.

AT THE FARM

I met Aunt Essie, Uncle Hess, and Ned at the airport. She didn't appear like a witch. But I felt she didn't like me. I tried to shake it off. Maybe I was wrong. She'd only met me a minute ago!

During our first interaction, Aunt Essie told me in private never to mention my mother. Ever. Period. She was a whore and a harlot, and I was never to speak of her in the house. I wasn't sure what a whore or harlot was. I'd figure it out when I went back to school and dictionaries. And the rule of not mentioning my mother only applied to me. Aunt Essie (or TheLady as I called her in my head) brought my mother up all the time. My mother's name always elicited insults and name-calling.

I'd been there a week the first time she backhanded me across the face. I was still getting used to being there, the meals, the rules, the undertones. When I first got up, I'd wander into the breakfast bar and say, "Good morning." If I came inside to go to the bathroom and TheLady was cooking, I'd say, "Hi, I'm going to the bathroom." If we met in a doorway in surprise, I'd say, "Oh! Hi."

That day I was on my way outside after cleaning my room. I passed her as she was sitting on a high-swivel stool, partly in the walkway. I inched around her and said, "Hi, I'm going outside now."

When the back of her hand crashed into the side of my face, my head jerked back and to the side. The world shook, and I put my left hand over my burning cheek and looked at her, wondering what I had done.

She answered that. "For God's sake, quit saying 'hi' every time you walk by. Bad enough we have to greet in the morning! You're here. I get it! You've arrived, so shut the hell up. You got that?"

I nodded and made myself take my hand away from my face. Should I walk outside now or wait? I decided waiting was the best bet.

"God help me," she muttered as she took a drink out of perspiring tin glass. "I'm realize who you are, Sadie. Don't you think I don't!" Her eyes bore into mine, and I looked back, waiting for her hand to rise again.

"You're exactly like your mother. A whore and a harlot. You'll spread your legs for anything that is male. You are a regular strumpet! God, what did I do to deserve this?"

At least I understood what a whore and harlot had in common, but now I'd have to go to the dictionary for strumpet.

Abruptly she grabbed me by the shoulders and violently shook me. "And show some respect and stare at the floor when I'm talking to you!" Quickly, she threw me aside and slumped onto the stool. "Get! Get out of my sight. You disgust me."

I walked until I'd eased the backdoor shut (as instructed), then I ran into the woods beyond the pasture, where I wandered, too anxious to sit down, and delaying going back to the house

WHAT'S LOVE GOT TO DO WITH IT

Being hit and backhanded in the face became part of the landscape. I lived with it like I did the sky, ground, or atmosphere around me. When she berated me, I continued to gaze at her and not at the floor. To peer down made me too vulnerable. I needed to know when she would hit me because then I'd move my nose and lips out of the way. Most times it worked, a few times it didn't. If I ended up with a swollen lip or bruised cheekbone. It was my fault anyway, according to her.

My punishments progressed quickly that first year. They went from getting slapped to getting backhanded two to three times a week and progressed to the leather cat-of-two-tails to the belt, to the buckle, and finally culminated, a year later, in being beaten black and blue with a piece of lumber.

I never cried. I hadn't done so since escaping Dale's apartment. He'd said, "You're made wrong, defective." Not crying illustrated another aspect of my flawed construction. I still tried to please her even while the physical punishments were escalating. I wanted her to like me, no, that's not the complete truth. I wanted her to love me.

Ned would come home from school and walk right into her hug. She'd take his books and direct him to the bar where our snack awaited.

Next, she'd say, "Sadie, put your books in your room and get to the snack bar."

By the time I joined Ned, she and he talked about what had happened at school that day. Or he'd tell her what grade he got on a test and she'd give him a rewarding hug. At breakfast they talked easily about the coming day. I desperately tried to eat the huge amount of food allotted to me. At first, I tried telling her it was too much to eat, but that brought about disastrous results.

"You'll sit there until you eat it and if you don't, you'll get a belting before school."

I hardly saw my father. He came in for coffee and disappeared into another room, where I was not allowed to go. The three years of our separation became a giant ocean between us, and the distance trounced us. He never inquired about me or my grades. He believed everything TheLady told him about me. Why did he never asked why I behaved so badly? She ruled her domain, and it was total domination.

Once she stirred a pot in the kitchen that smelled good.

"Oh, what's for dinner?" I asked.

"Don't ask that. You'll eat what I damn feed you, you hear?"

Seconds later, Ned came in from the porch, gave his mom a quick hug and said, "Mama, what's for dinner. That smells good."

"You're favorite, honey. Barbecued pork with red potatoes."

"Yum, good." He laughed, rubbing his belly.

TheLady looked over at me with a look I couldn't quite figure out, like she wanted to make sure I'd noticed the difference in her response to Ned and me.

Ned became a witness when she'd display the difference. At first, it made him nervous, but after a while it became the way our world worked.

I envied him, his ease around her and the love he elicited. I studied him and tried to do what he did. That never worked. I did chores and asked for extra. I got the added duties and never a thank you.

I laid in bed at night and craved hugging or to be held or to have a gentle word spoken to me. I tried a hundred ways to please her, but nothing worked.

"No one loves me," I'd whisper to myself. Saying it aloud, trying it on to see how it fit. "No one loves me."

Did anyone love me? I never heard from my mother. TheLady said she'd never cared for me, that she enjoyed whoring and having a nasty good time more than me. My mother had once loved me. Why didn't she try to reach me?

My father once loved me. Did he now? Yet he never so much as patted me on the back. I remembered hugs before the divorce. Was that a fantasy? He never said a kind or unkind word to me—few words, at all. Did I blend into the background like the table in the dining room or the couch in the living room, nothing to comment on? No explanation required, no need to figure me out. He never told me I looked pretty, never commented on anything I wore, and never asked me how I fared. I considered us alienated.

This kind of love was like the old jar of yeast the lady had in her pantry to make her bread rise. It wasn't unsafe from non-use. It hadn't turned green with mold but its prime was ancient history with no zest or rise left. If the yeast didn't make the bread rise, it presented no useful purpose. Was this love useful? This distant, disconnected love. A love that never noticed me. My presence needed no observation. I once thought my father had loved me. But could yeast-less love be love?

Diana, my best friend, loved me. Could people who didn't know each other genuinely love each other? She didn't fully know me. Did she only love me partially, the part she recognized? If love existed, I thought it breathed and lived. I watched Diana's love for boys. She thought it love if they wanted to have sex with her. To her, sex equated to love. But she was the center, the focus, of that love. Her love involved her ego with no room for anybody else.

Love had sex in it, but that wasn't the total. That love didn't interest me. I needed to be careful about wanting love and wanting attention. I didn't want to remind someone I existed. I wanted love to be mutual, respectful, and always in-sync or finding out why it was not. I wanted the desire to be intimate on all levels, to be organic and evenly divided. I pictured love as a tandem bicycle. I didn't want to be the one doing most of the pedaling or all the work. I'd seen my mother doing that.

I wrestled with my aloneness and what love might be into the wee hours of the night. Yet I came to no concrete definition or conclusion. If what existed between my father and me served as love, I wanted no part of it. Yet again, I must be careful and not form my decisions into concrete—as adults did. Once they decided someone was a loser, nothing would change that. They could become wealthy, but they'd still be losers in the adults' eyes, "lucky" losers but losers. Right now, I thought distant love bore a resemblance to love. But I'd keep my eyes and heart open to new and different definitions. My thinking kept me busy. It didn't help the feelings of abandonment and loneliness.

COMPLETED FIRST YEAR AT THE FARM

I completed my first year at the farm, along with the fifth grade. There had been losses and some gains. I lost my mother, although I desperately held on to her in my mind. I went over all the adages she'd dispensed to me over the years. I could no longer talk about her aloud. I had no pictures of her. She seemed extremely far away from the small dark patch of earth on which I now lived. But I'd gained an entire inner world in my mind. I had a cave I retreated to anytime I endured an attack. During punishments, I sometimes escaped. I became a huge lumbering animal walking over the scorched earth. I didn't will it, it happened. Also, I'd gained two friends: Diana, and I held on to her for dear life, and a pine tree on the backside of the pasture I called Ol' Pat for patience.

I'd passed fifth grade, and Ned had passed sixth. TheLady congratulated him and ignored me. And the three months of summer stretched out before us. I'd only experienced a few weeks of summer last year after my father dropped me there from the juvenile home. Ned was excited about all the time for play and no school. I didn't know how all that time would work out for me. Ned and I had different experiences in the same house.

I'd climbed out the window in my bedroom. Most nights I'd walk to the far end of the pasture and climb into the arms of my pine tree, Ol' Pat. The night before our summer began, I talked to my tree about TheLady. I told Ol' Pat things I could never tell Diana, like how I wanted TheLady to like me...to love me.

That night I told Ol' Pat one thing I noticed about the adults at the farm, my father included. They saw what they wanted to see. They were not honest with themselves and so not with anyone else. But they thought they were being honest because they believed their lies.

"So, Ol' Pat," I said. "TheLady doesn't like me." I wanted her to, and I tried to make myself into someone she would like. But the truth is—she doesn't. My mom used to say, "Quit tilting at windmills." TheLady is a windmill, and I've got to quit trying to knock down her wall. It's there. It's real; it's a thing.

I sighed. "I want someone to love me, Ol' Pat, and no one does. No one. That's how it is, except I know you love me. But I'd like some human love."

But I can pretend. I chewed on some sour grass I'd grabbed on my way over to the tree. "Okay, Ol' Pat. You keep me honest, okay? Honest with myself and you. I may have to lie here. But I have to acknowledge to myself that I'm lying." Before dawn, I crawled back in the bedroom window and slept till about 7:00 a.m. when awoken by TheLady.

SUMMER AT THE FARM

The summer was full of sun and chores. I turned pink, bubbled, and peeled—yet she repeatedly sent me out into the field and in the 2:00 p.m. sun to mow the lawn. TheLady liked to go to the beach now and then and sunbathe. Ned and I would also go. Ned would play in the water and build forts in the sand. I would climb the rocks in the jetty and try to find shade.

That summer TheLady also rented a cabin at a lake with a friend of hers who had a son of Ned's age. My favorite time to get in the water off the dock was the morning when the sun didn't bite as deeply as later. We, kids, had to stay outside while TheLady and her friend sat at the kitchen table, drinking and smoking. About three days into our trip, I woke up with an itchy rash all over my face, neck, arms, and legs. They severely itched, and I had a banging headache.

I went to the kitchen table where TheLady sat enthroned, talking to her friend over coffee.

"Umm, Aunt Essie, something's wrong. Look." I held out my arms.

Her friend exclaimed, "Ohmigosh, it's all over your face too, poor baby. Does it hurt?"

"It itches," I answered.

"Well, don't scratch it. Essie, are you aware of a doctor in these here parts?"

"Sadie, of course, you come up with a rash," she hissed. "No, there's nobody, but we'll go to the drugstore. Lots of time they know."

So we all got dressed and walked into the pharmacy. TheLady did the talking, saying I just woke up looking like this and we were from out of town.

The man in the white coat came out from behind the counter and examined my face, arms, and legs. "Do you have the rash on your belly," he asked gently.

"No, sir."

He nodded and turned to the two women. "She has sun poisoning. She's allergic to the sun. She hasn't the skin for it, and she never will have. Now, she has to stay out of it completely while the rash is active. And after that, she must wear a hat, long sleeves, and sunscreen when she gets in the sun."

"For how long?"

"The rash can last two weeks. But again, even after that she has to be careful in the sun."

TheLady pursed her lips. "Well, Sadie, you've ruined our vacation."

"Oh, Essie, it'll be okay. She can swim in the early morning and at night. The rest of the time she can be on the porch, listening to music, or drawing. It'll be fine."

The pharmacist listened to the conversation. Then he handed TheLady a bottle of cream to rub on the little clusters of blisters. "She can take aspirin for her discomfort and cold compresses could also help."

TheLady was slightly shaking her head, and the air tense.

As the man went back behind the counter to ring up the cream, he said, "You're lucky. This time it's only costing you the price of a tube of steroid cream. If she keeps getting in the sun unprotected, she'll be hospitalized."

TheLady looked surprised. "Well, that won't happen," she exclaimed. She paid for the cream and marched out of the store, with us three kids trailing behind.

Before exiting, I turned to look at the pharmacist. He gave me a friendly wave, which I returned by smiling and mouthing the words, "Thank you."

I didn't get cold compresses, but I got to stay out of the sun and use the tube of cream. Most of the time, I was in my room or on the porch while the boys played in the lake. That was fine with me. From then on, I got to wear light pants, a long-sleeve shirt, and a hat to the beach. And I got to cover up when I was mowing the lawn at the hottest time of the day.

When I was older, I worked in the medical field. I would ask doctors if they'd ever encountered a person being hospitalized for severe sun poisoning. None of them had heard of a single case. Had the kind pharmacist come up with a scenario that would ensure she kept me protected from the sun? I'll never know, but I like to think he was protecting me.

It was a long summer. I learned to stay out of her way whenever possible. I also knew I'd get in trouble for something at least once or twice a week, and there was no help for that. I learned not to let TheLady see my motions, to not let it telecast across my face. I became adapt at having a blank face. But the feelings rumbled underneath my skin. It made the monster in my belly claw at my stomach. It made me anxious, which made me want to talk and fill up the silence. But I learned to make myself be quiet. It made me angry, and I took that out on myself and would learn to displace it on others.

On August 12, I had my first menstruation period. When I told TheLady, she hugged me and said I was "a woman now." It was the first hug I'd ever received from her. She then sent me into the bathroom and directed me to the pads under the sink. It took me a while to figure out what to do with them. Then I retreated to my tree.

"I'm a woman now, Ol' Pat." I laughed. "Not really. I'm only twelve. Huh? How about that? I'll be glad when I can go to the school library and look some of this stuff up. Like how long does it last? And is there a comfortable way to wear these pads?"

That evening, as Ned was taking his bath, TheLady called me from the porch into the dining room. As I rounded the corner, she backhanded me across the face.

"I saw the way you were looking at Ned today," she hissed.

I arranged my face into a blank mask and wondered what she was talking about. Of course, I had talked to Ned that day. I talked to him every day.

"Your body's womanly now. Don't go imagining you can engage my son in your nasty sex behavior. You hear me?"

I nodded.

"When you get pregnant, don't you dare come home! You got that?"

I nodded.

"You run off with the guy or run away. You won't be welcome back here. And don't you dare get my son tangled up in your whorish ways. He's a good boy, and he'll remain a good boy. You understand! I swear, I'll beat you bloody if I find out you ever come at my son sexually. You hear?"

Again, I nodded.

Then Ned got out of the tub, opened the door, and walked through where we were talking in the living room. "Night, Mama," he said as he went by. She gave him a quick hug and told me to get into the bathroom.

As I soaked up to my neck in hot water, I again whispered, "Nobody loves me. I'm alone."

The water caressed me, and I let myself float. "But I can love me. I must love me if nobody else is going to...I love me." And that means I won't look for it from the grown folks around me.

Heck, they don't even like me. So that means I don't have to believe anything they tell me. If me and the Big Guy think I'm doing the right thing, I can disregard what the people here tell me.

I smiled as I soaped the washrag. "Somebody does love me! And it's me. I love me," I sang softly under my breath. It felt good, not only because I loved myself but also that I recognized that those adults around me didn't love me. And in TheLady's case, she didn't even like me, she hated me.

> Somebody loves me and it's me.
> Just as I am, just as I be.
> I am the someone who loves me.

This became my silent song.

RETROSPECT

I didn't realize at the time what a huge accomplishment this decision was in the course of my life. I had realized I was alone, and I vowed to love me even if no one else did. Also, by recognizing that I couldn't depend on their outlooks, opinions, and conclusions, I gave myself permission to follow my conscience. It's a twelve-year-old version of "to thine own self be true." As long as me and the Big Guy thought I was doing the right thing, to heck with the others. Of course, I made mistakes and had to make many adjustments. I got angry at myself. But I kept growing under the guidance of my conscience.

4

BEYOND THE FARM

ANOTHER YEAR AT THE FARM

IN SEVENTH GRADE, TheLady started talking about a dance Friday night at our junior high school. Would we like to go? I'd recently taught Ned to dance, so he was all excited. She and Ned discussed what he'd wear, what time we ought to get there, early or on time? Although, I wasn't asked these questions, she always said "ya'll" when she talked about it.

That Friday, as Ned and I exited the bus and walked into the dining room, he chattered about the dance. As soon as we walked in, I knew something was wrong.

TheLady sat on her chair by the window, blowing swirls of gray smoke over her head.

"Sit!" she barked.

We sat. Ned chewed his lip, and I put on my blank stare while the animal in my gut clawed at my stomach lining.

"Sadie," she started as she tapped her cigarette ash on the edge of the ashtray.

"Yes, ma'am."

"Do you wear lipstick at school?"

Oh, that's what this is about. Last week I had put some of Diana's lipstick on after lunch. Our class filed by Ms. Schmedley, the principal, to exit the lunchroom. She and TheLady were good friends, and she spied on me. As I came up level with her, she said, "Lipstick, Sadie?"

I smiled my best smile and answered, "Yes, it's called Pink Ice by Revlon."

Her face changed. "Are you smart-mouthing me, Sadie?"

"No, ma'am. I was answering your question."

TheLady slammed her hand on the table. "Sadie, do you wear lipstick at school?"

"I have tried some on."

"You know damned well that's forbidden. I won't have your whorish ways. You are grounded. You won't be going to the dance this Friday."

She watched my face, and I kept it blank and looked back at her.

"And you'll go to bed early. I won't have you acting like your slut of a mother. You hear me?"

I nodded.

"Good, now put your books in your bedroom, change, and go outside."

As I walked away, Ned asked in a little voice, "What about me, Mama, can I still go to the dance?"

"Of course, you can, honey. You have done nothing wrong."

I was glad Ned could go, and I was happy I was going to bed early. In my bedroom, I got to be myself and think my own thoughts. Ms. Schmedley and the lipstick incident had happened at the beginning of the previous week, and she was absent all this week for a conference. TheLady had set me up. Building my expectation about the dance and then dashing my hopes. I couldn't afford hope; it hurt too much. So I shoved it down like I had pushed fear down in the depths of my being. It hurt too much to feel.

AFTER HIGH SCHOOL/KELLY

I bounced between relatives in my teen years from Georgia and back to New York State, then back again. Sometimes I stayed with other relatives of my father, but not for long. My happiest year was living with my best friend, Diana, and her family. When I found out they would not continue to do that, I ran away (Diana came too). We got arrested for petty larceny (two forty-nine-cent records) and stayed four days in the adult Miami jail, one of my lowest points. But I'd promised the Big Guy after the car accident at fourteen that I wouldn't try suicide until ten years had passed. And I keep my promises.

Finally, I got kicked out of my aunt Essie's house (she had married my father) when I was sixteen years old. I worked at a five-and-dime store and rented a room in town. This was where the owner, an old man, met me naked as I came out of the shower, making me wonder if I had a "molest me" sign taped on my back.

At last, I graduated and moved into the YWCA. All the troubled times were behind me, right?

At the YWCA (Y) I met Kelly Carroll, who introduced me to her parents, Adrian and Rod, and younger brother by three years, Luke. That first Christmas at the Y, she made me go to Christmas at her grandmother's house.

I had lots of friends at the Y. I was well liked and would do anything for anyone. But I'd cut myself off from emotions, and if any of them had left the next day, I'd have waved and been okay. One day, a group of us girls were talking in the cafeteria of the Y and someone said something that made us all laugh.

"Now, that was funny," someone said, and everyone agreed.

Then Kelly commented, "Yes, but Sadie's laugh never reaches her eyes."

Everyone stared at me, and my roommate said, "Yeah, you're right."

I was scared and thrilled to have been seen. Then Kelly made it her mission to be my friend. I knew she'd only be there until I made her angry or she found someone more interesting. And I tried to shake her. I'd make lunch plans and never show up, forget to give her phone messages, and drive her car without permission. She always said, "I don't like what you did. But I love you now, and I'll love you more tomorrow." My reaction was "Gag me, you'll get tired and leave like everyone else." But she didn't

She accompanied me to California. I planned to find my mother and didn't. But I did reconnect with my older brother. Then one day, she wanted to take a walk at two o'clock in the afternoon, and I blocked her way, telling her she couldn't go. We tussled, and she asked what was wrong with me.

"You can't go," I said, "because you could get kidnapped (she rolled her eyes) or hit by a truck (she shook her head) or…or…you could keep going…"

"Ohmigosh," she exclaimed. "You care."

And my stomach clinched. *Shit!* I did care.

Kelly once asked me why I wasn't in college, and I told her I wasn't smart enough. She almost fell off her chair.

"Why would you think that?" she asked.

"The high school counselor told me so."

"Ohmigosh," Kelly snorted. "Did he notice how many schools you'd been to? How thick your file was? How it's a miracle that you passed grades and graduated?"

I shrugged.

"Doesn't it bother you? That he said you weren't smart enough?"

"No. I don't let it much bother me."

After that, she made it her mission to have me go to college. She arranged with her folks for both of us to go back to their house and enroll in school. I got student aide to pay my tuition.

"I want to prove to you are smart enough. And I want you to know what it's like to live in a Christian home."

Kelly's family was very traditional and went to church every Sunday. Rod Carroll, her father, was the captain at the helm, and his wife, Adrian, was passive and compliant. Luke was in high school and loved football and his guitar, neither of which his father endorsed. Kelly's relationship with her father was strange. He was critical of her in many instances and won every argument by getting her off track. He saw himself as the ruler and others would obey.

I felt the tension in the atmosphere when he was angry. No one dared talk back or even question him. Everyone walked on eggshells. But I had already lived a similar life with Aunt Essie, and while he wasn't abusive, he was hard to take. And we butted heads.

For example, he got up at 6:30 a.m. and thought everyone in the house should. Luke had to get up early for football practice, so it was okay with him. Adrian had to run the secondhand store they operated in town. She'd get up and get some housework done before she had to be there. Kelly and I, however, didn't have our first college class until 10:00 a.m. so we could sleep in. Except her father didn't think so.

He'd get up and bang on her closed door. Then he'd open it and flick the ceiling light off and on. Next was the TV that Kelly had bought herself with a part-time job in high school. He'd turn it on, loud. Finally, he'd exit and leave the door open so we could hear everyone's voices.

We'd tried to talk to him and explain when our first classes were, but he said his house, his rules. And Kelly agreed. I didn't. So one day I unscrewed and removed the bulb from the ceiling light.

Kelly chanted, "He's gonna be mad. He's gonna get so mad."

Next, I knotted the TV cord so that it would not reach the wall. I couldn't do anything about the door, but it'd be easier to go back to sleep without the light and TV blaring.

The next morning, he banged on the door and tried to flip the light off and on. Then he found the TV didn't work, and when he traced the cord, he found it wouldn't reach the wall socket.

"You girls think you're funny?" he growled as he exited, leaving the door open.

Rod Carroll didn't like it, but he no longer tried to get us up.

All day Kelly lamented about how angry her father was going to be. I shrugged. I could live through his anger. That night after he came home, he never mentioned it and no longer tried to get us up.

Then one evening during dinner, I excused myself to go to the bathroom. While in there, I heard him say, "It costs me five cents every time she flushes the toilet."

When I came out, I put a quarter down by his plate and said, "There now, I'm four flushes ahead."

Luke had to cover his mouth and pretend to cough to cover his laugh. Adrian took a drink of water and looked straight ahead. Kelly looked down. Looking back now, I think I was terribly disrespectful, but controlling behavior made the warrior rise up in me.

KELLY'S FATHER

I never mentioned the following in my first book because Kelly asked me not to do so. Her parents were still alive then, and she didn't want them hurt. I figured I owed Kelly, and I didn't write about it. But now I am.

Kelly and I rented a house in the same city as her parents. Not soon after this I bought my first vehicle, a twenty-year-old Italian car for $50.00. When we drove up to Kelly's parent's house, Rod came out and asked if he could take it for a test drive. I scooted over to the passenger seat, and he took the steering wheel. Kelly stayed home. He drove around a bit then pulled over into a subdivision that was being built. Plots had been staked out around a large pond. He told me the car seemed like it drove well. I nodded. Then he put his hand on the back of the passenger seat and turned toward the middle to look back to reverse the car.

"Hopefully, I'll miss the pond," he said.

I then turned to look backward over the center at the pond also. In the next moment, I was drawn up into a sloppy wet kiss. His arms held me in a vicelike grip. As his lips ground away at mine, I kept thinking over and over, *Ohmigod, this is Kelly's father! Kelly's father. Ohmigod.*

When the kiss ended, he reversed the car, and then drove forward toward his house. My mind kept looping the thought of Kelly's father kissing me. He mumbled something about being sorry but I was just so pretty and he and his wife weren't getting along.

I nodded and sat in shock.

When we finally got back, Kelly and her mother were in the yard. Rod got out and loudly said he thought it was a pretty good car. Adrian asked why we took so long. He said he'd wanted to give it a good test drive. She nodded, and they walked toward the house together.

Kelly knew something was amiss. She could read it on my face. "What's wrong" she whispered.

"Nothing. I'll tell you later. Just don't leave me alone with your father."

She gave me a funny look and said okay.

We went inside and watched TV with them, and I laughed at all the right times, and answered questions when asked. Finally, Kelly and I started back to our place.

"Now, what's wrong?"

"Your father kissed me," I answered.

"What?" Her face blanched, and her eyes got huge. Raw anguish.

It reminded me of the look my mother had given me when I ran into her bedroom after being kidnapped by Dale. I was immediately sorry I'd told Kelly. She was heartbroken. I never wanted to see that look on her face again.

We went into our place in silence.

"Really, Kelly. It's okay. It was nothing." I tried to downsize it, but she'd already seen my shock and fear. I couldn't minimize it now. That night in bed I asked the Big Guy questions. *Why does this keep happening? What is about me that causes this? I really* do *have a "molest me" sign on my back.*

I was angry at myself. Why didn't I say no? Why didn't I hit him or get out of the car and run? Why did I always freeze! His kiss brought back the smell of Dale and the calloused hands of my grandmother's friend. Any healing I'd done from previous sexual abuse was rendered null. Rob's molestation tore the bandage off, and it took the skin with it. I was back to an oozing, bruised, and frightened child with an open wound. *Defective...defective...defective.*

Also, I was alone because I would never share my fright and hurt with Kelly. I couldn't; she was gutted. So I didn't tell her of the many other times her father tried to put his hands on me. Eventually, Kelly forgot about not leaving me in a room with him. Mr. Carroll must have had some kind of radar because when I was alone, he made a beeline for me.

Kelly had become the friend I confided in, and now I couldn't do that. I had vowed to tell the truth, and now I was lying to her. I made excuses not to go with her to her house, but I had to be careful not to make too many or she'd start questioning. When she walked out of a room, I couldn't run and follow her or again she'd have suspected something was happening. I became evasive. It created a block in our friendship. I could feel it but felt hopeless about doing anything about it.

He'd try to put his hands up or down my shirt. He'd grab me for a kiss, or he'd pat my bottom. At least I'd found my voice, and I told him no repeatedly. This went on until I was twenty-nine years old. At Thanksgiving, I'd be at the table and he'd be beside me trying to work one hand up to my crotch. I loved Kelly, her mother, grandmother—her whole family. Without them I'd have had no place to go at holidays. I'd look over the table and know I couldn't tell them. I didn't think I'd be believed for one thing. How could his mother think this of her son? Why would Adrian believe me over her husband? And Kelly, she would have believed me, but it would have killed her. Even with my husband and kids sitting at that table, I fought off his hands and remained silent. I was defective. It was my fault and my shame. It was my price for having a pseudo-family and a place at the table.

DR. TNUH

I went to college intermittently because I found it hard to go for a full semester and work part-time. So I tried going one semester working and saving money and going the next. One day, I walked into the head of the psychology department's office and asked Dr. Tnuh if I could ask him a question. I'd had him in my first semester in college.

"Yes, of course."

"Could I be crazy?"

He paused and invited me to sit down. After I sat, he looked at me over his desk. "Why do you ask?"

"Because my mother was an alcoholic and heroin addict. She was in and out of institutions. And everyone says I'm just like her."

He nodded and tented his fingers. "Are you? Just like her?"

I paused before answering. "I look like her—fair skin, green eyes, and reddish hair."

He nodded.

"And I'm creative like her...but I don't know..."

"Do you think she was crazy before she became an alcoholic and drug addict? Or after?"

"I'd say after. Before I was five years old, I was close to her."

"So do you think drugs and alcohol could have made her less stable?"

"Absolutely."

"Do you use heroin and drink to excess?" He smiled. "You see where I'm going?"

"Yes."

"You know I've never talked to anyone who had alcoholism and heroin addiction growing up, and I'd like to know more. Would you be willing to come here once a week? We could have lunch together in the office and we could talk to each other?"

"Umm..."

"You must have more questions. I know I do. How about it? Next Wednesday at noon?"

"Okay."

"And"—Dr. Tnuh wrote on a notepad—"homework! Entertain these two questions, and we'll talk about it next week."

I looked at the paper he handed me. It had, "(1) Do you think you've been affected by your background? (2) How are you on trust?"

To answer his question of if my background impacted my future, I replied, "Yes and no." I didn't think it had because I was okay. On the other hand, I knew my non-trust showed that it had affected me. I concluded that I didn't want it to have influenced my life, but it had.

Trust? I said I trusted Kelly.

He asked if there were things I hadn't told her for fear of how she'd react.

Her father touching me and Dale jumped into my mind. "True. There are some things."

"That's good to recognize. So right now, you trust her as much as you can. Would you say that's true?"

"Yes, but I want to trust more. It'll take time."

"That's also good to know. Be patient with yourself. What kind of trust do you want?"

I'd thought about that. "The kinds I've seen are blind trust, naïve trust, reciprocal trust, and melding trust."

"Good list. Tell me about them."

"It may not be all of them, but those are the ones I've seen or thought about a lot." I smiled. "Naïve trust is often said to be the trust of children, but I don't think so. Kids have an innocent trust because they don't have enough life experience. Naïve trust is having some experience but choosing to read it in only a positive way."

Dr. Tnuh swallowed his bite of sandwich and said, "Example?"

"Like believing that all hippies are good and kind. Some are, some aren't. Just like anywhere. I'm seldom naïve. Next is blind trust. That's when you don't want to see the truth. I see girls living with a boyfriend who is obviously lying to her about seeing other women, but she refuses to see it. That's blind trust."

"Okay, and reciprocal and melding trust?"

"Reciprocal is mutual trust. It's not tit for tat, as in I'll trust you with this, now you trust me with that. It's the willingness to go deeper. It's a slow build, never fast, because it is constructed on risk and security."

"Do you have reciprocal trust with anyone?"

I thought of Kelly and Diana. "No, not yet. Kelly and I are working toward that, but it's still in the growing stage."

"Okay." Dr. Tnuh motioned with his fingers. "What's melding trust?"

"Hmm…I think that comes after reciprocal. It's based on eons of positive experiences and mutual trust."

"Eons?"

I laughed. "Well, that's what it seems like. Anyway, it takes a long time. And I've only seen it once. It's a circle where the people share and trust, share and trust."

"Do you think you'll ever have reciprocal trust with Kelly and melding trust with anyone?"

"I don't know."

Dr. Tnuh waited, tenting his fingers.

"I'm my own worst enemy. I learned not to trust, so learning to trust is…scary."

He nodded.

"But not as scary as not ever trusting. I am willing to trust…just taking baby steps."

"Ah, that's great. The willingness. With that, you'll get there. Not that there won't be bumps along the way, maybe even hurts. That's where self-trust comes into the picture. Trusting yourself not only to be willing, but knowing you will pick yourself up, and be okay if it doesn't work out."

I laughed again. "True. Self-trust. I hadn't thought about that one. That's the only kind of trust I had for years."

"Yes, I can see that," he replied. "And everyone over the age of twenty-one has experienced some kind of betrayal in trust. The key is to not label it as a failure but as a lesson and learn from it."

"I'll have to work on that. I'm good at calling myself a failure."

"Good to know. Good to work on."

"Learning lessons instead of failure. Hmm…food for thought."

BED WETTER

In one of our sessions, Dr. Tnuh asked if there had been abuse in my background. I told him about one of my mother's boyfriend's hitting me and a few incidents at the farm. I didn't go into any depth. I picked at my arms while answering and felt uncomfortable. I blamed myself.

He then asked me if I'd ever tried to hurt myself. As a kid, I did. Did I grind my teeth or wet my bed? I felt my face turn red and pulse with every heartbeat. I told him I'd seriously considered suicide at age fifteen. Then I clammed up.

He watched me for a while. I felt he knew there was more, and it made me squirm.

Finally, he said, "It's okay if you aren't ready to talk about it. I hope someday you do because it will free you."

I wondered what he meant.

That night as I sat in the dark at home, listening to music, I remembered how I used to wet the bed as a child. Even in the dark, my face burned. *I was a bed wetter.*

I frequently wet the bed when I was little. The last time it happened, I was eleven or twelve and wet the bed at the farm. That morning TheLady had marched into our Sunday school auditorium. She announced in front of everyone that we were late because I'd wet the bed and she had to clean up the mess.

After that embarrassment, I learned how to crawl out the window at night so I could get rid of the enemy, urine, in the woods behind the pasture.

I was ashamed. Wetting the bed had always been humiliating. Doing so at TheLady's was a million times worse. I felt I deserved the consequences.

I had dreamed I was on an airplane and had to go to the bathroom, which I did. I awoke from the dream and tried to stop the warm urine flowing from me, but it couldn't be stopped. I tiptoed into TheLady's bedroom where she was asleep with Uncle Hank. Gingerly, I shook her shoulder and told her what had happened.

She jumped up and put her finger to her mouth in a "shhh" motion. She marched me out into the hallway between the bedrooms and in front of the bathroom.

"Really! Wet the bed at your age! Get in the bathroom and hand me your stinking nightgown. I'll have to strip your sheets and turn the mattress."

I went into the bathroom and did as she said. I opened the door a crack and handed my wet nightgown to her.

"Now get your wash rag and clean yourself up. You smell. Stay in there until I tell you."

I did as she instructed, then wrapped my towel around myself. It was cold in January, and I shivered as none of the house was heated at night.

"Come on out," I heard her say.

I hesitantly stepped out, expecting her to have fresh nightclothes in her hand. Instead, she held a belt by both ends, making it half its length and thicker.

"Get in there." She motioned to my room.

As I went in, I noticed the window had been opened, letting in the frigid winter air. The mattress had been turned, but there were no sheets on it. *What's going on?*

"Turn around," she ordered. "And you'd better damn well be quiet. You wake anybody up, and I'll make sure you get belted every night for a week."

I had hardly completed the turn before the blows from the belt rained down on my back. I hunched over, and involuntarily, my feet moved forward until I was against the wall.

"You ruined my mattress! You little whore!" she whispered as she brought the belt down on my back. As I crouched, trying to make myself a smaller target, she grabbed the towel away from my body. I turned to get it back just in time to get a belt across my front, so I turned away again.

The blows kept coming. Each stroke stung, increased by the next and the next. I wasn't human anymore. I was a throbbing point of pain, especially when the belt landed on places it had hit before. My back, buttocks, and upper legs were on fire. On and on it went, with her whispering the words, "Bitch, whore, tramp" on the downswing. I don't know how long it lasted. Time became measured by the pause between strappings. I vacillated between being grateful the belt was withdrawn and dread of the next lash.

Finally, she stopped. Breathing heavily, she hissed, "Now you sit on this mattress and think about what you've done! And don't you dare close the window or get any of your clothes out of the closet."

I crawled up the end of the bed, and sat at the center, with my knees drawn up to reduce my nakedness.

She jutted her face toward me and drew her hand back with the belt. "Did you hear me, girl? Don't move from here until I come and get you. You hear me?"

I nodded.

Then she left and locked the door.

I sat on the bare mattress, shivering and naked, hugging my knees. Pain radiated all over my body, not just at the site of the belting.

Six hours later she came in and threw some sheets at me. "Make the bed. Get ready for church."

My fingers were so cold I had trouble fastening the buttons. *Hopefully, I'll catch pneumonia and die.* The thought comforted me.

FRIGID FLASHBACK

The six hours I spent shivering and hugging my knees for warmth, left me plenty of time to reflect on being hit, socked, and belted. I'd always been slapped and knocked about. My half brother was ten years older than me and I remember him hitting me out of frustration or anger. I adored him and seldom told on him because I recognized that my father would come down hard on him. In many ways, my father was not nice to him and his only guard was our mother.

Nuns in my kindergarten had permission to hit my hand with a ruler. No one in my family was Catholic. Before age eight I don't remember going to any church. But there I sat. In a classroom full of children and nuns in long black-and-white dresses floating about the room.

One day, I did something wrong and a nun marched over to me and ordered me to put my hand out. She was going to hit it with the wooden ruler she held in her hand. That seemed counterintuitive to me, and I refused to put my hand out. When she insisted further, I balled my hands into fists and hid them behind my back. I remember how quiet the classroom became as I defied the nun. Eventually, I was carried out by someone else, still with my fists balled up.

My mother and father spanked me usually with their hand. After running away from the Presidio in San Francisco, my father whipped me with the belt. After the divorce, my starving dog devoured my mother's diaphragm. She used a wooden hanger on me in anger.

All her boyfriends would slap me in the face. She was sitting right there, so they must have had permission. One of her boyfriends would tie my hands behind my back and push me in a closet. He'd smack me until I stood as high on my tippy-toes as possible. Then he'd insert a wire hook from wire hangers he'd twisted around the pole in the closet into each nostril. He'd leave me there for hours, until when let out, I couldn't put my heels on the floor. My mother knew of this, so he had permission.

My brother used to pick me up and stuff me under the mattress of his bunk bed. He'd force hot-sauce in my mouth and he and his friends would sit on top of me while my mouth burned and tears spilled. He also hit me out of frustration or anger. I adored him and had seldom told on him because I recognized that my father would come down hard on him. I sensed my father hadn't liked him.

It was so cold sitting on that mattress. I thought my bones would break from the quaking. TheLady must have had my father's permission to discipline me physically. The school too had permission to paddle me. They never did, but they had full consent if they wanted to do so. Being hit became a familiar violence. I pushed my toes into the mattress, hoping to warm them. I sighed. There was no getting away from it. Kids were punching bags for everyone. I couldn't escape it until I was eighteen. I vowed *never ever* to hit my children if I ever had any.

RETROSPECT

Dr. Tnuh counselled me for over three years. He challenged my way of thinking, seeing, and being. He helped me change: *fail to try*, being different to being unique, and being closed to being open. I never told him about any of the sexual abuse or molestations. I wasn't ready. But I did reveal my utter lack of sexual feelings, being dead from the nose down. He called it asexual. He helped me make peace with it. As my self-trust grew, so did my acceptance of myself. He helped me unpack some past terror that I'd rammed down into my interior over the years. We only touched on anger, an emotion I didn't want to have. However, his biggest gift was encouraging me to be open to change, that what is true today may not be so tomorrow. And being open changed everything.

5

MEETING, HAPPY, AND A MAN

AGE TWENTY-THREE AND HAPPY

I WAS TWENTY-THREE years old when I woke up one morning, stretched, smiled, and realized I was happy. It was a strange feeling. In the past, I'd been cheerful for a minute after something good happened. But this was different. Absolutely nothing had happened, except a good night's sleep, yet I was happy.

I woke Kelly up. "Kelly, I'm happy!"

She groaned and turned her head into her pillow. "I'm glad for you. Now go away."

So I did. I went in the kitchen and did the dishes that were piling up, made my bed, and straightened the house. When Kelly came stumbling out of her bedroom with her eyes half open, I handed her a cup of fresh hot coffee.

"What's got into you?" she asked.

"I'm happy."

"So I heard. Why?"

"No reason. I'm simply happy. If my life never changes from this moment on, I'd still be happy."

"Are you crazy?" she asked. "What about the future? Marriage, children, a fantastic job?"

"Hmm, I'm not ruling them out, but even if they never happen, I'm happy. I think it's the first time I've ever felt this way. Happy *as is.*"

"You take some happy pill?"

"Ha! No, if that were available, I'd have taken it long ago. No, this happy is from the inside out. As in *right now*, in *this place*, I am happy. If this is all there is, it's okay—and I'm happy."

Kelly sipped her coffee and shook her head. "Yeah, I think you've lost it."

FORETHOUGHT

It is strange that the minute I was okay with life as it was, I met someone who would change it forever. I'd been in love once. I didn't fall easily or quickly, even though I was much more open than in the past. Did I have to become comfortable with myself before meeting someone else? Was that a prerequisite for meeting someone special? I don't know, but I am grateful it happened that way.

TIMOTHY

One crisp October evening, Kelly urged me to go with her. She volunteered at a recreation night at a work center for adults with cognitive disabilities. It was part of her psychology class assignment. She knew I had worked with such adults when I was a fifteen-year-old runaway. She thought I'd enjoy it.

At the last minute, I decided to go. My waist-length hair needed washing, but there was no time. So I parted it in the middle, put it in braids. I put on an unflattering pair of brown pants with a matching vest over a shirt.

We drove to the center in Kelly's small red subcompact Gremlin. As we opened the double entrance doors, a man with longish blond hair was taking a drink from the water fountain. His hair fell around his face like a curtain. The door made a racket, and he swung his hair to the side, wiped some water from his mouth, and said, "Hi, Kelly." He was tall, blonde, sprouting a beard, and had light-blue eyes.

Kelly said hi and introduced me to Tim. My first thought was how much he looked like Ted, the first and only guy I'd ever fallen in love with long ago. My second thought was my unfashionable braided hair and terribly unflattering outfit. I didn't have time for a third thought because we'd walked into the recreation hall. It buzzed with activity, Ping-Pong, music, and dancing. The clients of the center were engaging and fun to get to know. I met so many clients and students that my head spun. But I remembered one name, Tim.

The next week as we left the center, Tim looked over the top of his green Volkswagen. "Hey, would you like to go get a beer at Lum's?"

Kelly had brought another friend named Susan, and we looked at each other. I had the Gremlins front seat pulled forward, ready to crawl into the back. When we agreed to go, I flopped the red seat back into its rightful position and said, "I'll ride with him." As I walked toward his car, I saw Kelly's mouth drop open. I'd never done anything like that before.

I got into Tim's car and started my twenty-one questions. I always asked myriad questions, and he didn't seem to mind. His blond hair sparkled in the sun, and his blue eyes had a twinkle. Tim was twenty-nine years old. He'd gotten out of the Air Force in June, was going to college, and letting his hair grow. He was separated, pending a divorce, from his wife and had three little boys, ages six to four. From the picture he showed me of them, they were all blond headed and adorable.

He sounded surprised that I was twenty-four years old. I laughed. "I know, I've been mistaken for eleven!"

At Lum's, we talked about various subjects, and on the way out, he asked me to go to a movie with him the following Wednesday.

"Yeah, I'd like that," I answered. As he and I walked toward the parking area, I said, "Hey, you don't think of me like a sister, do you?"

He tilted his head as he considered the question. "No, I don't think so. Why?"

"Because a lot of guys I know put me in the sister category and want to protect me or something."

"Protect you from what, them?" He laughed.

"Yeah, maybe. Anyway, I don't want to be your sister."

"Okay." He studied me for a minute. "I'll see you Wednesday."

FIRST DATE

Tim picked me up, and we went to see the movie *Billy Jack*. It was about a guy who was part Native-American and who stood in defense of a counterculture school. The kids in the school had been humiliated, and the female director of the school was raped (surprisingly, this wasn't the scene that got to me). Then the police surrounded Billy at the school. The school's director knew he would be content to let the police kill him. She pleads with him to turn himself in and live. She didn't want him to die and neither did any of the kids. She loved him and so did the students. Live. *Live* for them. (This was the scene that undid me.)

Tears welled up in my eyes. Tim was holding my hand with his hand on my lap. I didn't want to withdraw it and call attention to the tears. Instead, I opened my eyes real wide, hoping that would cause the water to drain. However, one errant tear got away, ran down my cheek, and fell off my cheekbone, and onto Tim's hand.

Startled, his eyes flew to mine. Then he took a handkerchief from his pocket and handed it to me.

"I'm going to get mascara on it," I whispered. (I'd never met a man who carried handkerchiefs.)

"It's okay." He smiled.

When I finished getting eye makeup all over his hanky, he took my hand again.

After the movie, we got something to eat at a fast-food place and sat outside. I gave him back his black-stained handkerchief.

"Thanks. I don't cry very easily. But when I do, like now, even for a few seconds, it'll be evident I've been crying for the rest of the day or night."

He peered at my eyes with his clear blues.

"Am I right?" I asked.

"Yup, you've definitely been crying."

I laughed. I liked this guy. He was honest. Another man might have said, "No, you don't look like you've been crying at all." But he hadn't done that.

We were together almost every night since our first date. We'd go to the Laundromat and wash our clothes. I wouldn't let my underwear share a dryer with his because we didn't know each other that well. Or we'd ride to the beach or walk on the pier and talk, talk, talk.

He waited three weeks to kiss me, and it was worth the wait. He drove up to a beach entrance beyond the pier and asked if I wanted to look at the stars. I said yes, and he went to the front of the VW and pulled a blanket from the trunk. *Uh-oh*, I thought.

But nothing untoward happened. We reclined on the blanket, and he pointed out various stars and their names. I knew the Big Dipper and could sometimes find the little one.

But he pointed to a bright star and said its name was Orion. Then he showed me three stars in a row, called Orion's belt. He told me that if I followed Orion's belt east, I'd find Sirius, the brightest star in the sky. Next, he pointed out the Seven Sisters.

"Wow, they are beautiful. Do the sisters have names?"

"Probably, but I don't know what they are."

"How do you know so much about stars?"

Tim laughed. "I learned what I know in school, but I don't know a lot, only a little." Then he got up and started walking in the sand.

I trailed him, stepping into his footsteps. His stride was longer than mine, and I had trouble keeping my balance as I'd sunk into his steps.

Suddenly he pivoted around, and we were face-to-face. Then he kissed me. I don't remember him reaching for me or me turning upward to meet his lips. The air was cool; his lips were warm. The kiss was not invasive; it was captivating. It was gentle but glowing. And it made me hungry for more.

He pulled away, and we walked back to the blanket in silence. We folded it up and returned to the car. On the way home, he held my hand. I sat amazed at the ease I felt being with him. There were two of me. One sitting comfortably in the front seat of Tim's VW, holding his hand. And another above me in awe of the kiss and the feelings it had invoked. I loved kissing him. It felt like I was falling into him when we kissed, although he had to give me lessons later on how to do it. I didn't mind; I wanted to learn and knew I didn't have much experience.

We started kissing a lot after that night. A week after our first kiss, we were standing in line to get into a restaurant when he said, "Once we're inside, I have something to tell you."

My stomach clinched, and I chewed the corner of my lip. "What? What is it? Is it bad?"

"No, don't assume it's bad."

"Oh, okay. So it's good then?" And I did a little dance.

"No. Don't assume it is either good or bad. It's just something I want to tell you, a statement."

"All right." I smiled, but my mind was jumping from question to question.

Finally, in mid-meal, I asked what it was.

"In July, my brother introduced me to a girl who works in the veterans office at the college. Her name is June. Anyway, she and I began seeing each other. She had already planned a six-month European trip, and she left in September."

"Oookay," I began. *September, a month before I met him.* "Are you in love with her?"

"I don't think so," he replied.

"Well, that's fine because I'm not going to fall in love with you." The minute this came out of my mouth, I knew it wasn't true. I was halfway there. I liked this guy. I really liked him.

"She and I had an enjoyable time. I expect to see her when she returns next year, but that's all." He looked at me steadily with his bright blue eyes.

"Why'd you tell me?"

"I just felt you ought to know."

"Okay, thanks." I did need to know.

But as I contemplated what he'd said that night after he dropped me off, I decided it would not make a difference. The only thing constant is change, so it's okay. All I had was right now, and right now I liked him a lot. It's been six years since Ted, since I felt this way. *I'll enjoy our time together until (and if) we had no time together.*

MEETING THE PARENTS

Tim and I left Pete's Pizza on Friday night and drove to his house, or rather to his parents' house (he had moved in after getting out of the Air Force and enrolling in college). He stopped the VW, turned it off, and said, "I've got a new candle, Pot-cha-poorie or something. It really smells good. Want to come in?"

We'd both had a few beers, and I wondered aloud, "Is this like asking me to come see your etchings?"

"I don't think so," he answered. "It's cold at the beach so we can talk here."

"Okay," I said, following him into the dark house.

In his room, he lit the blue candle. I couldn't identify its ingredients, but it did smell good. We sat at the foot of his bed and talked. Then leaned back, kissed, and talked…

The bright Florida sunlight streaming through his bedroom windows awakened me. I heard people talking beyond his bedroom door. *Oh shit. We fell asleep!* I shook Tim's shoulder and whispered, "Wake up! Tim, wake up! We fell asleep."

"Huh?" he groggily said.

"Please wake up. We fell asleep, and it's umm…" I looked frantically around the room and found his alarm clock. "It's ten in the morning! At your house! Your parents are up. Ohmigod."

He sat up on the edge of the bed then and ran his fingers through his hair.

"Listen, just let me hide under your bed until tonight, and after they're asleep, I'll leave. Please."

"No." He shook his head. "You can't do that."

"Yes, I can! Listen, I *cannot* meet your parents for the first time walking out of your bedroom, I can't."

"Wait, a minute. I'll think of something." Then he got up, went to the door, and said, "I'll be right back."

I wanted to sink into the floor, hightail it out his window, or get under the bed immediately. *Oh shit.* Oh no. No, no, no, no. And what was Kelly thinking? Since I didn't come home last night. *Ohmigod.*

I didn't hear yelling or anything being thrown in the other part of the house. I bit the side of my finger and waited.

At last Tim walked through the door, holding two steaming mugs of coffee.

"What happened?" I asked as he handed me mine.

He calmly said, "I met Dad at the coffeepot and told him I had a girl in the bedroom."

A girl in the bedroom! My mind flew in a thousand different directions. I really wished he'd let me hide under the bed. Finally, I asked, "What'd he say?"

"Nothing," was the answer.

Again, my mind zipped around with a million thoughts. I knew we'd done nothing to be ashamed of last night. But I knew his parents wouldn't think that. I almost wished I could call a doctor to make a house call, examine me, and verify that I had *not* had sex last night. This is *not* how I wanted to meet his parents, but this is how it was going to happen. *Shit.*

"Do you do this often? Have a girl in your bedroom?" Maybe he did, I didn't know.

"No," he answered. "You're the first."

I groaned.

He cleared his throat. "We need to go out there because my soon-to-be ex-wife, her boyfriend, and our kids are coming over at eleven o'clock. They are bringing over my stereo system. They'll be here soon."

You've got to be kidding me! Ohmigod.

He motioned me toward the door, and I followed. He took me to the living room where his mother was sitting in a rattan chair, smoking and drinking coffee.

"Mom, this is Sadie."

"Hi," I barely whispered as I sat in a big black recliner, trying to disappear into the cushion.

She nodded. Then the door burst open, and three little boys bounded into the room. They greeted their grandma and dove toward their dad for a hug. The screen door slammed open and shut, open and shut, as they ran back and forth. Then a very pregnant soon-to-be ex-wife walked inside. She was pretty with dark wavy hair and a nervous smile. Tim had already told me that she had gotten pregnant by another man and had demanded a divorce. Next, the other man walked in the door. Tim introduced them to me as Jeannie and Bob.

I nodded hello.

Next, a little lady swept in the door with a big voice saying hello to the kids. She was their great-grandma, Tim's mother's mother. The boys all hugged her at once and then bolted off in another direction. They were never still or quiet, and everyone talked at once. Tim's mother lit two cigarettes and didn't notice. The great-grandmother looked around the chaotic scene; saw me; and asked Tim's mom, EJ, "Who is that?"

EJ picked up one of her cigarettes, waved it my way, and said, "That's…that's…tha-tha…oh, I'll tell you later."

Ohmigod, I thought. *If they put this scene in a sitcom, people would say it was too outlandish.*

Tim and Bob took the stereo equipment into Tim's bedroom. Unexpectedly, Tim's brother came out of another room yawning and saying, "What's all this noise?"

The three boys screamed, "Uncle Tommy!" and fought each other to get to him first.

After greeting his nephews, Tommy looked around, saw me, and asked if I wanted to sit outside. *Did I ever!* He motioned me to the front door and got a lawn chair for me to sit on in the lawn. Then he got one for himself. "I'm Tommy, by the way."

He looked nothing like his brother, but Tim had talked about Tommy a lot. I could hear the love in his voice. Tommy had long brown hair and was also tall.

"Hi, I'm Sadie." I didn't know how to explain my presence and didn't try.

"It's so noisy in there, I thought you might want to sit outside."

"Yes, thank you."

Just then an older man walked up the driveway.

"Dad," Tommy said, "this is Sadie, and it's bedlam in there. You want to sit out here?"

His father nodded "hi" to me and continued inside.

After about an hour, the stereo had been delivered. The boys, pregnant wife, and boyfriend were gone; and Tim came out to take me home. I explained what happened to Kelly. She'd spent the night next door and hadn't noticed till she came home. Then she thought maybe Tim and I had gone some place early.

"Did you sleep with him?" Kelly asked.

"Yes, fell asleep on his bed and slept with him all night. But that's not what you are asking, is it?"

"No, it isn't," she sighed.

"I fell asleep and slept with him, but no, we didn't have sex."

Kelly smiled.

"But I would have done so. I want to…"

Kelly grimaced. "But you are a Christian! And you always said you'd wait until marriage."

"Yes, I am a Christian. But I never said I'd wait to have sex until marriage, mainly because I never believed I'd get married. I said I wouldn't have sex until every cell inside me wanted to do so. Which was pretty safe to say at the time because I was dead from the nose down. You were the one who said they'd wait until marriage."

Kelly looked worried. "But Sadie, it's forbidden in the Bible. It's a sin."

"Look, I've read the Bible several times, and nowhere does it give a clear ruling that premarital sex is wrong."

Kelly shook her head and started to talk, but I held my finger up.

"Wait, listen for a minute. God doesn't have concise rulings about premarital sex, but it does about adultery. It doesn't mince words there. Folks having sex with somebody who is married to someone else, that's condemned. That's the rule, according to the Bible, that I'm breaking because Tim is married, albeit in the process of divorce. But Jesus didn't believe in divorce, so according to the Bible, I'll still be sinning."

"Well, there you go." Kelly put her hands out palms up and said, "Why are you doing what you know is wrong?"

"Because I'm not sure it's wrong. I won't be having sex indiscriminately. I love this man."

"But you already said Jesus didn't believe in divorce. So you'll be sinning and damning yourself in God's eye."

I was quiet and tired. "Kelly, I believe that God looks at everything individually, and he'll see two people who genuinely care for each other and want to become more intimate."

"You're going to bet your soul on that?"

I got up to go into my bedroom. "Yes, but not on that. I bet on God being huge and compassionate. He knows we are imperfect people trying to find our way…" Before I closed my door, I added, "I love you, Kelly. And I know you don't understand and maybe you never will, but I am going to follow my spirit and heart."

As my door clicked closed, I heard her say, "I'll love you more tomorrow than today." It was something she used to say all the time when I didn't believe in love.

ALL SYSTEMS GO

After two months, I knew I wanted to have a sexual relationship with this man. I wanted him to teach me, to be my first. Late one night, he and I came home to Kelly's and my house, and we began making out on the couch.

After a while, Kelly's voice from her bedroom interrupted us. "Sadie, can you come here a moment?"

I excused myself and met Kelly in the hallway where she held a small lamp in the threatening manner. "I told you never to come here and do that!" she snarled. "I can hear you."

It was true she had asked me not to play kissy-face in her presence. The request came after Tim and I had gone to the beach and looked at the stars and I'd told her about the kiss. She'd been gathering our clothes to take to the Laundromat, and when she picked up my jeans, sand fell out. She looked stricken and said, "I am ashamed of you."

What? I looked at her in astonishment. "Kelly, you're not my mother. You have no right to be either proud or ashamed."

"Well, I am," she huffed. "Just don't ever play kissy-face around me!"

"I won't," I had said.

Now, it seems I had. She was livid. I went back to Tim and told him we had to leave. He didn't question why. We got in his car and drove to the beach and talked. I told him of my promise to Kelly and that I'd broken it.

"But it's your house too," he said.

"I know. But I did promise, but evidently, we were loud."

Tim looked doubtful and said, "Why didn't she close her door?"

"I don't know. It may have been closed. I just don't know."

Then he gave me a huge hug and said, "I'm sorry. I can see it upset you."

"It does, but I'm not sure why."

I forgot it and proceeded to fall into his kisses until I pulled back. "I've never made-out before."

He nodded.

I laughed. "As evidenced by you having to teach me how to kiss. But I sure am enjoying it."

He smiled. "Me too."

"And I've never done anything else either. Absolutely nothing. But now I want to, with you. I want you to teach me."

He looked surprised. "Are you sure?"

"Yes, I'm quite sure."

"Why?" he asked.

That stopped me. *Why*? "Because…um…everything inside me says I want to do this. For the first time in my life, I want this. And I want you to be my teacher…I don't know why exactly."

"I…I think I do," he whispered as he drew me in for a kiss.

After that we placed our hands all over each other every chance we got. And I finally understood what "petting" meant.

FILL-IN GIRLFRIEND

June's scheduled return was at the end of February or first of March. I could tell he liked her and was looking forward to it. At least it wouldn't be a total surprise. I planned on loving him right now. When June showed up, I'd shake his hand and ride off into the sunset or over the rainbow. I loved him, but I didn't own him.

Once he picked me up and as he walked me to his car, he told me I looked really nice.

"Thanks," I said, then I paraphrased a popular car ad on television. "When you're second best, you try harder."

"Don't say that," he said. "You're not second best."

"No, just second. And that's okay."

Another time, he came into a restaurant where I worked part-time and saw me hand a note to a single guy in a booth. "What'd you give him?"

"A note with my phone number. But I told him not to call until the beginning of March. Because I'm filling in for your girlfriend and won't be free till then."

He took his eyes off the road for a minute and glanced at me. "You said what?"

"That I'm filling in for June for now."

"Sadie, you are not filling in. We're seeing each other."

"Right, but just until June comes home."

"You don't know that. Heck, I don't even know that..."

"Look you told me as a kind of warning, and I appreciate it. I like knowing rather than not knowing. And knowing this means I know there is an expiration date..."

Tim shook his head.

"Okay, a *possible* expiration date on our seeing each other."

He sighed. "I've never known anyone else who thinks like you do."

"Really?" I asked, surprised. "I think I'm just being real."

Tim turned the car toward his house. "Well, maybe other people think like you, but they don't say it aloud."

"Hmm...why?"

"I don't know, not wanting the other person to know their game plan..."

"I don't know how to play games. I don't."

"Yes, I can see that."

"But it's a good thing, right?" I smiled.

"I think so," he answered. He said that a lot, but it wasn't annoying because I believed he really thought about it.

6 THERAPY AND THOUGHTS

FOREPLAY

IN HIGH SCHOOL, all the girls had made out and fell in love with someone different every week. It could be normal. And by doing it they learned about sexual sensations and their own reactions.

Tim and I went to his house to work on one of his papers, but that inevitably led to us making out on his bed. As he ran his hands over me, I just lay there, enjoying it. Then he put my hand on a very strategic part of his body. *Oh! Okay...* I explored the sword hidden among his pinions. Something I had never investigated before. Then I started giggling. I knew it wasn't an appropriate time to laugh, and I tried to stop. But that only made me laugh harder. I managed to keep most of the noise down, but my body shook with silent belly laughs.

Finally, Tim stopped what he was doing, leaned up on one elbow, and, with a bewildered look on his face, asked, "What's funny?"

Finally, the inside laughs escaped my mouth and came tumbling out. Each time I tried to catch my breath and answer, a new cascade of laughter began. Finally, I stopped and answered, "It feels just like a chicken neck. You know from a fryer?"

He looked bemused and nodded. "Hmmm…hold that thought," and he kissed me again. "No, forget that thought."

We hadn't been able to be completely intimate because we had no place to go. We couldn't go to mine and Kelly's house, and his parent's house also didn't feel right. I couldn't believe the electric feeling that ran between him and me.

IMPROMPTU MEETING WITH DR. TNUH

I dropped by the college to see Dr. Tnuh at lunchtime, hoping we could talk. He stood and gave me a big hug, saying, "This is a great surprise. What's it been a couple of months since we last talked? How are you?"

"I'm really good. And I'm ba-a-a-ack!"

He laughed and invited me to sit. "What's up?"

I shook my head. "No, that's my line. What's up, Doc?"

"True, I'm the Doc, but you've got a question, right?"

"Kind of… I've met somebody."

Dr. Tnuh nodded.

"A guy. And I really like him. And…ah…I'm no longer dead from the nose down."

His eyebrows rose. "I see. And how do you feel about that?"

"All tingly." I laughed. "I feel good about it. I'm glad to see that I do have sexual feelings. And I'm glad they were awakened by this guy."

"Why this guy?"

"Because he's a really nice person. Not just to me, but to everyone. We volunteer with mentally challenged adults. They love him. That's a true test of someone's inner being because they can uncover a fake faster than anyone."

"And?" Dr. Tnuh said.

"And all my systems say go—and none of my systems have ever fired before."

"We're talking sex. Intercourse, right?"

I felt blood rush to my face. "Yes."

"Okay, I can certainly understand how good this feels—to feel something. Any drawbacks?"

"Yes, his wife is pregnant with someone else's baby. They are divorcing. And he met a girl, before he met me, who is currently in Europe. She'll come back at the beginning of March."

One corner of the doctor's mouth hiked up in a half grin. "And then what? What does she mean to him?"

"What then? I don't know. He doesn't know. He likes her. They hit it off, but he's not in love with her."

"Are you sure?"

"Yes, I believe him, and he's still getting over his marriage."

"True. Okay, worst-case scenario—you let all your systems go with this guy and afterwards he goes back to his wife or with the other girl. How are you then?"

"I've thought about that, and I'd be okay. I mean, I would be brokenhearted, but that's better than being devoid of feelings like I used to be. I...it's...umm...," I stammered.

"Say what comes to mind. If it needs revision, you can do that later."

"I never thought about having an intimate relationship with anyone. I had no sexual urges. I always said that I'd be a virgin until I met someone who turned on all those feelings. That's how I feel now..."

Dr. Tnuh nodded.

"I want to experience sex with someone I trust, feel safe with, and can be honest with. That's him. Will our relationship last? I hope so. But as we've talked many times, there are no guarantees. If we were intimate, and he left the next day...like I said, I'd be sad. But I'd also have had one of the most exciting experiences of my life. One I never thought I'd ever have..."

Dr. Tnuh smiled. "Sounds like you've got your answer. Just as an aside, anything familiar about this guy?"

I laughed and shook my finger at him. "Yes, darn it. He fits the pattern of me choosing guys who are unavailable to me. The first guy I ever went with was a Marine and stationed in another state, as you well know. And the only guy I've ever been in love with was engaged and in the Navy. But, hey, this guy, while getting over a wife and having some kind of relationship with another girl, he's here. Out of the military and in the same state. He's a real living, breathing human man in the flesh…I'd say that's quite an improvement."

Shaking his head, Dr. Tnuh said, "My little student is growing up."

"Yes, I am!"

"You've come a long way from that young woman who walked in and asked me if she were crazy that first day."

"Yes, I have."

"And you've come a long way from that little girl who was physically, verbally, and emotionally abused."

"Ye…wait, emotionally abused?"

The doctor nodded, took off his glasses, and cleaned them with his handkerchief. "Yes, we didn't talk about it specifically but it's part of the other two. Emotional abuse is anyone isolating, confining, or verbally attacking." He paused to look at me. "Using intimidation, humiliation, and anything else with the purpose of crushing your spirit."

"Oh, I can see that."

"Well, think about it sometime. The more you know about what happened to you, the more you can counteract it."

"I will. Thanks so much. I'll be back to visit. You've been a lifesaver."

"No, we just talked. You saved yourself."

EMOTIONAL ABUSE

That night when I couldn't sleep, I thought about what Dr. Tnuh had said about emotional abuse. I reached behind the curtain in my mind and examined how it had happened to me. It was harder to access because it was the environment in which I had lived. It was all around, under, above, as well as pressing on me. It was emotional abuse when my mother pulled a carving knife on my father. In that moment, I was utterly alone. I had no one to turn to because the two most precious people in my world were at war, willing to kill each other. In this instance, my mother was poised to murder my father. However, I'd heard him threaten her many times in the wee hours of the morning. Who do you call when you are five years old? When and the earth under your feet suddenly tilts, splits, and threatens to swallow you whole? I had no one to call and no intrinsic life experience to draw upon. I was beyond scared, sitting in the middle of the sidewalk and crying. It was too much, too big, too scary. And although they immediately forgot their own argument and came to my side. I'd already experienced the fright. Instead of comforting me, they lied to me. They thought I was too little to see the lie. But that lie, "We didn't mean it. We were pretending," made me push the primal fear down, down, down into the depth of my being. I couldn't trust them, and I was too little to bear the terror.

I had to get up from that sidewalk and walk into the house with them. I had to listen to them blame each other for scaring me. All I wanted was someone to hold me close, envelope me in a hug, and tell me, "Everything is going to be okay." I wanted them to *see* my fear and soothe me.

Both my father and mother often told me how proud they were that I was older than my years, more mature. But sometimes I just wanted to be a five-year-old.

Their continual fighting only crystalized my fear. Placing me in the middle of their fights panicked me more. *Stop, stop, stop!* But I had to listen. I had to find the right moment to cry and thereby signal the end of their argument. Not too soon, surely not too late (I didn't want the knife to reappear). These almost nightly sessions added to my fear bank buried deep in my being. I couldn't show my fear. I had to keep myself safe, and I did that by repressing fear.

Then the divorce came. Halleluiah, Amen! Except they asked me to choose. My eight-year-old self was incapable of choosing. Choose my father who I loved but didn't know as well as my mother? Choose my mother who was capable of pulling out a knife when she became angry? Choose my father who never asked me how I was or any other questions? Or choose my mother who asked me how I was feeling? I wanted someone to know how I felt, so even though I couldn't tell her, I chose her.

My father had promised me a trip to Disneyland and a horse if I chose him. Oh, I wanted that horse. I was horse crazy. No one knows how much I wanted that horse. So it is an indication of how much I wanted to be heard that I chose my mother because she did ask how I felt.

She had promised me nothing. She told me to go with the parent I loved the most. So choosing her elicited overwhelming fear that my father would think I loved her more. I drew pictures of rainbows and houses with smoke coming out of the chimneys and give them to my father. My favorite thing to draw was horses, especially my herd that followed me everywhere. But I declined drawing them for my father because I didn't want to remind him of his offer and my refusal. I didn't want to hurt his feelings. I walked an emotional tightrope of trying to let my father know I loved him while not hurting my mother.

During this time, I suffered with frequent stomach-aches. It'd start with a funny taste in the back of my throat and usually end with me throwing up all my stomach contents. My mother would help me change clothes and make sure a trash can was near my bed. But that night they'd argue about who was making me sick. It was my father's fault for not coming home on time or coming home in a bad mood. It was my mother's fault for not taking better care of me. Because it made them angry, I tried not to get a stomachache but that rarely worked. It became all my fault.

My father left, and I was happy that the arguments and my late-night refereeing would end. And I felt guilty because I was glad. I already held myself emotionally culpable for anything bad happening in my family. And by eight years old, I was a veteran of shoving my feelings deep into my interior, where I thought they died. Wow, was I ever wrong!

PRE-CHRISTMAS SURPRISE

I chopped furiously at the base of a live Christmas tree with a steak knife. Kelly was out with friends, and as I waited for Tim to come over, I thought I'd get the tree ready for a stand. I saw the car headlights run across the picture window in the living room. Soon Tim walked into our entryway. My first glimpse of him often brought butterflies to my stomach, and it did this time.

"Hi," he said, jangling his car keys.

Suddenly, *I knew*. It wasn't a guess; I *knew*. I said hi back and hacked harder at the lower branches of the tree, glad I had something to do instead of sitting on the couch.

Tim sat down and asked what I was doing. He thought a steak knife wasn't the best instrument for the job, and I agreed, but we had no saw. Quiet overtook us.

Tim looked at his hands, and a strand of his golden blond hair fell into his face. Absently, he pushed it back behind his ear. I loved his hair, his mane of thick, wavy blond hair. I fully embraced the trend of men having long hair.

Finally, he cleared his throat and said, "I have something to tell you."

"I know. June's back."

His eyes opened in surprise. "How do you know?"

Slashing away at a branch, I answered, "I don't know how I know, but as soon as you walked in the door, I knew."

He nodded.

I jumped up. "Umm, want some coffee?" I went to the adjoining kitchen, put water in a pot, and placed it on the stove.

"No, not really," he answered.

I started to take the pot off the stove; then stopped, sloshing water; and said, "Oh, maybe I'll have some." And I slammed it back on the burner.

Tim came over and wrapped his arms around me. "You never drink coffee at night."

I turned and hugged him. "I know."

He smiled. "Glad you put the knife down."

I nodded. "Yes, but you were never in danger. However, I did try to butcher the poor tree."

He tightened his arms around me. "Want to go for some ice cream?"

"Sure," I answered.

I locked up the house, and we walked to his VW. I got in, and as he turned on the engine, the song "Cherish" came on the radio. I associated the song with my first love and loss. Tears came to my eyes.

Tim glanced at me and said, "What's wrong?"

I pointed at the radio. "Th…th…that song."

He jabbed at the dial and changed the channel. Then "One Is the Loneliest Number" blared through the speakers.

He punched the button to turn the radio off. He peeked over at me and said, "It'll be okay."

I attempted a wobbly smile and nodded. We got ice cream, drove to the beach, and parked where we could see the waves.

"It's okay," I said, turning my ice cream cone. "I knew this day was coming. Now, I'll shake your hand and say, 'It's been nice having you and it's been nice being had.'"

Tim looked stricken.

I laughed. "No, not the 'being had' part. I've enjoyed every moment, and I'm ready to ride off into the sunset and over the rainbow. Like I said, I knew this day would come."

"Don't ride off so fast. I want to keep seeing you."

"You do? What about June?"

"I'll see her too. But something has changed. I sensed it at the airport. I picked her up, and we kissed, and I don't know. Something has changed."

"Changed with you or her?"

"Her, I think. But I don't know, it could be me."

"Okay." I watched the waves run to shore with their bright foam fringe and then scamper back out to sea.

Tim pulled me onto his lap. "You okay? You're quiet."

"Yeah, I'm okay. I just never saw past the sunset and rainbow…"

He looked puzzled.

"The one I was planning to ride off into. I thought June returning was the end…of us. And now…"

"Now?" he prompted.

"Now, I guess it isn't. And riding off into the sunset and over the rainbow will have to wait, and I don't know what that means."

"I'm glad you're staying on this side of the rainbow, and I don't know what it means either."

Then I threw away all thoughts of the rainbow and endings and returned his kisses.

EARLY DECEMBER

The loose group of people who had started volunteering at recreation night decided to form a group. We called ourselves Reach Out. Everyone showed up and brought refreshments for recreation night every Friday. And we committed to having a picnic or an outing once a month and a big event, like a prom or a visit to a theme park, once a year. We held car washes and other events to pay expenses incurred by the group. Tim was voted in as copresident along with another girl, and Reach Out met once a month to plan events.

Tim continued to see both June and me. I kept chanting that the only thing permanent was change and trying to enjoy the moment.

One Monday night at the pizza parlor, Tim told me he had asked June to a play on Wednesday evening. Some expression must have crossed my face because he asked, "What's that?"

"What's what?" I hurriedly answered.

"Your expression, like you were upset or something."

I tore my napkin into little balls and made smiley faces out of them. "No, it's nothing."

Tim lowered his head and looked directly into my eyes. "No, it was definitely something."

I shook my head and tried to stop the increased beating of my heart. My mouth dried up. I thought of Dr. Tnuh. We had talked about my apparent lack of anger, and how he thought it was another emotion I didn't want to feel. I'd vowed not to be like the folks who raised me—and they were all angry. But Dr. Tnuh said anger itself is a feeling and neither good nor bad. It was how you exhibited or acted out your anger that was important.

"Sadie, there are no good or bad answers here. No, good or bad feelings. And I saw some emotion cross your face, and I'd like to know what it was. Please."

Did he just echo what I remembered Dr. Tnuh saying? Ohmigosh. I took a drink of water and licked my lips to stop them from sticking to my teeth. "You're telling me you are taking June out on Wednesday, and that's fine. But I never know what you have planned for us, or even if you do. You just show up that day…"

Tim was quiet. I watched his face, expecting it to turn dark, for heated words to fly out of his mouth or for him to slam his hand down on the table and leave. Instead, he took my hand and squeezed it. "You're right. I have been doing that, and I'm sorry. I'll tell you ahead as much as possible."

I sat stunned. He wasn't angry. He wasn't defensive. He'd listened. "Oh, wow, okay. Thanks."

Then he laughed. "But you are so easy to be spontaneous with…"

I leaned over and gave him a quick kiss. "Yes, and I don't want that to end, but if you know ahead of time, it'd be great if I did too."

"Deal," he said.

I'm in love with this man. I knew he didn't know I was in love with him and he wasn't in love with me. I had no idea where this was going or when it would end. For the first time in my life, I was just going to go with the flow until I found out.

LESSONS FROM AN EX-WIFE

Tim told me his divorce would come through around the first of December. They were parting amicably and neither had lawyers. Jeanne only wanted him to pay $50 for child support. I urged him to get a lawyer or at least get that agreement in writing. In my experience, feelings and agreements could change.

Jeanne and Bob went to the hospital to sign preadmission papers. When circumcision papers were presented with "Baby boy Keyser" on them, Bob became enraged. "It's not baby boy Keyser—it'll be baby boy Lloyd." However, the hospital wouldn't budge. It was policy.

As soon as the divorce was finalized, he and Jeanne applied for a marriage license. They could pick it up after three days. While they waited, Jeanne went into labor. Bob was beside himself because he knew the baby would be registered under Keyser. Jeanne finally got her doctor to give her a couple of shots to stop labor, and it worked. Bob and Jeanne got married as soon as the small waiting period was over. Now, the baby would be a Lloyd.

CHRISTMAS PARTY AT SADIE'S AND KELLY'S HOUSE

Tim picked me up from work, and we rode to his house for him to get ready for the party at my house. I sat in the living room with his parents while waiting. Since waking up in his bedroom a couple of months ago, I felt too embarrassed to say much around them. If only I could have gone to a doctor and gotten a certificate saying I hadn't had sex that night. But now, because I wanted a sexual relationship with him, the point was moot.

I really liked his parents. His dad possessed a quiet strength, and his mother was gregarious and fun. The TV was tuned to some channel that had the Doors featuring the lead singer, Jim Morrison, singing.

"Do you like that singer?" EJ, Tim's mother, asked me.

I glanced at the TV. "He's okay. I saw him live in San Francisco, and he was so stoned he stumbled around the stage and could hardly get the words out."

EJ laughed. "Did anyone demand their ticket back?"

I shook my head. "No, nearly everybody else was stoned too. I wasn't though. But I didn't care as long as I could dance."

Then I found myself comfortably talking about my visit to California. EJ wondered how it compared to the East Coast.

Tim appeared, and I whistled to tell him he looked sharp in his red, white, and blue bell bottoms and blue shirt. He smiled.

"Say, Tim, has Jeanne had her baby? She was due a week or so ago, wasn't she?" EJ asked.

"I don't know. She had the contractions stopped about two weeks ago, so she's overdue. I'll call over there and find out."

He turned to the phone, and his mother said, "I know she really wants a girl this time."

Tim nodded to her, then talked to someone on the other end of the receiver. After he hung up, he shook his head and said, "Yes, she had the baby yesterday. A boy."

EJ said, "Oh, I know she's disappointed. She's wanted a girl ever since your first boy, hasn't she?"

Tim nodded. "Did Sadie talk your ear off while I was getting ready?" he kidded because he knew I'd been tongue-tied around them.

EJ laughed and said, "This is the most I've ever heard her say."

I knew that was true and blushed.

"Ready?" Tim asked, jiggling his keys.

I got up. We said good-bye to his parents and off to the party we went.

Kelly and my house buzzed with music and people dancing and talking. Everyone from Reach Out had appeared. Sometime during the evening, I noticed that Tim was missing and went in search of him. I found him in our laundry room in the dark. I reached my hand up to his face to guide my lips to his mouth, when I found his cheek was wet. *He's crying? Ohmigod...*

"What's wrong?" I whispered.

"I just wish Jeanne could have had a girl. It would have completed her life."

At that moment, I knew what a nice man Tim was. No one would have blamed him if he'd been happy that she had another boy. That after getting pregnant by another man and blowing up the marriage, she didn't get what she wanted. Yet here he was fervently wishing she'd given birth to a girl because it "would complete her life." A million thoughts and feelings ran through me. How could she have ever let him go? I hoped whoever he ended up with in life, even if it wasn't me, would be someone who would be honorable and faithful to him. He deserved that. I'd never met anyone like him before. *I love this man.*

7

CHAPTER

INTIMACY

NEW YEAR

AFTER A ROLLICKING New Year's Eve party, Tim had agreed to drive me to the farm. I needed my father's signature on a paper so I could continue to get financial aid in college that year. I'd gotten my father to sign it last year, and he had grumbled about having to document the fact that he hadn't supported me since the age of eighteen. In reality, he hadn't supported me since I was sixteen years old.

Tim picked me up in his VW. I threw my peach-colored nightgown on top of a case of beer he'd gotten for the party. We planned to spend the night on the way back. It was a relief to be in the car with someone I trusted behind the wheel. Cars were lightweight missiles flying along roadways. Tim had an easy command behind the wheel that relaxed me.

We arrived at the farm; and Aunt Essie took Tim into the living room, handed him a newspaper, and went back to the kitchen. I was told my father was in the bedroom. He sat beside a little table, reading. He put the book aside as I walked in and didn't get up, so I didn't try to hug him.

I handed him the paper. "Don't see why I have to sign this again. I signed it last year."

"Red tape," I offered.

He huffed. "You know, if you'd been a different kind of person, I could have sent you some money now and then."

I nodded and shifted my weight back and forth on my feet. *God, get me out of here!*

He scribbled his name on the appropriate line and handed the paper back to me. "What are your plans now?"

His question confused me. Now, as in now? Or now, as in college? I chose college.

"I plan to go another term and work part-time."

He nodded. "You should think of getting married. You're not getting any younger."

I shook my head.

He stood, "It's true. You'll be twenty-five years old this year. Betty's been married for years and has three or four kids."

I can't believe I'm having this conversation! "I'll marry, or *not marry*, when I decide to do so. Not because of my age, not because of the time or convention, and certainly not because someone else thinks I ought to do so."

My father sighed. "There you go, getting all riled up, and all I did was make a suggestion."

"Well, here's *my* suggestion. I suggest you make none in the future." I glared into his eyes.

He looked away. We walked out and into the hallway as my father hissed, "Might as well not make them. Words are wasted on you. You always do as you please. Go your own way."

We'd reached the living room. Tim stood up, and I introduced him to my father. I could feel he didn't like Tim's long hair and beard. Tim held out his hand to shake my father's, and though he hesitated, my father did shake his hand.

My father and Aunt Essie walked behind us up to the car. I watched Tim get in, turn to the back seat, and move something to the front. I opened the passenger door, and my father spied the case of beer.

"Hope you don't drink that on the way back."

Lordy that! Said by a man who pops his first beer before noon. I didn't answer. Instead, I waved to them. "Thanks for signing the paper. I'll write next month." I had continued to write letters each month to make sure he was okay and so he'd have my address.

They waved as we drove down the driveway to the road. I exhaled as we exited the farm. It felt claustrophobic there, and the air still swirled with anger and angst. Tim dug my nightgown out between his left thigh and door and handed it to me. "Didn't think you'd want him seeing your nightgown strewn over the beer in back."

I blushed. *Ohmigod.*

HOUSTON, WE HAVE TOUCHDOWN

We drove halfway back and stopped for the night. My stomach had butterflies, and my heart raced. *Tonight.*

We ordered Chinese takeout and talked quietly. I asked what he thought of my father and Aunt Essie.

"Didn't have much time to form an opinion," he answered. "Your father sign with no problem?"

"No more than usual. He doesn't like signing it, like he's embarrassed that he hasn't supported me since I was sixteen. But then he said that was my fault because I never listen and always go my own way."

"Yeah, I think I heard the tail end of that as you came down the hall."

"He's right. I do always go my own way. But wrong that I don't listen. He never offered any input when I was younger."

"Why not?"

"Ah, that's the million-dollar question. I don't know."

After eating, Tim turned on the TV and watched the news while I showered. I came out in my peach, empire-waisted, thigh-length gown.

"Umm, you look nice," he said, giving me a kiss on his way to the shower.

He came out of the bathroom with steam streaming off his body, wearing a little red towel wrap I'd given him for Christmas. He sat on the side of the double bed, his honey-suckle hair hanging to his shoulders. His blue eyes were clear with dilated pupils looking at me.

I stood between the curtain and the TV, looking at him…this man I loved. His eyes had no guile. His face held no expectation. His skin was rosy, steam still misted from his shoulders. His chest was muscular and broad. I twisted my hands together and chewed the side of my lip.

"Sadie, nothing is going to happen, unless you want it to happen."

Just the words I needed.

I went to him, pushed him down on the bed, and kissed him. We caressed each other. His hair smelled like fields of wildflowers, his body was fur and fiber, and his kisses were hungry. He'd brushed his teeth, and his mouth tasted like mint. I heard the music of little moans come from both of us. I responded to his touch in ways I never imagined. I tasted his ear, his face, his chest. I felt my skin swelling as his hands explored me. At the last moment, he pulled me over on top of him. I wanted him. I wanted all of him.

Then the buildup heat detonated. My world exploded. My body became its own agent. The fluttering within my center became wings—beating, thrumming, drumming, and pulsing to a crescendo…and gradually subsiding. *Ohmigod, I'm not defective!*

I slid down to Tim's side, cradled by his arm, my head upon his chest. I listened to his heartbeat slow down to a regular rhythm and knew my heart was doing the same.

Ohmigod, my body works! It actually works!

He gave me a sideways hug. "You okay?" he whispered.

"Better than okay," I answered. *Much better.*

RETROSPECT

I'd heard many dreadful stories of many women's first sexual encounter. I know how fortunate I was with my first sexual experience. I don't know if it was the buildup, or if it was because Tim had been married for seven years and knew what he was doing. If my first sexual experience had not been good, it would have proven to me (again) that something was wrong with me. And out of fear and embarrassment, I'd have never tried it again. I hadn't even been aware that I still thought of myself as defective until I silently rejoiced that I wasn't. Again, I was two people. One basking in the afterglow of great lovemaking. The other, apart and in awe of what just happened, grateful for it, and not assuming it always happened that way. Today, I am still grateful, in awe of it, and never take it for granted.

INTIMACY COULD EQUAL PREGNANCY

I wondered how having a sexual relationship might impact us. Being a keen observer most of my life, I'd noticed that when most couples started having sex, they talked less. That didn't happen with Tim and me. We talked just as much as before. He always entertained all of my many questions.

Both of us understood, I could have gotten pregnant that first time. So I immediately made an appointment with a gynecologist to get birth control pills. The thought of having a pelvic exam scared me, but that was the price of obtaining the pills. I got through the exam by pretending I'd done it before. If the doctor didn't know it was my first visit, and my fear, then I could pretend it wasn't—and I felt more in control. It worked because he wrote me out a prescription for birth control pills. The problem with that approach was that I didn't ask any questions. And there was a lot about taking birth control pills I didn't know.

For example, during my first month on the pill, I felt nauseous, especially in the morning when I sometimes threw up. When my first period came, it came like a tidal wave. I bled through a tampon in an hour or less. It was like a faucet had been turned on. The first two days of my period were usually heavy, but this was different. I asked a couple of friends if this had happened to them when they first started taking the pill, and they said it hadn't. I called the prescribing doctor's emergency number. He told me to put my feet up as much as possible and to go to the emergency room if it didn't stop tomorrow. He also changed my birth control prescription to the minipill. I thanked him and asked no questions. The problem resolved itself the next day.

At the end of March, I couldn't afford to buy my birth control pills until I got paid. The next morning I opened the pack and counted. I was five days late. I wanted to be protected, so I took all five pills at once to catch up. I turned on the top left stove burner in preparation for boiling water for coffee, and I quickly got dressed for work. I came back to the kitchen and filled a pot with water, pivoted to put it on the stove, and got dizzy. To brace myself and not fall, I placed my right hand on the red-hot burner. The emergency room said I had second-degree burns and one small area that was third-degree on the edge of my palm. They covered it with a sterile cloth bandage and told me to see my general doctor in a week.

"How'd you fall onto a burner?" the doctor asked.

"Umm…I took five birth control pills a little before it happened."

"Five? All at once?" the nurse asked.

I nodded.

Both the nurse and doctor stopped what they were doing and looked at me, an incredulous look on their faces.

"Why would you do that?" the doctor questioned.

"To catch up. I was five days late."

"What type birth control pill do you take?" the doctor asked.

I rummaged through my purse and brought out the pink round pill holder. "This one."

He looked at it and turned it over a couple of times. "You do know you can't catch up on birth control pills?"

I stared at him in disbelief. Hadn't I just told him I caught up by taking the ones I'd missed?

"What we mean," the nurse began, "is once you've missed a pill, you've thrown the entire menstrual cycle off. And you are unprotected for the rest of the month. There is no catch up."

I looked at her dumbfounded.

"Other things can render you unprotected too. Like forgetting to take one or taking them too far apart. If you usually take your pill at 7:00 a.m., then you need to take it as closely as possible to that time every day. Didn't your pre-scribing doctor tell you this?"

"No." I shook my head. "I never asked."

She patted my hand. "Well, now you know. Don't ever take more than one pill at a time and try to take them every day at the same time."

I nodded.

"I don't think you'll have any ill effects from taking five, but only because you are on the minipill. On the full-strength pill, it'd have been a different story. Never take more than the prescribed dose of *any* medicine without checking with a physician. Even, over-the-counter drugs. It can be dangerous."

I nodded. "Yes, sir. Thank you."

I told Tim about taking five pills at once, and even he knew it wasn't a good thing to do. I warned him that it also meant I was unprotected, pregnancy wise, for the remainder of the month; and we tried to be careful.

CONTINUING AFTER INTIMACY

Tim continued to see June and me, but she moved to Maine in mid-March to work at a ski lodge. After that, we went everywhere together. Before spring break, Tim asked if I wanted to go to Panama City. We'd stay there through the weekend and meet his best Air Force buddy. Of course, I did!

He drove up to my place the morning we were to leave and found me hopping about with two different shoes on my feet.

"I can't decide which to wear. What do you think?" I asked, pointing to my toes.

He studied my feet. The left one wore a white sandal with straps around my ankle. The right one displayed a black minimal sandal with straps across my instep and over my big toe.

"I don't know." He laughed. "Why not wear them like that!"

I looked down. "You know, that would be fun. Why do shoes have to match anyway! Why does anything? Who makes those rules?"

When I looked up, I saw Tim giving me that "*Don't do it*" look. "I was kidding."

"I know. But someday, I hope to have the courage to wear two different shoes if I want." I went into the bedroom and came out wearing the black pair.

Tim gave me a hug.

I met his best friend, Butch, and his girlfriend, Andy; and we played on the beach. I stayed in the shade while Andy had no problem tanning in full sun. At night, being at a motel, with no roommates or parents in the next room, made our nights a virtual sexual playground. Tim had awoken my hidden sexual desire, and I reveled in the awakening.

Either Kelly had become accustomed to Tim and I being in an intimate relationship or she resigned to it. But it was now okay for Tim to sleep over occasionally. Kelly often spent the night next door, with a friend of ours who was divorcing her husband. She had air-conditioning, something our house lacked. Likewise, Tim's parents accepted that he and I were together and let us be alone in his bedroom. We tried not to overstay our welcome at either of these places.

MAY DAY

One May day Tim and I sat in the college cafeteria talking. The side wall was a bank of windows, and the sky was a backdrop of azure blue with a few wispy white clouds daubed in the background. The sun streamed through the windows and into my face. I squinted and tried to dodge the rays, but there was no place to hide.

Unexpectedly, Tim said. "You have green eyes!"

I laughed. "Yes, and they've been green the entire eight months you've known me!"

His face reddened a bit. "And you have red in your hair. I hate red hair."

"Hello, my names Sadie. Nice to meet you, Tim," I said, holding out my hand. "Are you just now seeing this?"

"I guess so. I never noticed before."

"You hate red hair?"

"No, not hate. Never found it attractive."

I studied him. "Well, I guess it's a good thing that my hair is brownish-red or reddish-brown. It only screams red in the sun. In most light, it appears brown."

He nodded. "Your hair color is fine. I meant the screaming orange type of red. That doesn't appeal to me."

"Well, I only had orange hair when I lived with TheLady, Aunt Essie, I mean. She would cut it, perm it, and then send me out into the sun, which resulted in my hair turning orange."

"Perm?"

"Yeah, a permanent to create curls. I got one once a year before school started."

"Why?"

"You know, I could never figure that out. She usually didn't like spending money on me. And she absolutely hated my mother's auburn hair. So why would she do anything to bring out the red in my hair! It's beyond me. She might have done it because I hated it so much. I never wanted false curls or short hair. I wanted enough hair to put in a ponytail."

"What was her reason? I mean, what'd she tell you?"

"Well, she didn't need a reason. But she said she permed it so it'd be easier to keep clean."

"Keep clean?"

"Right. Ridiculous! Because she authorized when I could wash my hair. I didn't dare use her shampoo without permission." I shook my head. "I've stopped trying to figure out her motivations."

"Probably a good thing," Tim said.

ROUND TRIP AWAY FOR ONLY ONE

Tim had planned to drive around the USA after college was out in the summer. I wanted to go with him, but he hadn't asked, and I would not invite myself. He thought he'd drive up to Richmond, Indiana, where he'd grown up and visit his aunt and uncle in Dayton, Ohio. I'd been with him almost every day since October the previous year. His absence would create a sizable hole.

I worked in the parts department of a car dealership, and I got him four new tires with my discount. He wrote me a check for $70 for reimbursement. Something told me not to deposit or cash the check, and I didn't.

I watched him pack his suitcase in his bedroom. I snuck a note into one of his socks that said, "Miss you," for him to find later.

"What time do you think you'll leave?" I asked.

"Oh, probably around nine or ten o'clock. Why?"

"Well, if I know the approximate time, I can run down to the gas station. You know, the one a block from my house on the main road? It's the only road out of town, and I'll watch for you so I can wave to you as you drive by."

Tim stopped packing and searched my eyes.

His look made me uncomfortable. *Did I say something wrong?*

"Sadie," he said softly, "I'm going to come by to say good-bye to you."

Oh! That thought had never occurred to me. I assumed he'd just leave. I remembered a few months back. Reach Out was going to canvass neighborhoods and hand out car wash flyers. Captains had been picked to choose team members, and Tim was one of them. I had stood nervously, twisting a strand of my hair, my mouth dry, and my stomach knotted. *Would he pick me?*

When his time to choose came, he looked over at me and slowly said, "Saaaadie."

Everyone smiled, like it was a foregone conclusion.

Why hadn't I believed he'd come by on his way out of town? Hmm…this, I knew, was all about me and not him. If a close friend had told me her boyfriend was driving right by her house on his way out of town, I'd have assumed he would stop at her place. But not when it's me. I decided to drop by and talk to Dr. Tnuh about it.

The first leg of Tim's trip took him to Atlanta, where he visited his best friend, Butch. A week after he was gone, he asked if I wanted to fly up to meet him. I used my tax-return money to do it. We went to clubs dancing, and he drove me around Atlanta looking at the sights. But all too soon it was time for another good-bye. I flew home on the red-eye with red eyes.

I found it hard to sleep while he was gone, so I took a second job. In the daytime I worked at the car dealership, and at night I worked at a pizza parlor a bicycle ride from my house. It meant peddling down a busy causeway, but I was determined to do it. Unfortunately, it didn't help me sleep. I'd get home after 2:00 a.m. and lie awake. The best sleep came about an hour before my alarm went off. Then I'd drag myself out of bed, jump in the shower, and go back to work.

I did go see Dr. Tnuh one lunchtime. He agreed that me not knowing Tim would choose me or come say good-bye was about me. Life had taught me not to have any expectations or to have low ones, if any, Dr. Tnuh said. But I didn't want to stay hostage to my past; I wanted to change that. But how?

I decided to design a litmus test for myself. What would I tell a friend? I'd bestow whatever problem I'd encountered onto a friend of mine. What would I tell them? When I projected my dilemma onto someone else, I could see the soundest course of action. All my life experience and observations came together when I took me out of the equation. I called it my life litmus test. Dr. Tnuh thought it was an excellent plan.

Dr. Tnuh added. "You won't have to do this forever, Sadie, just until you trust and value yourself as much as you trust and value your friends."

Summer dragged on, hot and heavy. My Reach Out friends knew I was hurting and stepped into the gab, asking me to accompany them here and there. I still went to recreation night at the center, and someone always took me with them to Pete's Pizza. One guy told me he hoped his girlfriend would miss him, if he was gone, as much as I missed Tim. Missing Tim infused the surrounding air. I was like the character in the newspaper comics who walked around with a cloud over his head. My cloud was missing Tim and could be felt by everyone.

Tim wrote me letters. And when he had a return address, I'd reply. He also called occasionally, usually late at night. Toward the end of July, he telephoned from Uncle Phil's house in Ohio and told me he was running low on money. He said he had planned to go to Maine and see June, but now with expenses low, he would not do so. Without doing that, he'd be back by the beginning of August. My heart soared at the thought of seeing him in August, just a week away!

After we hung up, I went back to bed and thought about what he'd said. *Go see June! Hell!* It was the first I'd heard her name since she had moved. The bedroom had one small window, and it was hot. I threw off my sheet, beat my pillow into submission, and planted my head in the middle of it. There was enough moonlight for me to see the ceiling. *Shit!* I didn't want him to go see her! It was too scary. What if he found out he preferred her? What if he stayed there...*shit!*

Finally, I dragged out my newly formed life litmus test. What would I tell a good friend in this situation? I sighed. *Damn.* I'd tell her she needed her boyfriend to be sure, that she wouldn't want him with her if he was still hung up on someone else. I'd tell her that she would want him to be with her only by choice and not by default. *Let him go, and if he comes back, then I'll know.*

I got up, scrambled through my purse, and found the $70 check Tim had written me. I tore it in half and taped it to a piece of paper. Then I wrote him a letter around the check, telling him he had the money now—to go see June in Maine. I sealed, addressed, and stamped the envelope. *I'll see you the end of August, or not.* Then I waited for my alarm to go off. There was no sleeping.

He called the next week to tell me he was driving home the next day. He'd decided not to go to Maine. *What?* He might even get home in time to go to Reach Out's recreation night Friday. *Ohmigosh.* My heart fluttered. I felt giddy. *One week.*

That week took two years! I needed a new outfit and had no money. So I tore my curtains down and made a wraparound pair of pants with a matching halter top out of it. It also felt like I was getting a summer cold. *Can't get sick now!* Kelly offered some leftover antibiotics she had, and I gladly took them.

Friday finally came! Nancy, our neighbor, offered to take me to the rec-center as Kelly would get there late. I put on my new "curtain" pants and top and got in, and we started down the roadway. It was August in Florida and hot, so we had our windows rolled down. I looked over in traffic, and who do I see? Tim in his VW! *Ohmigod!* My heart flew up to my neck, and I danced in the seat. "It's Tim! Look! It's Tim!"

Nancy maneuvered to the lane beside him and waved him over. "You'd better pull up or Sadie's either going to have a heart attack or make me wreck!"

Tim pulled over and got out. And I flew out of the front seat and into his arms, almost knocking him over. *Ohmigod, I can't believe it!*

After I let him go, Nancy gave him a hug. "You coming to Reach Out tonight?"

"Yes, my plan was to go home, take a shower, and head on over there," Tim acknowledged.

"Everyone will be so happy to see you." She looked at us and paused. "And I'll see you *both* at the rec-center because I'm pretty sure Sadie isn't getting back in my car."

I laughed, nodded, and gave Tim another squeeze.

"Yeah, I'll see you there," Tim said as he opened the door for me.

Nancy drove off, and we went to Tim's house where he greeted his parents. They hadn't known he was coming back and were pleasantly surprised.

EJ looked at me. "Sadie, you look like you are about to burst with happiness."

I nodded. It felt like I'd been in a desert walking for a long time and had now found an oasis. Tim and I unpacked his car, went in his bedroom, and closed the door. And kisses led to making love.

"Now, I really need a shower," he said.

"Me too, but I'll make do with a turn at the sink in the bathroom. I'm so glad you're home."

"Me too. Now listen to this song I recorded." He handed me a small recorder. "I really like it," he said as he disappeared into the bathroom. The song was "Too Late to Turn Back Now" by the Cornelius Brothers and Sister Rose.

I listened to it over and over as I waited for him to get out of the shower. What did it mean? Was it a message? A sign? I shook my head. It's a great song, and he likes it. That's all. That's it. It's just a song. I'll know he loves me when he says he does.

I worked hard at not leading myself on by seeing signs and cues everywhere. In the beginning of our relationship, I knew I loved him and he didn't love me. Then I felt as if he loved me but didn't know it yet or hadn't acknowledged it. Then there came a time, before he left, that I felt like he loved me and knew it. But those were just feelings and sometimes feelings lie, so I didn't put them in stone. The only thing I knew for sure were my own emotions, and I loved this man.

He came out of the shower, and we arrived at Reach Out recreation night before it ended. The clients of the center were as joyous seeing Tim as I had been. They all crowded around him and got their turn hugging him. Then the members of Reach Out also hugged him. Afterwards, we all went to Pete's Pizza for beer, food, and camaraderie. I looked around the table of smiling friends and had that feeling, again, that there were two of me. One me was sitting among a group, beside the guy I loved, and another me watching it from above in awe and gratitude. *All is right with my world.*

8

TURBULANCE

MY WORLD CHANGES

OUR NEIGHBOR, NANCY, now divorced from her husband; Kelly; and I were all moving in together. We'd rented a house in a subdivision. I wouldn't be there to help with the move.

Tim and I planned a trip to Juniper, Florida, where my aunt Ruby and uncle Frank now lived. It'd be a good getaway, and I wanted Tim to meet them.

College would begin when we returned. Aunt Ruby and Uncle Frank greeted us with open arms. We spent Labor Day weekend with them. In the evening, Tim would have a beer with Uncle Frank, and I'd talk to Aunt Ruby on the couch.

"You really like this guy, don't you?" Aunt Ruby asked.

"I do. He's a good fella. Wears a white hat."

"I can see that. Has your father met him?"

"Oh yeah, back in January. Tim drove me up to the farm to get a paper signed for college. My father didn't like his long hair. Or maybe he didn't like him because I did."

"Sadie," Aunt Ruby reproached, "don't think that way about your father."

"I'm not angry at him over it. But he…um…and TheLady, I mean Aunt Essie…" I took a deep breath. "I've been talking to a psychologist who has helped a lot."

"Oh, that's good, hon. I was hoping you'd go back. You went to see one once at my house. Remember?"

A wave of disappointment ran through me. How could I forget? I had told him about being raped. He told Aunt Ruby (which I now knew was unethical). And for some reason, Ruby told my father…Oh yeah, I remembered. I shook the feeling off. That was then; this is now.

"I remember." I nodded.

"Couldn't understand why you refused to go back." Aunt Ruby shook her head.

"Well, with this current psychologist, I learned about cognitive dissonance."

Uncle Jack and Tim interrupted us, loudly laughing over something. Aunt Ruby turned back to me. "Cognitive dissonance? I think I've heard of it…what is it?"

I took a breath. "It's when someone, in this case my father, holds two or more contradictory beliefs."

"What belief is that?" she asked.

"In my father's case, he has two contradictory people in his life, myself and Aunt Essie. He gets conflicted pictures of who I am. Am I the blackhearted person Aunt Essie describes? Or am I the girl who has supported herself since she was sixteen, never asks anything of him, and never causes him trouble?"

"Of course, he knows who you are."

I shook my head. "It's not about how well he knows me. The two pictures of me clash in his head. He can't hold both of them in his field of vision. So he goes to great lengths to believe one over the other. To resolve the conflict, he'll choose a vision and ignore anything that challenges that belief."

"Oh, I don't know about that…" Aunt Ruby mused.

"I do. It's the only thing that makes sense."

Uncle Frank stood, loudly yawned, and said, "I'm gonna head to bed."

"Me too." Aunt Ruby added. "It's been a long day. You guys know where you are sleeping?"

"Yes, ma'am." I was in the second bedroom. Tim was on a couch in their sun porch.

"Okay, all your bedding is out there, Tim." Aunt Ruby motioned toward the back of the house.

"Yes, thank you."

We decided to go to bed as well. I went into the guest room and saw Tim's shadow on the window that looked out into the sunroom. After I changed into my nightgown, I opened it. "Hey, stranger."

Tim stood in his underwear with the light behind him. He took my breath away. His hair looked like a golden halo around his head, and his body seemed etched in a gold-leaf outline. He looked like a young Greek god Adonis.

An electric current reverberated between him and me. We were two magnets lured toward the pull. "You'd better crawl in this window," I said. "Now."

Never taking his blue eyes off me, he slowly and quietly made his way inside the room. We fell on the bed and made love. This night was different. We made love in slow motion with a soft glowing mist around us. I asked Tim if he saw the mist. He shook his head no. What was I seeing? It surrounded us and made everything else out of focus. For one tiny moment, I concentrated on the blurred bedside table. It became sharply visible again. But once I shifted my attention back to Tim, everything else blurred. *Maybe this is what high means*, I thought. *I'm high on love.*

Afterwards, I fell asleep with my head on his shoulder. In the wee hours of the morning, he covered me, crawled out the window, back to the sunroom, and went to sleep on the couch.

The next day Aunt Ruby and Uncle Frank drove us around their small town. We had lunch and went back to their house where we watched TV. In the middle of a program, a woman turned to a man and said, "You are madly in love with me." It was a funny line, and we laughed. Then I turned to Tim and said, "You are madly in love with me," meaning it to be the same funny line. But Tim turned to face me and quietly said, "Yes, I am." That scared me into silence.

The next day, driving home, I asked if he remembered what he'd said. He did. He meant it. This should have made me incredibly happy. It was confirmation. It wasn't me leading myself on, yet I felt…I couldn't put my finger on how I felt, but it wasn't happy.

A visit to Dr. Tnuh is in order.

College started the next day, and I ran in to see the doctor at lunch. He motioned me in with a smile as always and waited for me to tell him why I was there. I told him about the whole interaction with Tim, the "You are madly in love with me" line.

"Why am I feeling like this?" I asked him.

Looking over his glasses at me, he asked, "What do you think it means?"

I twisted a piece of hair between my fingers. "I love him. I know that…"

Dr. Tnuh nodded.

"I believe he loves me. I've felt that for a while, but hearing it…" I trailed off.

"Yes, hearing it?"

"It scared me. I think it means I don't think I'm worthy of love. Isn't that sick? Something I've always wanted, now it's here, and I don't think I'm good enough for it! Shit!"

"No, it's not sick. It isn't even unusual coming from your background. You know the answer to this…go on."

"I'm scared."

"Right, what else?"

"Umm, do my life litmus test?"

In my peripheral vision, I watched him nod. "Okay…" I took a deep breath. "I'd tell anyone else to ignore their fear and go with what they know, *love*."

"You don't need me anymore, you know. You've got the tools you need."

"Maybe." I smiled.

"Definitely," he countered. "Now, go live *as if* you believe you deserve this love. Don't let fear make you walk away."

I stood and smoothed my shirt. "I'll do that. And thanks."

THE FLU

I got the flu I had hoped to avoid it. The next morning found me bending over the toilet. I couldn't afford to miss my beginning classes, so I went to school. A friend of mine brought me a soft drink to soothe my stomach, but one look at it made me run for the ladies' room. I could no longer even stand the thought of drinking cola.

Midweek, my period didn't come. I had always been quite regular even before the pill; but now, on the pill, it certainly should have come. *Probably because I'm sick.* Mornings were the worst up until late afternoon. In the evening, I was still nauseated but could function better.

The next week I felt worse. I continued to vomit, and my body ached. My breasts in particular were tender. I could hardly stand to have my shirt or bra touch them. I continued going to school and Reach Out since I no longer thought it was the flu.

Still no sign of my period. Tim was concerned.

"Maybe you are pregnant," he suggested.

In horror, I said. "Oh no, I took all my pills this month and at the right time!"

"Well, you'd better make an appointment with your ob-gyn doctor. You had trouble with the first pill, and maybe something about this pill has caused you to skip a period."

"Right, I should."

"Are you still taking them?"

"Yeah, I didn't know what else to do. I didn't take them for the allotted time. Then started again last Monday when it was time to resume."

"Yeah, you better ask about that."

I made an appointment two weeks ahead with another ob-gyn doctor that a friend had recommended. His office was closer. The lady from the doctor's office didn't think continuing to take the minipill would be a problem.

In the beginning of the next week, I had a two-hour earth science class at eleven o'clock. I felt so tired that I could hardly keep my head up. I sat near the door because the pictures of dissected frogs made me run to the bathroom and heave.

After class, a guy I had helped draft an English paper the previous year ran to catch up with me.

"Are you all right?" he asked.

"Yes, well, no. I'm not feeling that well, but it's not contagious."

"You got a ride home?"

"Not until after 4:00 p.m. when my roommate gets off work. I usually study till then."

"You don't look like you feel like studying. I'll be happy to take you home."

"It's way out Bingham road."

"That's okay. No problem." He pointed toward his car. "I'm parked over there."

I laid my head back on his front seat and concentrated on not getting sick. Finally, he pulled up in my drive and let me out.

"Thanks," I called as he left.

The house was cool, dark, and no one was home. I reclined on the couch and tried to sleep. I must have dosed because soon Nancy and Kelly walked in the door, laughing and talking. They stopped as they saw me sit up.

"Geez, you don't look so good," Kelly said.

"Matches how I feel then."

"You need to eat something, Sadie. You've hardly eaten anything lately," Nancy said.

"I know, but food makes me sick."

"Still, you have to try. It's my turn to make dinner. Think you could eat some chicken and mashed potatoes?"

My stomach lurched at the thought of chicken. "Maybe potatoes."

"Okay, I'll call you when they are ready."

I rested until she called me to the kitchen. I put some mashed potatoes, minus gravy, into a small bowl and went back to the couch. "I can't sit there and smell the chicken."

"Sure, that's okay," Kelly said as she and Nancy brought their plates to the table.

Two bites into the mashed potatoes, and I knew I had to get to the bathroom quick. The closest one was through the kitchen in the garage. I ran out there with my hand over my mouth. Kelly and Nancy followed me. I didn't have time to shut the door before I emptied my stomach of the two mashed potato bites, then came a series of dry heaves.

Kelly handed me a wet washrag when the spasms subsided, and I stood to run cold water in the sink to rinse my mouth.

"Ah, Sadie," Nancy said, pointing to the toilet. "Have you been throwing blood up?"

I looked, and amid the milky substance were strands of bright red.

"I don't think it's blood."

Nancy disagreed. "I think it is. Kelly?"

Kelly peered into the bowl and said, "Yes, it is definitely blood. My father has a stomach ulcer and used to throw it up."

I flushed the toilet. "Well, I see the doctor in another two weeks or so…"

"You need to call him tonight." Nancy pointed to the phone in the kitchen. "Doctor's usually have after-hours answering service. So call."

I went to the kitchen counter, took out the telephone book, and looked up the new doctor's number, Dr. Jones. I took the yellow receiver off the hook of the telephone mounted on the wall and dialed the number.

Kelly and Nancy watched as I told the doctor what had happened and answered his questions. I told him I had an appointment in about two weeks.

I listened to what he said, nodded, said, "Yes, sir," and hung up.

"Well?" Kelly asked.

"He told me to call the office tomorrow, and they'd squeeze me in…"

"Good," Nancy interjected.

"He said it probably is blood…and…" I quit, unable to go on.

"And what?" Kelly asked, looking concerned.

"He said I'm probably not late with my period. I'm most likely pregnant, and my throat lining has thickened due to that, and I've been vomiting so violently it's torn some off." I slumped against the counter.

Kelly looked stricken. "Pregnant."

I shook my head. "I don't think I am. It's got to be something else."

"Well, we'll find out tomorrow."

I nodded and rinsed out the washrag in the kitchen sink to use as a cold compress. "I'm going to bed. See you in the morning."

"Yeah, I'm off tomorrow, and I can take you to the doctors, or you can drive my car," Kelly offered.

I stopped in my tracks and turned around. "Oops, I'd better call Tim and let him know what's going on."

I woke up around 9:00 a.m., and Kelly was already up, drinking coffee.

"Want some?" she offered.

Coffee, like my favorite cola, now made me sick; and I shook my head no. I went to the kitchen, found Dr. Jones's number, and called the office. Kelly followed my every move. I told the receptionist that I'd talked to Dr. Jones last night and he wanted me to be worked into his schedule today.

To my shock, the woman started yelling at me, saying, "How dare you think you could get an appointment the very same day." I started crying. "We're booked up weeks ahead." I gave the phone to Kelly.

She told the woman the doctor had *told* me to *call* today. The lady wouldn't have it and hung up on her. I sniffled, turned to leave, and jumped as the phone rang. I motioned that I wasn't answering it, so Kelly did.

I could tell she was talking to the doctor's office again. She kept saying, "Okay, okay," and finally handed me the phone. I shook my head.

"I don't want to talk to her."

Kelly said, "It's not the same woman. Talk to her. She's going to get you in today."

Tentatively, I said, "Hello?"

"Hi, I am so sorry you were talked to like that. Dr. Jones said someone would be calling to have themselves worked in today. Please, come in to see him, say at 1:30 p.m.?"

"Will I have to talk to *that* lady?" I sniffed.

"No, no, we'll make sure you don't. Come in and sign your name. What is your name?"

"Sadie Brooker."

"Okay, Sadie, come in, sign your name, and I personally will deal with you—front and back office. My name is Sonya, deal?"

"Yes, ma'am," I answered.

"Good, see you later."

NOT THE FLU

At a little before 1:30 p.m. I walked into the crowded doctor's office. There were three women behind the counter. I went to the window and signed my name. And before I could even sit down, a nurse came over to me.

"Hi, Sadie. I'm Sonya. I'll take you to Dr. Jones's office and let you fill out the papers there."

I followed her into an office with a heavy dark desk and two brown leather chairs. She handed me a clipboard with a couple of sheets of paper. All had new-patient information typed across the top. I filled them out and read the print at the bottom. If you had no insurance (and I didn't) and you were pregnant, you would pay $600 to the doctor before delivery. *Six hundred dollars! That's more than I make in a year! Good thing I'm not pregnant.*

Sonya came back in; took the papers; and escorted me to a room, where I sat on the end of an exam table. I bit the skin at the side of my fingers and waited.

Finally, the doctor walked in with a big smile, and I immediately liked him. He had scruffy brown hair, beard stubble on his face, and round glasses like John Lennon wore.

"Hi, Sadie." Glancing at my papers, he said, "So you are almost two weeks late with your period and have hematemesis…"

"Hema—what?" I asked.

"Oh, sorry. Hematemesis is extreme vomiting."

"Right. Yes. I definitely have hematemesis then."

He smiled. "Okay, I'm going to run some tests before I examine you. The nurse will be in to draw some blood. Then I'll get back to you. Okay?"

"Yes, sir," I answered.

"Yes, is good enough. No need to say 'sir' to me. Back in a jiffy," he said as he closed the door.

Sonya drew my blood and handed me a magazine to read while waiting. "Are you okay right now? Nauseated?"

"Yes, but I haven't eaten, so I ought to be okay."

"All right, it won't be long."

I became engrossed reading an article about the Beatles.

Rapidly, Doctor Jones opened the door, swept in, and smiled. "Congratulations, Sadie. You're pregnant."

I froze midway, turning a magazine page. "No, I'm not."

"Yes, you are," he countered.

"No, no. I'm not…" I set the magazine behind me.

Doctor Jones sank to his wheelie-stool, looked at me with concern, and said slowly, "Sadie. I just took your test. The results came back positive. You *are* pregnant."

"No. I can't be. I'm on birth control pills."

"Ah," he said. "Do you have them with you?"

I did, and I handed them to him. "I'm still taking them."

He looked up over his glasses at me. "Well, you can stop now because you *are* pregnant."

I nodded.

"Why are you on the minipill?"

"Because I hemorrhaged with the big one."

"While on the mini, did you have any problems?"

"No," I shook my head. "Well, once I was late buying them and I took five at once to catch up, but that was over six months ago."

His brown eyebrows shot up his forehead. "Hmmm… how were your periods before taking either pill?"

"Good. Timely. If I started on a Tuesday at 2:00 p.m., I'd start my next period exactly four weeks later, on a Tuesday, around 2:00 p.m."

He nodded. "Did you ever have cramps?"

"No, not with my period. Sometimes, I'd have cramping in the middle, between my periods, for no reason at all. But it went away pretty fast."

Dr. Jones nodded again. "Did your cramps originate from the bottom, lower part of your abdomen? Or on the side or what?"

"The side usually." I unconsciously put my hand on the right side of my stomach. "But it could be either side. And like I said, it never lasted long. Sometimes only ten minutes. Why? Is it a sign of something bad?"

"What?" He rolled over and patted my hand. "No, nothing bad. Something pretty natural actually. It sounds like you continued to ovulate while taking the pill."

"But wasn't the pill supposed to stop ovulation?"

"Yes. But birth control pills are relatively new and being improved all the time. The first pill was too strong and caused harmful side effects. The minipill might not have been enough. Also, there are so many interactions that can render the pill void. Like taking some antibiotics…"

I flushed, remembering I'd borrowed Kelly's leftover pills. Tim was due home and I thought I was getting a summer cold. "I took some of those too." I groaned.

"Well, however it happened. It did. You are pregnant, and I'd like to examine you now, if that's all right."

I said yes, and he went to get the nurse.

I was verifiably pregnant. I had a long, narrow pelvis, which could be a problem if the baby was too big; but he'd watch that. I weighed 101 pounds and was 5 feet tall. He gave me a prescription for vitamins and pills to help alleviate what he called morning sickness.

"Will it also help all-day sickness?" I queried.

Dr. Jones laughed. "Yes, it should help that too. On your way out make an appointment for next month. I'll see you each month until you give birth."

I left his office dizzy. *Pregnant. I'm pregnant. Ohmigod, what now?*

Driving home in Kelly's car, I was pulled over by a policeman who said he'd been following me. Not only had I driven through one school zone, I'd blown past *two* different school zones.

I looked at him, standing beside the car with his ticket pad in his hand, and burst into tears. "I just found out I'm pregnant," I wailed.

He took two giant steps back, wrote out the ticket, and stretched his arm to hand it to me like I was contagious.

I tiptoed into the kitchen, went to the wall phone, and called Tim. He answered on the first ring. I could hear music coming from Kelly's bedroom.

"What'd the doctor say?"

"That I'm pregnant."

Silence followed. I waited. I bit my tongue. I wanted to fill in, explain, decipher, or untangle what I'd just said. *Pregnant.*

"Okay. And are you okay? What about throwing up blood?"

"Yes, I'm okay. Some people throw up so much that they rupture part of their esophagus. But he's given me pills that are supposed to help morning sickness, even if it lasts all day."

"Okay, you get a good night's sleep. We'll talk about this tomorrow at school."

I said, "Okay and good night." But sleep wouldn't come. It couldn't because of the barrage of questions in my mind. *Ohmigod, I don't have the flu. I have a baby. I'm in uncharted waters.*

BIG MOVES

Tim and I talked the next day. He wasn't angry. He made plans for us to move in together. He made good on that promise by renting a one-bedroom apartment over a garage on a crescent-shaped road by a school. I packed all my belongings into Tim's VW and moved in the beginning of October.

Everyone in Reach Out congratulated us. We were the first in the group to get pregnant, and all were excited. The clients at rec-night wanted to know where the baby was, and I'd indicate my tummy. Some knew what I meant, and others would shake their heads and walk away.

I went back to Dr. Jones for my second visit in mid-October. Sonya told me that the woman who had yelled at me on the phone no longer worked there; she'd done the same to other people. Sonya weighed me and took my vitals. Then Dr. Jones came in the room with my chart in his hands.

"Sadie, you weigh ninety-six pounds. You've lost weight."

I nodded. "I know. The pills help, but I'm still nauseated, and still get sick a lot. I'm never hungry and even the thought of eating makes me sick."

"Sadie, this is really serious. You cannot lose weight. You should be gaining a couple every month. If this continues, I'll have to put you in the hospital."

"The hospital!" I thought of the $600 we were paying for delivery in monthly installments. I couldn't go in the hospital. "What can I do?"

"You are going to have to eat. Isn't there a period after you get sick that you feel okay until the nausea builds again?"

I nodded.

"Then eat during that time. Eat all through the day and never let your stomach get completely empty. Something will stay down. Think you can do that?"

"Yes," I sighed. "I'll do that, promise."

"Good. I'll see you in a month then with a weight gain."

I continued to go to school, but I made sure I knew where all the bathrooms were. I was taking algebra this term, and math had always been hard for me. The teacher offered to tutor students who needed extra help in the evening. The first night about six of us turned up in his classroom. He began his extra instruction and came to each of our desks to see how we were doing. About fifteen minutes before the end of the session, I had to make a bathroom run in the middle of an algebra problem. After being sick, I walked back into the class nibbling on some crackers.

"Everything okay, Sadie?" he asked. "You sick?"

I nodded. "Well, not sick exactly. Pregnant. I'm pregnant."

The teacher, a tall good-looking man with dark hair and eyes, said, "Pregnant! I thought you were a good girl."

All eyes were on me now. My face heated up, and I knew I was bright red. "I am a nice girl, sir."

He turned toward his desk and said, "Not if you're sleeping around."

I felt sick again but furiously dug more crackers out of my purse.

Finally, class ended. I grabbed my books and made my way to the door with everyone else. One of the guys in class patted my shoulder.

"Sadie, he shouldn't have said that."

I nodded and whispered, "Thanks."

The next week, in my work-study office, as I was filing folders, the lady in charged mentioned that I looked better.

"Better?" I asked.

"Yes, it looks like you've gained some weight. Your face isn't so thin."

"I'm pregnant," I answered.

"Pregnant?" she echoed.

"Yes, and hopefully gaining some weight."

She nodded, and we kept working.

ALTERNATIVES

At the end of my shift, I was called into the dean's office. He sat behind a large desk and motioned for me to sit in front of him.

"Mrs. Galley has told me that you're pregnant. Is that true?"

I nodded and twisted a strand of hair.

"What are your plans? For this baby?"

"Umm…" I began. "Uh…we, the father and I, are living together. The baby's due the twenty-second of May, so we have time to figure this out, I think."

"Are you getting married?"

"No. No, I don't think so…"

His mouth turned down slightly. "Having a baby is serious. You are bringing another life into this world."

I nodded.

"A baby has many needs. Many. And one of them, the most important one, is two stable parents. A father and a mother. Not two grown kids making their way through college, who got together in this 'if it feels good, do it' kind of way. You want the best for your baby, don't you?"

I didn't trust my voice, and my face pulsed with blood. I knew it was bright red. I nodded.

"Studies show that kids grow up best when they have two permanent, grounded parents…married, committed parents in it for the long haul because it takes years to raise a child to adulthood."

I looked at my lap.

"Have you thought about adoption? You could adopt the baby out to a solid and established couple who could give your baby everything it needs?"

My head swung up to meet his eyes. *Adoption…*

He stood and swept his arm toward his door. "Think about it. It'd be for the best."

I stood and backed toward the door.

"If you need any help, I could direct you to some adoption services."

I was at the door now. I nodded, turned, and ran down the hallway in tears. I went out into the grassy public area, found my favorite tree, and sat under it. *Adoption! Shit.*

My stomach churned, and my face burned. Adoption. He talked about it like it was nirvana. But I knew it wasn't always a pot of gold at the end of a rainbow. Aunt Essie had adopted Ned. He'd had two parents until his father died, and she was manipulative and controlling. Diana was adopted, and her parents drank and fought regularly. *Shit.*

I could feel my heart beating furiously within my chest, and I knew my baby could feel it too. I put my hand on my abdomen and lightly rubbed it. *Sorry, baby.* What is best for you? I love your father. I believe he loves me, but is that enough? We are starving college students…I don't want to get married. But will you be called names if we don't legalize it? Hasn't society grown up enough for that to not happen? I hoped so but couldn't count on it. If I can't rely on society accepting you, how can I subject you to it? *Baby, what am I going to do?*

Shit! Then there's me, baby. I'm going to be a mother. Your mother. And I don't know how to be one. I have no models and no guides. Does that mean I have no chance?

Psychology says that if you've been abused as a child, you'll abuse your child. My child. You! I don't want to hurt you. I do want you to have the absolute best...*Oh God.* I put my face in my hands and cried. *Baby, I'm so sorry. I don't know what I'm going to do...* Except I'm not going to adopt you out. Nope. Not doing that...then what? Take a chance on myself as a mother? Can a motherless child ever parent well? I didn't know. I'd never read anything about it other than abused kids becoming abusers. Dr. Jones had mentioned that abortion was now legal...*shit.*

ANOTHER ALTERNATIVE

The beginning of November, I told Tim I needed to talk to him. He could see that something was troubling me, and he pulled me onto his lap.

"What?" he softly asked. I twisted my fingers together until he placed his hand on mine. "Just say it. Whatever it is..."

"I think I ought to get an abortion."

"Abortion? Have you thought this through?"

Had I thought it through? Indeed I had. I knew I'd have to go to New York to get an abortion. A friend of ours had gone earlier. I envisioned taking the train to NYC and getting the abortion. Then coming halfway back and getting off the train. I'd get off in Richmond, Virginia, leave everything and everybody behind and start over. I knew I couldn't come back to *this* city—where I'd fallen in love, where our love had started growing on its own, and where I had decided to kill it.

Tim waited for me to answer. I nodded that I had thought about it.

"I'll support you whatever you decide to do."

"If I have an abortion?"

"You won't do it alone. I'll be with you."

Whoa. That threw a wrench in my plan to get off the train on the way back. "Umm…I'd rather go alone if I do this."

Tim's blue eyes peered deeply into mine.

I was afraid he saw all my scattered thoughts and the outline of my escape or runaway plan.

"No, I won't let you do it alone. We're in this together. But what you decide is entirely up to you. But I'll be beside you every step."

Every step. Ohmigod.

I decided to cross the bridge of going to New York alone later. First, I had to call Dr. Jones's office, which I did, and they made me an appointment for that week. Again, I was ushered into his office. I squirmed in the leather chair in front of his desk before he came in. When he did, it was with a genuine smile.

"Sadie. How are you feeling? Better? Less sick?"

"No, but I'm pretty good at eating anyway now."

"Good, good. Now, Sonya tells me you've decided on an abortion."

"Yes, sir." I answered, my stomach clinching.

He gazed at me through his hippy glasses. Then he glanced at my chart. "This is the beginning of your third month, so we'd have to hurry. Get it scheduled in the next two weeks." He looked at me.

I clawed my forearm and nodded.

"You'd have to go to New York City."

I nodded again.

Then he folded his hands together on his desk and sat back in his chair, studying me. "Let me ask you, Sadie. Will you be aborting a fetus or a baby?"

My eyes filled with tears. "A baby. My baby."

Dr. Jones leaned forward and said softly, "Then you shouldn't get an abortion, Sadie."

I looked into his eyes, and relief flooded my body. I had needed someone to say that. *No abortion.* "Okay. Right. No abortion."

He smiled. "So I'll see you next month? And if you need anything before that, just call."

I said okay, and as I walked down the hall, he called after me. "And relax, Sadie. You look like you are carrying the weight of the world on your shoulders."

"Yes, sir. I mean, yes. Thank you," and I walked to Tim's VW a lot lighter than when I had walked in his office. *I'm sorry, baby, for even thinking of abortion. Forgive me?*

When I got home, Tim was waiting, and I told him what had transpired, that I wasn't getting an abortion. He smiled and gave me a big hug. "Whatever you decide, I'm here."

FIRST BIRD

Right before Thanksgiving, I weighed 103 pounds. So the eating-all-day plan was working although I felt awful all the time. Tim decided we would cook our own turkey that Thanksgiving. Although we would still go to his parents' house in the evening, I felt relieved I would not have to fight Kelly's father's hands at their Thanksgiving table. It would be the first Thanksgiving in a long time that I would not be there.

I knew nothing about cooking a turkey. Tim read the instructions as I faced a bald bird in our kitchen sink.

"Now, put your hand inside the bird and pull out the bag of entrails."

"Are you kidding?" I asked.

"No." He smiled. "The heart, neck, and kidneys are in a bag. Pull them out."

If I'd felt better, I'd have made a joke about the turkey neck, but I didn't.

"Why would they put the poor thing's heart and stuff in a bag?" I said as I hesitated, looking at the turkey, not knowing which end he was talking about.

He pointed and said, "Put your hand in there. And we'll use them to make the dressing and gravy."

"Couldn't we just buy gravy?"

"Buy?" He pretended shock. "No faking here. Go on and pull it out."

Finally, I did, but as I slid the bag out of the cold insides of the bird, my stomach revolted. I ran to the bathroom and threw up. I brushed my teeth before returning to the kitchen.

Tim laughed as he saw me emerge from the doorway, and he handed me a couple of crackers. "Here."

"I'm glad you think it's funny."

"It was kind of."

"It's not. I can throw up water."

"I know. You are in the champion class of vomiting." He laughed again.

I wanted to throw the turkey at him. But doubted I had the strength. Besides, I didn't want him laughing at my ill health. I wanted us to be "super couple." We would be happily ever after. We would be an exceptional twosome. So I reverted to old ways of coping and shoved my irritation down, swallowed it, and pretended it didn't exist. *All is well in my world.*

9 CHAPTER

SINGLE TO MARRIED

FLEEING

AT THE END of November, Nancy and a couple of friends came over for a visit. We sat on the daybed in the living room and laughed and talked. Then Nancy asked Tim if we were going to get married.

Married! No, we're going to live happily ever after.

Tim looked at me and nodded. "Yes. After the college semester is out. Sadie's on a work-study scholarship, and we can't get married until the term is over or else pay for it."

I sat across from them with my legs drawn up with a notebook in my lap and a pen in my hands. I'd been writing a letter to my father. But now I started writing, "No, no, no, no, no," over and over.

"When's the term out?" Nancy asked.

"December 20, I believe."

Nancy took out a purse calendar and looked it up. "Well, the next Saturday is the twenty-third. Right before Christmas. I'll help with plans if you want." She looked at me.

"Plans?" I echoed.

Tim interjected, "Nothing big and very informal. And we'll invite the recreation night clients."

"Okay. Sounds good," Nancy said. "Let me know when you know more."

Tim agreed and walked them to the door. Then he returned to the kitchen table where he was studying.

Married? We can't get married. Why can't we just live like this forever? I tore the paper out of the notebook, wadded it up, and threw it away. I was getting a headache.

"I'm going to bed," I said. I gave him a kiss and went into our bedroom. Thankfully, being pregnant was extremely tiring, and I went to sleep.

In mid-December, Tim told me to call around to churches to see if we could be married in any of them on the twenty-third. I called various denominations. But they wanted us to take some classes or counselling before they'd preform a marriage ceremony. In a way, I was relieved. We could just stay like we were.

Then I remembered his ex-wife and how a baby born to an unwed mother would have the mother's last name. *Maybe it's changed.* I called the hospital affiliated with Dr. Jones, and they informed me the law was the same. Any baby born to an unwed mother had the mother's last name. Period. *Heck!* I didn't want my baby to be born a Brooker. I hadn't had a good time with that last name and didn't want to burden my baby with it. I wondered how one changed their name all together. I had no idea.

That evening Tim started talking to me about getting married. I said I didn't want to.

"Let's just stay like this." I offered, shoving down the thought of my baby's last name.

He pulled me into the bedroom and reclined, holding me in his arms. "We would probably have gotten married a couple years from now anyway," he offered.

"Well, let's wait till then." I smiled.

"No, let's not," Tim said.

"I don't want to get married now while I'm pregnant. People will think you were forced into it. A shotgun wedding."

"We'll know it's not. Our friend's will know. And nobody else matters. Okay?"

I shook my head.

"How about Saturday the twenty-third? At the park. The Indian Mound. We'll ride around, and invite everyone we know. I've got an insurance guy who will marry us."

The whole time he was talking, I was thinking of all the reasons not to get married. I couldn't do this to him. I couldn't get married while pregnant. I had never thought much of marriage. But I'd always said that *if* I married, I would never divorce. Never. Some part of me knew the only way to be sure you'd never divorce was never to marry.

"What do you say?" Tim prompted.

"I say I've never seen any good marriages."

"Not even one?"

Kelly's aunt Ann and uncle Harold came into my mind's eye. "Maybe one."

"That's good enough odds for me then! And we'll have a good marriage."

"I don't want a good marriage," I countered. "I want a great one, otherwise why bother."

"Okay, we'll have a great one then."

I couldn't talk him out of it, so I nodded. Then I went to the couch, got my notebook, and started writing him a good-bye note.

He came out and said, "Hey, I think I'll go get us some ice cream? You okay?"

I could tell he felt my unease. I quit writing and smiled big. "Yeah, that'd be great! Always have room for ice cream."

As soon as he left, I quickly finished my note, placed it on the kitchen table, and grabbed my coat and hat as it was a frigid wintry night. Then I walked down the twenty-three steps of our apartment. I had no plan and no idea where I was going. I wandered down back streets trying to figure it out. *Brrr, it's cold.*

I could pass time in a movie. It'd be warm and give me some time to think. No, I only had $5.00 to my name and couldn't spend most of it on a ticket. Everyone I thought of calling was in Reach Out and friends of both of us. They'd try to talk me out of it and tell Tim where I was.

I know, I'll go sleep on one of the benches at the park. Crestlake Park. It was a long walk, but I could make it. I shivered in my coat. No, I can't. I could freeze to death. And although I might not mind, I did have a baby to think about. *Sorry, baby.* I seemed to be apologizing a lot to him/her. *Sorry.* And the park has alligators. And I thought I could get arrested. My mother had gotten arrested for sleeping on a park bench. But that was California. Still, I didn't want to chance it. Finally, the cold forced me into a diner close to our apartment, where I ordered a cup of tea.

As I warmed my hands on the cup, I looked at the other diners. Most of them were elderly. I watched a couple who held hands across the table. Was it true that love could not only last but grow through the years? I didn't know. My mother had always said never to be afraid to try. Dr. Tnuh, what would he say? Oh right, my life litmus test. I sighed. What would I tell a friend in my position? I'd tell her to go for it, to believe him, to not think of failing but of trying.

I finished my tea. It was time to go back, go home to Tim. His car was in the parking spot, and I quietly walked up the stairs to our door. Through the window, I could see him, his back to me, talking on the phone. I took a breath and opened the door while removing the hat from my head. He turned around with his face twisted in distress. As he saw me, he absently hung up the phone.

"Sadie," he said, at the same time I said, "I had nowhere to go."

In two steps he reached me and enveloped me in a bear hug. "What's wrong? I thought we talked it all out?"

He let me go and helped me take my coat off while waiting for an answer.

"I know. Sorry, I just kept thinking of all the reasons we shouldn't marry while you were listing all the reasons we could."

He smiled and led me to the couch. "And now?"

"Now…" I gulped. "I don't know." I twisted my hands together and started to bite my fingernail.

He drew my hand into his. "There are no guarantees. But if we both give marriage our best…"

"Yes," I agreed. "We have to give it our best. For us and for the baby." I patted my abdomen.

"We will," he confirmed, then drew me into a hug.

Ohmigod, I'm in uncharted territory again.

KISMET

The next day, two things happened that if they'd happened the day before, I'd have been gone. First, as we drove to Tim's parent's house, I saw a bunch of young people outside planting a sign in a front yard. It was a shelter for young people who had nowhere to go. If I'd known about it the night before, I'd have walked there.

Second, came a letter from my brother with a one-way ticket to California in it. We were in the car when I opened it.

"Ohmigod, Tim, look at this! Dan sent me a ticket to California!" I waved it in the air.

"Really? What's he say?"

I scanned the letter. "He invited me out to his house with him and his wife, Jane. They could help me until I had the baby and got on my feet." I put the ticket in the envelope with the letter. "This is your chance, Timothy. If you don't want to get married, it's okay. I can go to California and have this baby. We could be happy there."

He glanced over and took my hand. "Nope. Come the twenty-third, we are getting married. That was nice of your brother, but your home is here with me."

I believed him and tucked the letter away.

I called my father eight days before our scheduled wedding at the park on the twenty-third. I used the office at the recreation center. Surprisingly, he answered the phone. Usually, TheLady answered.

"Uh…hi," I stumbled. "This is your dau…this is Sadie."

"Hello."

"Yes, well," I continued. "How are you?"

"Good, and you?"

"I'm good too. Umm, how's Aunt Essie?"

"She's fine. What's this about, Sadie?"

I took a deep breath. "I'm getting married a week from tomorrow, at four o'clock in the afternoon…"

"Oh? That's great. I wish you all the luck in the world."

"Thanks. Do you think you could come? On the twenty-third?"

"No, no, I don't think so. But we wish you well. We really do. Thanks for calling." His usual line before hanging up.

"Wait! Wait," I blurted out. "Don't you want to know who I'm marrying?" I was gripping the receiver so tightly that my hand hurt.

After a pause, he said, "Yeah, who?"

"Tim, Tim Keyser. You met him last January. When he drove me there to get the paper signed."

"Oh, okay then. Well, like I said, good luck. Thanks for calling."

He'd hung up. I hadn't expected him to come. *So why am I disappointed?* I chewed my lip and wondered what I was going to tell Kelly and Tim when I left the office? I knew he wouldn't come to see me get married. But I had thought he'd at least be interested in who I was marrying, ask some questions, have a comment…something.

When I closed the office door behind me, Kelly and Tim were waiting in the hallway.

Tim gave me a questioning look, and Kelly rushed forward, saying, "What'd he say?"

I squared my shoulders. "Oh, they are busy next weekend and can't make it. Maybe if I'd asked earlier…"

"Oh, that's too bad," Kelly said.

Tim said nothing as we walked back into the rec-hall. *And they really are busy next weekend, busy not coming.*

> December 23, 1972, Timothy L. Keyser and Sadie Brooker married, and she happily took his last name. She wore a long yellow dress with orange and red flowers. Many friends and clients of the rec-center surrounded her. The only person she didn't know was the insurance man who pronounced them husband and wife. They were the last to leave the party given to them at Nancy and Kelly's house.

A new beginning, but I would be dragging the past with me.

RETROSPECT

Looking back, it looks as if something, the fates, the gods, or kismet wanted us to get married. Did God or the gods go out of their way to encourage this scared young woman to marry? There may be many who would disagree, but I can't see it any other way. I met the most remarkable man ever, Tim. And my first time making love to him was phenomenal. How fortunate that I met a man who was kind and patient. How auspicious that I could allow myself to open up and be vulnerable with him. I don't see that as luck. It seems divine.

I ended up marrying this wonderful man. Something I'd have never done if I had not become pregnant. I know folks are objecting. Saying God would not condone a young woman getting pregnant out of wedlock so that she would wed. Again, I can't see it any other way. That's the way it happened, and it was to my betterment. God sees our hearts. God certainly knew mine. And I am so grateful.

FORETHOUGHT

I didn't know how to be a mother or how to be a wife. So I did what I'd done in the past: I reverted to pretending. Just like I used to do when I'd walk in a new school with "new girl" written all over me. Just like I did when I went to the first gynecologist. I had learned to do it as a kid, and I did it well. Now, I applied that to becoming a mother and a wife. From the outside I looked like still waters, like I knew what I was doing. On the inside, I was a churning, rapid waterway, always thinking, double-guessing, and doubting. If few people saw this, it was because I'd become good at pretending and I didn't want them to see.

FEAR AND REGRESSION

Tim went to school in January after we got married. I'd lost my work scholarship, and I went to work. After many conversations with Tim, I applied for a job at a small community hospital. I told him I wanted the job but didn't think

I could get it. I wasn't sure I could do it and was afraid being pregnant would also be a reason they would not hire me.

Tim became my Dr. Tnuh, listening to my self-doubts and challenging them.

"You've done that kind of work before. That's good because they will want someone with experience. Of course, you can do the work. You've done it before, and any details specific to that hospital, you'll learn. As for being pregnant, let them tell you they do or do not want you…don't pre-decide a negative."

"Pre-decide a negative?" I asked.

"Don't fail to apply because you think you'll know what they decide. Give them the facts and let them decide."

"Oh." I smiled. "Like turning fail into try."

"Exactly."

I got the job.

Our first fight was the stereotypical one about toilet paper. I used the last of the roll and congratulated myself on remembering to put another one in its place. Something I didn't always do.

I was in the living room when Tim came barreling out.

"Did you see what you did with the toilet paper?" His face was flushed, and his nostrils flared.

"I put a new one on the roll."

"Yes, but did you see how you did it?" He pointed toward the bathroom.

What, did it fall off the holder after I left? I went into the small room with Tim right behind me. The toilet paper was still on the roll, hanging from the wall. I couldn't understand why he was so upset. "What?" I asked.

"You put it on backwards!"

"Backwards?"

"Yes, you put the loose end facing the wall. It's supposed to face outward!" He pushed past me and jerked the roll off the holder.

I went into our bedroom, laid down, and pulled a pillow over my face and cried. *Ohmigod, he's so angry.* When I finally removed the pillow, he was standing by the window.

"I shouldn't have gotten so mad." He sat on the end of the bed. "I'm sorry."

"That's the way I was taught to put it on," I sniffed.

"It's just easier to find the loose end if it faces outward. I should have asked you about it."

I sat up. I smiled at him. "That's okay. I'll do it like that from now on."

"Again, I'm sorry," he said, walking out of the room.

He meant it. But I never wanted to make him angry again. *See! I don't know how to be married.* From there on out, I vowed to anticipate his every need, to stop any annoyance, he might have before he had it. I'd have to watch myself.

ONWARD

I grew more pregnant with each month that passed. In December, I felt the baby move for the first time. I was ecstatic. Tim took it in stride. *It's because he's already had three babies; he knows the ropes.* I tried to rein in my excitement around him.

In January, I started wearing some maternity tops. I still felt nauseated every day and still fought a war with eating and keeping it down. In February, I could still wear some of my old clothes but I was definitely growing out of them. I had one pair of maternity pants and three tops, and that would have to do.

In April, we went to Panama City again and met Butch and Andie. I didn't play on the beach this time. I hid in the air-conditioning and slept. The baby kept getting hiccups, and I would unconsciously drink more water when it happened.

I started having less morning sickness by the end of April. But then I started fainting and feeling faint. In my May visit to Dr. Jones, after my exam, when he told me my baby hadn't dropped yet, whatever that meant. I told him how I was feeling. He had Sonya take some blood to run some tests. As I walked down the hall to exit his office, Dr. Jones yelled from one of his exam rooms. "Take your iron pills, Sadie. You are anemic."

I hurried out. I tried to take those big old horse-sized pills, but the aftertaste made my stomach hurl. But I assured Sonya I would faithfully take them now. She said anemia was causing me to feel faint.

The beginning of May, Tim got a job surveying for the summer and had to be up at 5:00 a.m. I jumped up the first few mornings with him, asking if he wanted me to make his lunch. He told me he could make his own lunch and to go back to bed. But I still woke up every morning in case he needed me for something. *That's what wives do.* After he drove off, I'd go back to sleep. I was now on maternity leave from the hospital.

The second week in May, I called my father to tell him he was going to be a grandfather. Aunt Essie answered, and I told her they would become grandparents later in the month. She thanked me for waiting until the end to tell them.

May 22 came and went, and I was still pregnant and not feeling happy about it.

Friends would see me and say, "Oh, you're still pregnant."

And I'd snap back, "No, I had the baby last week! But I want to look like this, so I stuffed a basketball up my shirt."

Word got around our group quickly not to ask me that.

Once, I got up in the night to go to the latrine. To get to the toilet, you had to make a sharp right turn between the tub and sink to reach the toilet at the end. That night, I turned too sharply and fell into the bathtub, butt first. My feet were sticking up in the air, and I could get no leverage to crawl out. I was stuck! I called and called Tim to wake him, but he could sleep through a cattle stampede. Finally, I grabbed the shower curtain, pulled on it; and as it tore and went snap, snap, snap, I managed to get myself out.

As soon as Tim opened his eyes, I apologized for the shower curtain, promising to buy another one out of my next check. He groggily nodded, then went in the bathroom. When he came out, he said, "Wow. I had no idea what you were talking about."

"Yes, sorry."

"You got stuck in the tub?" He was starting to laugh.

"Yes. I turned too quickly."

He burst out laughing. "Sorr…ha-ha, sorry…," he tried to say.

I guessed him laughing about it was better than being angry, and I shrugged.

"You've got to admit, Sadie. The picture of a very pregnant you, stuck in the tub, with your feet sticking up is funny."

I nodded and made a chuckling noise. I could see how it could be funny to him, but to me it had been seriously scary because I'd been afraid, he'd be angry. So, while it wasn't humorous, it was a relief.

Tim graduated from junior college in May, and I (with Kyle in utero) cheered him on. I had mixed feelings about him graduating. I was glad he had but wished I was as well. Yet another part of me was relieved, I wasn't going because I was still afraid of being stupid.

JUNE FIFTH

I woke up at 5:00 a.m., Tuesday morning, when Tim did, but stayed in bed and pretended to sleep. He kept insisting I did not need to get up with him in the mornings. He was perfectly capable of getting himself off to work. But I thought good wives stayed alert to their husband's needs. So I silently stayed awake and waited for some time when he might need me.

He quietly closed the door, and I heard him start the car and drive away at 5:30 a.m. My abdomen had been contracting irregularly for a couple of hours. *It can't be labor.* It didn't hurt, but it was uncomfortable enough that I couldn't go back to sleep. I got up and wandered around our small apartment. I felt my stomach becoming hard and then relaxing now and then, along with a dull ache in my lower back. I rubbed my back and wished I had someone to call who'd had a baby so I could ask about this. I looked toward the ceiling. *This is when I could use a mom.*

I didn't want to eat or drink anything, so I brushed my teeth and paced the living room. *Who can I call?* No one in Reach Out had delivered a baby, and I didn't want to ask Tim's mom because I wanted her to think I knew all about this. I had read *Dr. Spock's Baby and Child Care* book over and over. I'd dog-eared pages and highlighted sections; still, I felt unprepared.

At 6:00 a.m., I called Dr. Jones's emergency number. Because I might be in labor, the service connected me to him at his house.

"Hello? Dr. Jones, I'm sorry to be calling you so early."

"It's okay, Sadie. I'm due to get up now anyway. What's happening?"

"Well, my stomach has been getting hard, then relaxing for hours now. And my back aches, I don't know what it is.

But I can't be in labor because I'm not screaming and crying like they do on TV."

"Hmm, Sadie. You are two weeks overdue. Why don't you go to the hospital and let us determine what's happening?"

"Oh, okay. I'll have to call my husband's supervisor to go get him out of the field so he can come home and drive me to the hospital."

"That's fine. I'll see you there."

"Umm, okay, I guess."

"Sadie, everything's going to be okay. Don't worry. I'll see you in a couple of hours."

"Yes, Dr. Jones, I'll get there. Bye."

I sat on the daybed with the phone beside me. *I'm scared. Shit, I'm so scared.* I swallowed my fear and dialed Tim's work number.

A man answered with the name of the company.

"Hi, my name is Sadie Brook...Keyser, Sadie Keyser. And I might be in labor and need you to tell my husband so he can drive me to the hospital."

"Ohmigod, okay. Right. Tim Keyser. I'll have to drive over to where he is and get him. Ohmigod. Will you be okay while I get him?"

"Yes, I think so." I felt compelled to reassure him. "Listen, I'm fine. I've got plenty of time. No problem. Just get him to come home."

"Yes, yes, I'll do that. Right now. Ohmigod. Okay, you take care now."

And with that, he was off to find my husband. I lay back in bed and tried to rest, but mild cramps and my backache wouldn't let me. I got up and paced some more. I checked my small suitcase with clean underwear, a nightgown, and Dr. Spock's book nestled inside it. *Yup, I'm ready.*

An hour later, around 8:00 a.m., Tim walked in the door.

"Phew," he said, "I heard a baby crying as I came up the walk, and it scared me for a minute. I thought you'd had the baby alone in here." He eyed my huge stomach beneath my caftan.

"Nope, no baby here. Yet. I'm not even sure I'm in labor. But Dr. Jones told me to go to the hospital."

"Okay," he said, picking up my suitcase. "You got everything you need?"

As we walked out of the apartment, I answered, "Yes, except for a name. We haven't decided on one."

"I thought we'd settled on Cierra if it was a girl."

"Yes, but we never came up with a boy's name. And you tend to throw boys."

We got in the VW, and we drove out of our crescent road onto the small two-lane road that would take us toward the hospital.

"Yeah," he answered, taking my hand. "We didn't, did we?"

"Nope, and all the good names are taken by your three boys—Michael, Jeffery, and David. And you don't want Timothy…"

He shook his head. "No. No juniors."

"Right. So we are without a name." Just then I saw and pointed to a billboard advertising Kyle's Clock Shop. "Oh, look. I like that name. Kyle. What about that, if it's a boy."

"Kyle," he tried it on his tongue. "Kyle Keyser. Yes, I think that would be good." He smiled.

"Now, middle name. Your brother or mine, Dan or Tom?"

"Kyle Thomas…Kyle Daniel. Nope, doesn't fit. How about your father?"

I looked at him askance. "No."

We drove into the hospital's parking lot.

"Well, we don't have to decide right now."

I got out of the car, took his arm, and waddled toward the automatic double doors. "Except I want to decide. How about David? After your father? I know one of your boys is named that, but this would be a middle name."

"Sure." He nodded. "That would be fine. And Mikey, his name is Michael David, then there is Jeffery Scott, David Patrick."

"Well, I still like it and it's only a middle name. Your dad should feel flattered having three of your kids named after him."

We went through the door, told the receptionist why we were there, and I was put in a wheelchair. I told them I could walk, but they said it was policy. The intern holding my chair told me to tell my husband good-bye, that I would see him later.

Tim leaned down to give me a kiss. "Okay, Kyle David if it's a boy."

I nodded. Then I was whisked back to a room with an exam table. Nurses busily got me in a gown, took my vitals, and helped me lie down.

I answered questions, signed my name, and watched the bustle.

"Dr. Jones will be here shortly. If you need anything, push that button." She pointed to a rectangular box hanging from the top of the table.

"Okay," I answered.

Dr. Jones walked in the door with his customary smile. "Sadie! How are you?"

"I guess you'll tell me."

"Okay, put your feet in the stirrups," he said as he put gloves on. "Let me take a look."

Obediently, I planted my feet in the cold metal. The entire lower part of my body was shaking. I put my hands on my thighs to try to stop the quaking.

Dr. Jones turned around, looked at me, and walked around to the head of the table at eye level with me. "Sadie, are you okay?"

"Yes, sir," I said through clenched teeth.

"Are you in pain?"

"No, sir."

He watched me for a minute. "Sadie, I've delivered many babies. And you are going to do fine. Don't be scared."

"I'm not, really, I'm not."

He watched me for a moment, then patted my hand. "It's okay if you are. As a first-time mother, you are entitled. Just remember, you are in good hands...these hands." He held them up. "Now, let's get this baby born. Okay?"

"Yes, sir."

He examined me. Then stood up and said, "I'm going to break your amniotic sac. Nothing to be afraid of. You'll feel a rush of warm fluid, that's all."

I clamped my teeth together, determined not to make a sound. *I'm going to white-knuckle myself through all of this.*

I felt the gush of water and hoped baby and I were on our way to meeting each other.

"Okay, now we'll admit you to a labor and delivery room. Anything you need, just ask. The nurses will keep me appraised of your progress, and I'll be checking on you." He smiled, turned his gloves inside out, and threw them away. "It's a fine day to have a baby," he said as he left.

A nurse came in, put me back in a wheelchair, and pushed me into a room with one bed.

"Here you go, upsy daisy. There's the nurse call button. Now we wait."

I nodded and arranged the surrounding sheet, and my hands shook.

"You cold? Want a blanket?"

I nodded.

Time passed without me being aware of it. Cramps eventually turned into contractions, but worse was my backache. I felt attacked from the front and back. My back pulsed with soreness between contractions and burst into severe pain during them. I constantly twisted my hand around to rub it. The nurse asked if I was experiencing back pain. When I nodded, she rubbed the small of my back. That felt so good. It felt like my baby was fighting to come out of my back, which I thought was a little misdirected.

I heard women coming into the room next to mine. They were usually screaming, cursing, and crying. Two of them came in and went out while I was drifting in and out of sleep. I heard the nurses tell them to stop bearing down. Usually right after that, they were wheeled into the delivery room where they had their baby. I heard a third woman being wheeled into the next room, and I fell asleep.

I awoke to find Dr. Jones reading the newspaper by my bed. When he saw me awake, he stood and came over to my side. "Your contractions have slowed down. We're going to give you Pitocin to help speed up your labor."

I nodded.

"You may have to have a cesarean section. The nurse will bring you the papers to sign."

Again, I nodded.

"I'll keep checking on you. Don't worry." He smiled. "Try to relax. I know that's easy to say, but the psychological stress from being acutely afraid of labor can slow it down. That stress could be caused from just fear of pain to sexual abuse in the past. We don't want it to slow down, so again, please try to relax. This is all normal. Okay?"

I nodded and flashed a weak smile.

The nurse put the new drug in my IV line. "That should help, hon. And I'll get a hot water bottle for your back."

Oh, that would be heaven. I heard the voices in the next room tell the lady not to push. I had absolutely no urge to do so, but the other women who had pushed had already delivered. So I pushed, but only when the nurses were not around.

The drug started my contractions and back pain again. *Good.* About three hours later, my bed was being pushed down the hall to the delivery room. I watched the lights zip by overhead. I didn't know if I was having a cesarean or natural birth. My heart was racing, and I would not unclench my teeth to ask.

In the delivery room, I was asked to move over onto the table, which I did. Then they grabbed my feet and tried to put them in stirrups that were way too far apart. I couldn't flex out that far, but I wouldn't open my mouth to say anything. Finally, I heard another woman's voice say, "Bring the stirrups in." That solved it, and my feet were planted firmly in the metal cups. I could feel myself trembling. I heard the anesthesiologist at my head say, "Now, I'm going to put this mask on your face to help you sleep. Breathe deeply."

As his hand was coming toward my head, I grabbed it and the mask, placed it on my mouth, and sucked in big gulps of air.

I can still hear voices! Ohmigod, I'm not out yet.

A voice awoke me, for what seemed like a short time later, saying, "Hey, wake up. You have a baby boy." I registered that. Then the voice said, "She could care." And I went back to sleep.

Later, I woke up in another unit of the hospital. A nurse welcomed me back to the world and said, "You are in intensive care. You had a rough time and have had to get some blood transfusions. She pointed to the IV pole. This is your second one. Your baby is fine, and we'll bring him to you shortly. Any questions?"

My mouth was dry. "Where's my husband?"

"He's here. We'll let him come in to see you if you feel up to it."

I nodded.

Quickly, Tim was beside me. Groggily, I asked if he'd seen the baby.

"Yeah, he's cute. A little beat up, but fine. Eight pounds! Wow!"

"Yes, wow. Ouch."

"I know, Dr. Jones said you had a very hard time in there."

I'd been asleep, but waking up in the ICU made sense now. I nodded. I kept falling in and out of consciousness. I couldn't seem to stay awake.

He said he was going to go, and gave me a kiss. "I'll tell Nancy and Kelly."

It was impossible to rest because nurses would push on my abdomen every fifteen minutes or so for the next three hours. The goal was to get my uterus to shrink from the size that holds an eight-pound baby to the size of a cantaloupe. *Ohmigosh! Painful!* If I could have gotten up, I would have punched them and left.

Finally, a nurse brought me my baby. She held him up for me to see. They didn't want to chance me holding him. He had a black eye and a swollen face.

"Is he okay?" I asked.

"Yes," she said. "He's fine."

"Let me count his toes." That was something mothers always did on TV.

She carefully unwrapped his feet.

I would count to six or seven and lose count and start over. Finally, I asked, "Can you count for me?"

She touched and counted each little toe, reaching ten. "See, they are all there."

I nodded.

"What did you name him?"

"Kyle David. We saw a sign for Kyle's Clock Shop while driving to the hospital, and that's where we got it."

The nurse looked surprised. "Really? I'm engaged to the son of the man who owns that shop. It's their last name, but it makes a good first name too."

"Wow, well tell them they have a baby named after them."

"I will." She laughed. "How odd that we'd connected the dots, huh?"

I nodded and yawned.

"Okay, they are done pushing on your stomach. You rest. You'll be needing all your strength soon to take care of this little guy."

I peered at the little guy and started to ask about his APGAR score but stopped. I was too tired to talk. I closed my eyes and fell into oblivion.

The next morning, I was moved to a regular semiprivate room. Ward nurses would walk in and say, "Oh, you are the one! That was one hard delivery." An orderly cleaned my room and told me the labor and delivery room had looked like a war zone with blood all over it. Even though I'd been asleep during the event, all the after tales frightened me.

Dr. Jones came in the evening and sat on the side of my bed.

"Wow, you gave me a scare, Sadie. You had a tough delivery, and you'll need to take it easy."

"So what happened?"

"You lost a lot of blood. I made a Y-shaped episiotomy, and you still tore in three places. You have 150 stitches. You'd have had fewer stitches if you'd had a cesarean. For the next two weeks, take small steps, don't climb up on things, take it easy, and rest every chance you get."

I nodded.

"Part of the blood loss was because of anemia, but also because you tore. And as you know, we are giving you iron shots."

"Yes. Ouch. They hurt going in…"

He laughed. "And no intercourse for six weeks. Not until your next visit with me."

"I'm never doing that again!" I said in horror.

Dr. Jones laughed again. "I hear that a lot right after birth. Just take it easy, Sadie."

"I will," I promised.

Tim took Kyle and me home the next day. It took me fifteen minutes to walk up our twenty-three steps. But I got there. We had no bed for Kyle. So we improvised and put the baby-sized box the hospital sent him home in on our dresser. The baby's nook was complete with a small lamp with a colored bulb in it.

10 INSECURE

BABY AND ME

I HAD DECIDED to breastfeed my baby. That meant I didn't sleep a lot. My mind was hardwired to hear Kyle's even slightest whimper. So when he started fussing two and a half or three hours after his last meal, I got up and fed him again. He'd suckle for about forty minutes, then fall asleep, and I'd take that time to change his diaper and put him back in his box. Then two hours later, we'd repeat the process. There was no equipment needed but me and my baby, but it was tiring to an already exhausted mother. Plus, I could never tell how much he drank. Was he getting enough? That worried me.

Everything about Kyle worried me. I'd never been around a lot of babies. How would I know I was doing it right? Tim was my go-to guy for baby advice. He'd had three before and knew a thing or two. He told me babies like to be wrapped snuggly in a blanket. He showed me how to do it, and sure enough Kyle liked it. But Tim couldn't help with breastfeeding.

Dr. Jones suggested I drink a beer before a feeding to relax me. I'd put a beer on the table beside the daybed, then put Kyle on the mattress, and, finally, carefully sit on it and back up until I was against the cushions. I'd put a couple pillows on my lap and then Kyle. I'd take sips of the beer while I talked to him. Coming from an extensive line of alcoholics, drinking a beer while talking and feeding my baby did not make me feel good.

One day, while I was sitting on the couch breastfeeding Kyle, the phone rang across the room. Tim was at work, and it might be him. I threw the pillows to the side and pulled Kyle away from my breast. *Ohmigod, that hurt.* I bent over in pain. When I got to the phone, the line was dead. No one, not even Dr. Spock, had told me to break the suction before pulling my baby away. Lesson learned.

One night I got up to change Kyle's diaper and feed him. I turned on the little lamp with the blue bulb. It provided just enough light to see but not enough to wake my sleeping partner. As I opened Kyle's diaper, I saw green poop. I was horrified!

Anxiously, I woke Tim up. "Tim, our baby, we have to take him to the hospital immediately!"

"Why?" he asked as his eyelids fluttered open.

"He has green poop. Dr. Spock said that if your baby ever had green poop to take him immediately to the hospital."

He closed his eyes again. "Okay, if he still has green poop in the morning, we'll go." Then he resumed snoring.

I took Kyle in the living room, did the routine with the pillows, and breastfed him. I apologized to Kyle. "I'm sorry, little man, that your dad won't wake up. That he doesn't care enough! I'm so sorry." I rocked him until he went to sleep, then just held him for a long time, amazed he was mine.

The next morning, as soon as light hit our room, I was out of bed ready to take Kyle to the hospital. I hadn't thrown the diaper away, figuring I might need it. And as I picked it up and unwrapped it, I was shocked to see not green poop but yellow. *Yellow?*

I looked at the small lamp. Yellow + Blue = Green. *Ohmigod.* If Tim hadn't turned over and gone back to sleep, I'd have subjected our baby to all kinds of tests and anal probes. "I'm sorry I judged you," I whispered to his sleeping form. *I am so lucky to have a levelheaded man!*

TIM AND ME AND BABY MAKES THREE

Tim found a two-bedroom duplex, and ten days after Kyle's birth, we moved. Kelly had bought Kyle a white crib, so he had a bed now. Sometimes, Kyle cried for no reason that I could figure out. He was fed, he was dry, he was swaddled, his crib mobile was playing soft music; yet he cried.

I had started writing the baby letters the minute I learned I was pregnant. The first line in Kyle's book of letters was "A fourth of an inch you are." Now, I sat biting the sides of my fingers because my baby was crying. Tim told me to give him ten minutes. If he didn't stop, go in and pat him on the back or rub it lightly, then leave. Then wait fifteen minutes. Within two time periods, he stopped. We were teaching him we were there, but also showing him that he could self-sooth. Tim was invaluable to me as a guide.

When Kyle was a month old, I took him out in our backyard and sat in a chair. It was a warm July evening in Florida, and the stars were out. Kyle looked at me with his huge wise blue eyes. He looked like he was born with the knowledge of the ancients. I held him up and introduced him to my mother.

"This is Kyle, your grandson. This is who you are missing because somewhere down the line you chose drink and drugs. Damn it! Why aren't you here? I'm a new mom with a baby and no one to ask advice. I love you, Mom. I miss you, and right now I'm really pissed at you."

When I looked down, Kyle was asleep. I took him inside to his bed. As I closed his door, Tim asked me what was wrong.

"Nothing. Why?"

"You look like you've been crying or something."

"No, I guess my allergies attacked me in the backyard."

"Oh, okay." He smiled.

I didn't tell him because the wives on TV never burdened their husbands with problems. And I was determined to be a good wife.

VISIT FROM MY FATHER AND THELADY

The next day TheLady called saying they were in town and would like to come for a visit. *How bizarre!* I told them to come that afternoon when Tim was home. I examined the house. It was neat and clean. We didn't have much furniture—a bed in our room, a crib in Kyle's, and a small table with two chairs, and Kelly had given us an old daybed.

When they came in, Kyle was asleep. Tim sat in one of the dining room chairs; and my father, TheLady, and I sat on the hard daybed.

"Kelly called us right after you had the baby. She said he looks just like your father."

I smiled. *Kelly! Ever the salesperson.*

Kyle squeaked, and I jumped up to get him. TheLady oohed and aahed. When I spoke, Kyle turned toward me, and she excitedly said, "Look, he knows your voice!"

"What'd you name him?" my father asked.

"Kyle."

My father and TheLady gave each other a look. One of those exchanges that alerts you that something is going on.

"Why? You don't like it?"

"No, no," TheLady said. "We have a friend who has a teenager named Kyle, and he's giving her a lot of problems."

"Oh. It's Kyle David Keyser."

They nodded.

"Your place is nice. Maybe tomorrow we could take you out and get you some stuff for it." TheLady smiled.

Who is she? Why's she acting so nice? "Umm, yes, that'd be okay." I looked at Tim, and he nodded. He'd watch Kyle while I went. It was Saturday, and he didn't have to work.

The next morning, they picked me up and took me to a thrift store. TheLady bought me some bowls, silverware, and a spoon holder for the stove.

"Spoon holders are so useful. Now that you are married maybe we could exchange recipes when you write your father."

"I'm just learning to cook."

"Then mine will help you out."

It was like she thought now that I was married, I had joined the same club as her. The married women's club. Or it was because she felt my father was off the hook and I was Tim's liability now. *I don't trust her.*

My father went ahead to the car, and as we stood in the checkout line, she said, "I told you that you'd get pregnant. Out of wedlock."

My face burned; the clerk had heard her. I turned and said, "Yes, you told me since I was eleven that when I got pregnant to not come back, and I didn't. I went home."

She looked confused. "Home? What are you talking about?"

"I went home, to *my* home with Tim."

"Yes, it's a good thing he married you." She smiled.

I looked at her. She wasn't saying this in meanness. She was just conversing and had no idea that she was being offensive. *This is who she is...*

That night, they took us out to dinner at a fast-food place. Tim talked to them easily. I noticed that my father and I got along better when other people were around. Still, I'd be glad when they left.

After they dropped us off, we waved good-bye to them from our driveway.

"God, I'm glad that's over." I sighed.

"It was tense at first."

When we went inside, I told him about her remarks at the counter and how it felt like she thought I'd joined her club.

"Married woman's club? I can't figure it out," I concluded.

"Quit trying. It doesn't matter. She can't bother you now unless you let her."

"True," I said, giving him a hug. I always tried to discern what was going on in the world around me. My head was full of hypothesizes. I'd done so since I was a little girl. If I could determine what had happened, I could predict what came next and keep my world safe.

DIFFERENT LIVES

I discovered that having a baby meant that Tim's life went on as before and mine changed completely. He went to work as he usually did. At night, he might help me with Kyle until he went to sleep. But I was the psychological parent who woke up the second Kyle cried. He also continued going to Reach Out rec-night on Fridays and to Pete's Pizza afterwards. I stayed home with the baby.

Soon, it was time for me to go back to work. In preparation, I quit breastfeeding and made a follow-up appointment with Dr. Jones.

His nurse, Sonya, led me to an exam room.

"I heard about your baby. You are so lucky Dr. Jones is skilled in high-forceps delivery."

"I know, several nurses at the hospital told me the same thing."

She smiled, handed me the paper gown, and told me the doctor would be in shortly.

"Hi, Sadie, how's that eight-pound baby boy?"

"He's ten pounds now and already smiling."

"Say, that's wonderful. Now let's see how you are."

I got in position on the table and discovered that after having a baby I was no longer self-conscious.

"You are healing well, Sadie. That was a lot of stitches. Now, let me see." He was quiet as he examined me, then he sat back and told me I could sit up.

"Sadie, I see some abnormal tissue on your cervix. Probably due to your difficult delivery. Nothing to be alarmed about. We can do a procedure called cryosurgery. It's just a small area and won't take long. Cryosurgery uses a very cold chemical to freeze the bad cells and remove them. Then you'll have to wait an additional six weeks before you and your husband can have intercourse."

"Oh, my goodness. Are you going to do it today? Because if so, we'd better schedule it for as late in the afternoon as possible and let me run home and make love to my husband. He's already waited one six-week period."

Dr. Jones let out a whooping laugh. "Sadie, didn't you tell me at the hospital you were never doing that again?"

I felt my face turn red. "Yes, I'm afraid I did."

"That's okay, I've heard it before. No, we'll do this in two weeks. You and your husband will have some time before the other six weeks starts."

"What about returning to work?"

"That should be okay. What are you doing for birth control?"

"Oh yeah, I need some pills, but not the mini one. How about a medium pill?"

"I think we've got just what you need. I'll write a prescription and leave it at the desk."

"Can we wait six weeks? I'd like to know how the new pill is going to work with me."

"Yes, that's fine. I'll see you in six weeks."

SIX WEEKS LATER

I had already taken and quit one job and was applying for another. I'd needed a job quickly, so I chose to waitress at a fancy restaurant. That way I would work evenings and nights and be able to be home with Kyle in the daytime.

However, my back betrayed me. I thought I would magically be completely recovered within six weeks of birth. That's the time allotted by physicians and maternity leave. But within a half hour of bending, lifting, and walking on concrete, I'd have pain. It started in my lower back, ran down to a specific spot on my buttocks, and down my leg. The longer I worked, the more severe it became. By the end of the shift, I was panting in pain.

Shit. My mother had had back pain. That's what started her down the road to addiction. The doctor prescribed phenobarbital, and she took it and drank right up until she met Mr. Heroin. My back also hurt when leaning over Kyle's crib to change his diaper. Tim bought me a changing table and that helped. He also said his mother had pain like that, and it was called sciatica.

I didn't care what it was called. I wanted it to go away, and I wanted no drugs. I waited until my appointment with Dr. Jones. Plus, I needed to tell him taking the pill was making me suicidal. I'd told Tim that if I ever committed suicide, it would be the night before my period started. The medical examiner could confirm it. He thought I was kidding.

Dr. Jones asked about the pill.

"Yes, I wanted to talk to you about that. I get up in the morning and say, 'Oh shit' and then the day goes down from there."

He nodded. "Yup, you need to get off it then. I'd say you are not made for birth control pills."

"What will I do?"

He smiled. "Well, there is foam and condoms."

Condoms I knew about. "Foam?" I asked.

"Yes, it's a spermicide. It contains chemicals that kill sperm."

"Gosh, it sounds dangerous, like chemical herbicides. They're meant to kill weeds, but they'll kill flowering plants too."

He laughed. "Well, spermicide will *only* kill sperm, nothing else. The drawback is that it's only about 70 to 80 percent effective."

"Oh, great!"

"However, if you combine it with condoms, it goes up to about 97 percent."

"I guess those are better odds, even though I got pregnant while on the pill."

"Yes, the minipill, which in your case, didn't stop ovulation. This in combination will work."

"How do I do it? I mean, how does it work?" *I didn't ask questions when I got birth control pills, so this time I am!*

"You spray the spermicide inside your vagina. Try to get it as deeply into it as you can, then wait ten to fifteen minutes before having sex. But after thirty to sixty minutes it can be less effective. So there's a window of time to aim toward."

I sighed. "There goes spontaneity."

Dr. Jones laughed. "Everything has its price."

"As I'm learning."

Next, he treated me for the abnormal cells. The cryosurgery wasn't too bad, but the aftereffect was. Sonya had said that sometimes, it caused a hot flash. She had me recline on the treatment table for a while afterwards.

In a few minutes, it felt like an army of fire ants was crawling up my legs. They marched in columns that created waves of heat undulating up my body. When the advance hit my face, it became a pulsing, throbbing concentration of heat.

Sonya opened the door and said, "Just checking to…oh yeah, you are having a hot flash." Then she closed it and left.

My heart sounded loudly in my head, and I felt dizzy. *Ohmigod, if these are the hot flashes that come with menopause, I don't want them.*

In a short while, the heat and pounding dissipated. *Phew.*

Dr. Jones came back and told me again to refrain from sexual intercourse for six weeks. Then asked if I had any questions.

"Yes. One more. I ask a lot of questions."

"I like them. Fire away."

"I'm having back pain that my mother-in-law says is sciatica. What can I do about it?"

After describing the pain, Dr. Jones agreed it was probably sciatica. "Well, the only thing that can really help it is rest."

"But I have to work."

"Try to get something that doesn't have you lifting or standing for prolonged periods."

I nodded. "What causes sciatica?"

"There are many variables that could cause or create it. In your case, it was probably delivery oriented. You had back labor, yes?"

I nodded.

"That could create it. And you had a hard delivery—all of this could have contributed."

"I thought I'd be all better at six weeks, now it's been twelve and I'm still reaping the…"

"The aftereffects of birth. Yes. But six weeks is arbitrary. It is six weeks for some and a lot longer for others. There is no hard and fast rule."

"Will the sciatica go away?"

"It should. It usually does unless it's a herniated disc. Time will tell. But there are other reasons…"

I sighed.

"Sadie, remember when I told you that you looked like you had the weight of the world on your shoulders?"

After our discussion of abortion. "Yes, I remember."

"You had a surprise pregnancy. Then a marriage. Then a baby. You've had a lot happen in a relatively short time. I've been doing labor and delivery for a few years now. And I've noticed that women who are under stress or anxious have more serious morning sickness, like you did."

What's this got to do with my back? I nodded.

"Stress exacerbates everything. My patients who were the most pressured also had more sciatica, and that doesn't mean it's all in your head. It means your body is reacting to constant stress with physical pain. Do you feel stressed?"

I hung my head and nodded.

"How?"

"Like you said. New baby. New marriage. Have to get a job. Life is very serious to me."

"I can tell." He smiled.

"You can go to counseling to help control your anxiety."

I thought of Dr. Tnuh, but I didn't want to go to him because I wanted him to believe I'd made the right choice. I nodded.

"I can prescribe some pain pills for your back, Sadie."

I shook my head. "No, no thanks. I'd rather have pain."

His eyebrows rose.

"My mother was a heroin addict, and she started down that path by taking pills for her back."

"Okay," he said. "I understand. If you change your mind, just call the office. And think of seeing a counselor."

"I will," I promised. But I walked out of the office, knowing I wouldn't. We couldn't afford one. I needed to get a job and pull my weight. I didn't want to burden Tim any more than I already had.

But my mind wondered that if stress could cause sciatic pain, then letting go of stress could remedy it. Somehow, I was going to have to de-stress myself. I got another job standing up at a manufacturing plant but was laid off. Next, I applied to be a telephone operator, and I got it. I worked shift work; and a Reach Out friend, Ruthie's mother, agreed to watch Kyle until one of us could pick him up.

By Christmas I was free of back pain. *Was it stress or something structural with my back?* Tim and I had a child-care routine established. Life had settled into a predictable schedule. When I worked, Tim changed diapers, did laundry, and kept the house as well as I did. I was grateful but also didn't want him to have to do those things. He kept saying he didn't mind. But wives on TV never had their husbands do the laundry. *I'm one lousy wife.*

Six months after working at the telephone company, I obtained a better job at one of the large hospitals. I liked the work and made two friends, Judy Hoo and Judy Vee, who I called Hoo and Vee. Hoo was five years younger than me, very levelheaded and ambitious. Vee was six months older than me, a single mom with a four-year-old and flirty. Hoo and I could talk about issues as well as personal situations. Vee and I talked about personal stuff, childcare, and lighter things. Both thought Tim was quite a catch. Having girl-friends felt good, to hang around with, confined in, and talk with endlessly.

RETROSPECT

Tim and I again settled into a routine. He went to school and worked part-time. I worked full-time, and we both did childcare. It should have been a relaxed time for me. But I judged every single thing I did or did not do. I had hated verbal abuse at the farm. Yet here I was continuing it. In my mind, I was verbally abusing myself.

VERBAL ABUSE

Before my parents' divorce, I experienced my parents slung belittling and insulting words at each other. My older brother would sometimes call me names when he was frustrated with me, but I gave as good as I got.

After the divorce, there was myriad verbal abuse flying around the house. Nasty words flew from the other druggies who moved in, my mother's boyfriends, and her. People in the house would try to bully me into doing what they wanted. I didn't do as they asked, which sometimes earned me a punch.

My mother's boyfriends made fun of me, telling me how ugly I was. I didn't believe them until after my kidnapping. Then, because I thought badly about myself, I let in more outside negative comments.

TheLady had always had a steady barrage of verbal aggression aimed at me. By the time I figured out that she hated me, I had become adept at repelling her curses. Like Wonder Woman and her golden cuffs, I could deflect her attacks. It's surprising, in retrospect, to realize what messages did get inside and become part of my own belief.

Once, Ned and I were outside acting out parts from a play I'd checked out from the library. TheLady walked by and asked Ned what we were doing. He told her I wanted to be an actress when I grew up and he was helping me by practicing acting. She laughed and looked at me, saying, "You'll never be an actress. You're not pretty enough. You're not even cute." Then she walked on into the house. Ned and I continued in our playacting. But later I took the play back to the library and never thought of being an actress again.

Another time, Ned and I were at the breakfast bar talking about what we wanted to do when we grew up. I never gave growing up a thought. I couldn't think beyond the day I was living. Sometimes I couldn't think of being alive an hour later. Because if I'd let myself think there would be twenty-four to forty-eight hours, months, or years like I'd just endured, I'd have rather died, broken my agreement with the Big Guy, and found a way to check out of the world. Yet, when he asked, I knew I had to sound "normal" so I chose something of interest to me. He wanted to be an engineer. I said I wanted to be a psychiatrist. TheLady looked over and said, "You're not smart enough to be one, Sadie." I believed her and gave up that notion before I even had it.

Now I realize that for those comments to make that impression on me, that I already had some doubts about myself. I didn't believe I was pretty or even pleasant looking. I was defective. The same with my intelligence. I didn't believe in it. My half brother (ten years older) had always been deemed the genius. Ned was also called a genius. Me? The few things said were not complimentary.

When report cards came, TheLady signed them. I'm not even sure if my father saw them. He never commented. In fact, I seldom saw him, let alone talked to him. Ned was congratulated on every good grade. I was lectured or congratulated on grades. When Ned hit seventh grade, he became more interested in girls than grades. I remember he had no interest in civics and didn't score well on report cards. I was a year behind his grade, and when I hit civics, I loved it. I memorized the Preamble, and the first part of the US Constitution. It was interesting to hear about our government and foreign ones. I made all A's and B's in that class, yet there wasn't one comment from TheLady. She just handed me back my signed report card. My father never signed them; she did. Did he see them, or did she tell him her version of my grades? Since he lived elsewhere and I only saw him on occasional mornings when he walked in for coffee, I didn't know. The absence of comments regarding my grades was also abuse.

Verbal abuse is always a sidekick to the others: physical, emotional, and sexual. And its impact is just as deadly. Had I married before therapy, before the age of twenty-three, I'd have married someone who would have verbally, emotionally, and physically abused me.

11 CHAPTER

LIFE GOES ON

TV WIFE

DR. TNUH HAD talked about my condemning inner dialogue. Back then, I'd tried to stop doing it and largely succeeded. But those were heady times. I was madly in love, surrounded by a great group of friends, and had not a care in the world.

Since getting married and having a baby, I never made demands of Tim. I made it a point not to sound like a wife. If he got invited to one of his brother's parties, I pretended I didn't mind that he went. I'd rearrange my schedule to make sure he got to do as he would have been able to do if he hadn't married me. I was not going to be a burden. This left me harboring resentment and pushing it down. There was static in the "perfect married couple" picture that I pretended I didn't see. I started having bouts of depression, which I'd try to hide because TV wives never got depressed.

Consequently, I exhausted myself. He'd come home; and I'd have Kyle bathed, fed, in his crib, and dinner on the stove, even though I too worked. I'd defaulted to old behaviors. I no longer tried. I failed, over and over. I graded my mothering and wife abilities against the moms on television. I always fell short. I resorted to calling myself "stupid, ugly, and substandard." I had true compassion for everyone else but never myself. I wouldn't have called my worst enemies the names I called myself.

LIVING IN SEPARATE PLACES

Before graduating from junior college, Tim had applied to transfer to a four-year university. He received an acceptance letter from Oshkosh University in Wisconsin. It had a program he liked. But he had signed a year's lease for our duplex, and that wouldn't be up until May of the next year.

We discussed and discussed. He thought the Wisconsin winters would be hard on Kyle and me; neither of us had warm clothes. It was finally decided that Kyle and I would stay in Florida, and he would go to Wisconsin alone. After the lease was up, we would make another decision. I'd work and find childcare down south. He'd find a room to rent and be a married college student up north.

The decision scared me. But because I had decided never to burden Tim, I kept my fear to myself. But it swirled around my mind at night. Would it be good for our marriage? Would he meet someone else? We'd only been married a little over six months, had only been together a year and ten months. Would I be able to cope without him? I'd have to, but I remembered how much I missed him when he went away that summer.

Kyle wouldn't grow up around his dad. This dynamic hadn't worked out well with Tim and his father. Right after EJ got pregnant, his dad went overseas for four years during WWII. When he came home and met his son, Tim ran away from him. His father never tried to breach that gap, and as a result, Tim felt uncomfortable being in the same room with his dad. Actually, Tim's grandmother and grandfather raised him. They lived next door to EJ, and they did all day-to-day interactions with Tim.

In August, Tim packed the VW for his trip to Wisconsin. By now, my grandfather had given me a huge white 1950s-something four-door station wagon. So I had a means of transportation. My heart sunk with each parcel put in his car. My stomach hurt, and I wanted to cut myself. Something I hadn't done in over a decade. Inside I was screaming! But no one could hear it or see it. I wouldn't let them. My heart throbbed in my ears, irregular and loud. I drown it out with refrains. I would not suffocate him. I would not inflict my needs on him! After all, I was the perfect wife and as such, of course, I'd let my husband go over one thousand miles away to pursue his dream. He would leave in the morning.

I went in the house to feed Kyle while Tim made last-minute adjustments to the car. After a little while he came in; and Kyle, bouncing on my knee, laughed and held out his arms to his dad. Tim picked him up and sat opposite me. Because of the look on his face, my stomach tumbled downward and my heart froze.

"What's wrong?"

He thumped a letter across his leg. Kyle tried to grab it, but he handed it to me.

"What's this?"

"It's an acceptance letter from South Florida. Tampa. I don't know what to do."

My heart fluttered, beating rapidly. I didn't trust my voice and waited.

"I'm all packed for Oshkosh."

I nodded.

"What do you think?"

"I, umm, I think you have a big decision to make."

"I already know that—how do you feel about it?"

"About Wisconsin or Tampa, Florida, less than a half-hour away. How do you think I feel?"

"You want me to stay." He looked into my eyes.

"I want you to stay if you want to stay."

He shook his head. "What's that mean? Of course, I want to stay."

I searched his eyes. "You do. Okay. Then what is the decision? Can you get the degree you want in Florida?"

"Yes, a comparable one."

Kyle fussed.

"Here, let me feed him." I took Kyle, got his bottle, warmed it, and gave it to him.

We watched Kyle for a few minutes in silence.

"I think I ought to stay here and go to South Florida," he finally said.

"Ohmigod!" I screeched loudly. "You're gonna stay? Really?"

Kyle started crying, and Tim's eyebrows rose.

"Yes, I am. You seem pretty happy about it."

"I am!" I patted Kyle to quiet him. "Omigod, I am."

"So you were upset when I was going?"

I nodded. "But I wanted you to do what you wanted."

"Sadie, I need to *know* how you feel. I could have still decided what I wanted knowing your feelings."

I shrugged and gave Kyle back his bottle.

"We're a couple. We decide things together, with full disclosure. Okay?"

My face flushed. "Yes. Okay. I'll try."

He reclined on the couch. "Now I've got a car to unpack that I just spent all day packing. Awe, heck, I'll do it tomorrow."

"And I'll help you," I offered. *Staying! He's staying with us.*

RETROSPECT

Once again, fate intervened. Had we gotten the acceptance letter the day after, Tim would have been gone. He would have called when he got to Wisconsin. After I told him about the letter, would he have come back? I don't know. Since he would have been at the college of his first choice, I doubt it. However, I do know it happened this way. Some people would call it coincidence or luck; I call it divine.

Why didn't anybody back then tell us that Tim going without his family was a terrible idea? Somebody should have given us a reality check. I wasn't going because Wisconsin winters were cold. And? So? Because we didn't have winter clothes? Thrift stores were an alternative to that. No one talked sense into us. That appalls me. That I was so dedicated to pretending scares me. Looking back in hindsight, I thank God that at the last minute another alternative, a better one, appeared.

SURPRISE!

Tim started driving to school. He carpooled with another girl. I worked at the hospital, and Kyle was safe with Ruthie's mother while I was gone. Hoo and Vee and I went to movies, picnics with Kyle, and hung out at each other's house. When Tim wasn't going to school, he was working part-time and still going to Reach Out Friday nights, the monthly outing as well as the once-a-year event. When I could bring Kyle, I would come. But he was happier sleeping in his own bed.

The March after he started going to college in Tampa, Tim, Hoo, and I visited his brother, Tommy, who now worked at a newspaper in Sanford, Florida. Kelly watched Kyle for us. We took off Friday night and got there after dark.

177

The next day, Tommy showed us around his area, and we ate dinner out. That night we drank a couple bottles of wine, listened to music, and talked in the living room. Tom was the first to retreat to bed. We had insisted Hoo have a bedroom, so Tim and I were on the couch.

In case we were intimate, I had loaded myself up on foam during one of my bathroom breaks while talking in the living room. The couch was not meant for sleeping; it was less wide than a single bed, Tim and I were smushed together. I held on to him so I wouldn't fall off the edge. We started fooling around, giggling, and trying to be quiet.

"I don't have a condom," he whispered.

"It's okay, I'm at the very end of my period, and I used foam."

As we wiggled around on the couch and I fell into his kisses, I saw the mist again. I vaguely remembered I'd seen it before but couldn't remember when.

"Mist…"

"Yeah, I've missed this too, just you and me and a bed."

I shook my head. *I must be drunk.*

We made love, and I didn't think about it until the next month.

Hoo, I, and another girl had booked a hotel at Disney World. But the Wednesday before we were to leave on Friday, I spiked a fever, had a sore throat, and went to the emergency room at our hospital. Lucky for me, the ER attending had been an ear, nose, and throat doctor in his past. He read over my vitals and examined my throat.

"Ah-ha," he said. "I would usually say this is just a virus and send you home, but I think you have strep throat."

"Strep throat?"

"Yes, you have all the markers. A temp over 101, red spots on the back of your throat and the roof of your mouth, plus your lymph nodes are swollen."

"Oh, are you sure?"

"Yes. Do you have any other symptoms? Headache?"

"Yes, and I'm dead tired all the time and a little nauseous."

"All in line with strep."

"Is it dangerous?"

"No, no. I'll give you an antibiotic and you'll feel better in no time."

"In time to go to Disney World in two days?"

He looked up from writing in my chart. "Two days? No, I wouldn't recommend that. You need to help the antibiotic work." Glancing at my chart, he continued, "And you're allergic to the best one, penicillin. But don't worry, I'll prescribe you an alternative."

"Thanks." I smiled.

The day before we were to leave for Disney World, I still felt no better. I had stayed out of work Thursday and intended to do so on Friday as well. My headache lingered, I had no appetite, and had a terrible burning in the middle of my chest, which I learned was heartburn. I called Hoo and told her I couldn't go. I felt terrible about it, but she only wanted me to get better.

I went to work Monday, although I had not improved. I couldn't wait to hear about their good time. During lunch, I ran to the bathroom and lost the little I had eaten. Hoo and Vee came in.

"Are you okay?"

Rinsing my mouth out, I said, "Yeah, just strep."

Vee eyed me. "When was your last period?"

"Period? Oh no, I'm not pregnant, just sick." But she got me thinking. I tried to visualize the calendar in our bedroom where I kept track. Then I realized that my breasts felt tender, like they did when I was pregnant with Kyle. *Oh, no.*

Shit. I called Tim to tell him I'd be a little late and went to the ER after work and asked a friend there for a pregnancy test.

I drove home carefully, making sure to obey all traffic signs and school zones. I pulled into our driveway and saw the light on the porch. I loved seeing that light. At the farm, TheLady used to turn it off if I was coming home at night. But here I was home, and the light said, *Come on in. You are welcome.*

I walked inside. Tim had put Kyle to sleep and was studying at the dining room table. He was getting better and better at reading me, and it was getting harder and harder to hide.

"Are you okay?"

I put my purse down, flopped on the couch, and said, "Kind of…"

He looked at me, and I pulled a pillow on my lap and twisted the corner. He came over and sat beside me. "Sadie? What is it?"

I shook my head. "I'm so sorry! I know we just made the last payment on Kyle's delivery hospital bill…and ohmigod…"

He stopped my hand twisting. "What?"

"I'm pregnant."

He looked stunned.

"I'm so, so sorry. Really, I…"

"Sadie, don't apologize. We both had something to do with this. How…when do you think?"

I remembered the surrounding mist at Tommy's. "In Sanford, during our visit with your brother."

"How?"

I felt my face turn red. "I'm not sure. Foam? But it was the end of my period so there should not have been an egg! But, but…if I'd been more, um, perceptive, I'd have known we shouldn't have been doing that, make love, I mean."

"You couldn't have known."

"But maybe I did. Remember the white mist around us at Aunt Ruby's when we made Kyle?"

He nodded.

"Well, there was white mist around us at Tommy's. I should have known what that meant!"

He half-laughed. "What? That we shouldn't make love when we are away from our own bed? Sadie, again, you couldn't have known. Maybe the mist just shows up when we are out of town or when it's a particularly wondrous love-making session."

"What are we going to do?"

"Have a baby."

"Ohmigosh. But I can save us money this time because I know we just made our last payment on Kyle. If I deliver at the hospital I work at, it will only cost us $25. Total."

Because of my stay in intensive care, Kyle's bill had been over $1,000.

"Dr. Jones practice there?"

"No, I'll have to change doctors." I sighed. I hated doing that. I liked him, and he had saved our lives, Kyle and me. "I'll start looking tomorrow."

"Okay." He smiled. "I think your white mist means don't drink wine and make love away from home. Both were elements of your aunt Ruby's and Tommy.

"Maybe." But I didn't think so.

CHANGING DOCTORS FOR PREGNANCY NO. 2

Changing ob-gyn doctors ought to be easy. I worked in a hospital. Hoo and Vee made lists of prime affiliated doctors. Luckily, doctor number 1, Dr. Linson, could see me that Thursday, the same week.

The office staff was friendly, and it wasn't too long before I was in a gown with my feet in stirrups. In walks Dr. Linson.

He had a head of white hair, dark-rimmed glasses, and a friendly manner. As he began my pelvic exam, he cheerfully said, "Wonder is my assistant." I looked around the room for the nurse, but there wasn't one. I heard scratching and looked down beside the table to see a small black-and-white dog with its feet up on his knees. "She's my supervisor." He laughed. *A dog? A dog is in here?*

After the exam, I answered a few questions and bypassed the checkout desk. I would not be signing forms to have my medical records from Dr. Jones transferred to him. Nope, that wouldn't be happening. I wouldn't be going back. Tim shook his head in disbelief when I told him what happened.

"Yes, absolutely mark him off the list."

A week later, I had an appointment with Dr. Swan. This office wanted me to sign a transfer authorization for my records before I saw the doctor. I said no. I'd do it on the way out. That earned me some funny looks, but they said okay.

Dr. Swan walked in as I assumed the position, my feet in stirrups. I leaned up to say "Hi." He sat down and inserted the metal speculum. Abruptly, one of the office workers interrupted to tell him he had a phone call from his wife. He stood, took off his gloves, patted my knee, and said, "I need to take this," and off he went. *Are you kidding?* I thought about getting up and leaving, but I didn't know how to take the instrument out. I breathed deeply and waited. Finally, he came back in, gloved up, and said, "Sorry. We're redecorating our house and she wanted my input." I left that office without signing the transfer forms.

The third time must be the charm. Vee found me a doctor who everybody liked. Hoo had personally talked to two of his patients. A week later, I was in stirrups again when Dr. Henry stepped into the room. He was tall and in his forties. He washed his hands before gloving up and came to the head of the table to introduce himself. *So far, so good.* He examined me. Then told me to sit up. He opened the door, stood in the doorway, and asked if I had any questions.

"Yes, I'd like to get my tubes tied after delivery."

"Oh?" He busily looked over my patient intake sheet. "You only have two children?"

"Yes, and I am sure I don't want any more."

"You cannot be sure at twenty-eight years old. You never know what's going to happen." He shifted his weight back and forth on his feet like he couldn't wait to leave.

"True, we never know the future. However, I am sure I only want to have two kids, and only be pregnant two times because I am not a good pregnant person."

"I won't do a tubal ligation on a woman with only two children."

"I am paying for five! My husband has three from his first marriage."

"Divorced? No, you should have thought of that before you married him. Any more questions?"

"No, I've gotten my answer."

"Okay, stop at the desk and fill out the forms."

I did stop at the desk to complain about his attitude.

"Oh, he's Catholic. And he'll only hire Catholics."

"Well, maybe he should only *deliver* Catholics. I won't be back." I left in tears. I felt like I was submitting to rape by speculum before deciding if I even liked the doctor.

That night I told Tim what had happened. "I've been to three! Three pelvic exams! Now, I'll have to have a fourth."

Tim quietly said, "Go back to Dr. Jones."

"But we just got Kyle paid off, and I can have a baby for $25 if I deliver at my hospital."

"So? You have confidence in Dr. Jones. He did an excellent job with you and Kyle. We can pay for this baby in installments too."

I exhaled and relaxed on the couch. "I will. I'll make an appointment tomorrow. Thanks."

DR. JONES PART II

Dr. Jones gave me his usual smile as he came in the door. "Sadie! So good to see you."

My first question was how I could have gotten pregnant when I was at the end of my period and had used foam.

"Well, I told you it's only about 70 to 80 percent effective. As for the end of your period, boy sperm swim faster than girl sperm. But girl sperm can last long and swim further. If you ovulated early, either could have reached an egg. There are many variables that could impact birth control."

"Okay. I'm thinking of having my tubes tied after the birth of the baby."

Dr. Jones nodded. "It would mean a longer hospital stay. I'd be doing it a couple days after delivery."

"Oh, you can't do it at the same time?"

"I can with cesarean sections but not natural births. And we would want to see how much blood you lose this time."

"Okay. Thanks."

Dr. Jones was gentle, caring, and intuited how scared I was. "Sadie, your second delivery can be polar opposite to your first. So don't worry."

THANKSGIVING: EIGHT MONTHS PREGNANT

Tim, Kyle, and I went over to Kelly's grandmother's house for Thanksgiving. In the afternoon and that evening we'd go to Tim's parent's house. Grandmother always made me my favorite vegetable, field peas. There were over ten of us at the table. I waited to see where Rob sat, then I chose a chair catty-cornered away from him at the far right near the end. Right after Rob said grace, he stood, put his hand on his hips, and stretched backward. He said that chair hurt his back. Could he trade seats with, and he pointed to the person sitting at the end of the table, right by me. I fought his hand all through the meal with my husband sitting next to me. I would give birth in three weeks. *Really!*

12

CHAPTER

BABY, ABUSE, AND QUESTIONALBE FRIEND

SECOND BABY

I FELT JUST as ill as I had with Kyle but threw up less, which I wasn't sure was a good thing. At least after regurgitating I felt well for a while. I had strep four more times during the pregnancy. The only good thing about being pregnant, I told Tim, was that I couldn't get pregnant.

Dr. Jones said my due date was December 24. *I do not want to spend Christmas in the hospital.* Dr. Jones shrugged when I told him. "The baby will come when the baby is ready."

I'd been two weeks late, last time, maybe I would be this time too.

Around the first week in December, I went on maternity leave. All I'd wanted to do since getting pregnant was sleep. Now I did so. On the sixth, Hoo had a "naughty" Christmas party. Everyone was to bring a naughty ornament for her tree. All of Reach Out would be going, along with Vee, in addition to some other hospital friends. I asked Hoo if she minded if I stayed home. She understood.

I painted a Christmas bulb for Tim with a naked man on it (resembling him) with a bow hiding his private parts. I was asleep when he came home. But the next day, I'd played twenty-one questions to find out how the party went. It was an enormous success. Still, I was glad I'd decided to stay home and sleep.

A week later, December 14, I started feeling my abdomen tighten and loosen. *Braxton Hicks.* I'd been having those contractions since the beginning of December. Tim talked to his boys and his ex-wife on the telephone. She asked to speak to me.

"You're having contractions?" Jeanne asked me.

"Just Braxton Hicks."

"You know the second baby comes faster than the first one."

"I hope so," I sighed.

"You won't have a girl, will you? You won't do that to me."

"I don't know what I'm having." I felt uncomfortable with the question.

After I hung up, I told Tim I was going to bed. I lay down and put my hand where I felt the baby on my stomach, and the baby startled away. I smiled. This baby was shy. Finally, I fell asleep.

I felt Tim crawl into bed at about eleven o'clock. As soon as he pulled the covers up, the baby kicked me out of bed, or that's what it felt like. I had a massive and painful contraction. I went to the bathroom and found I'd lost the cervical plug that Dr. Spock and Dr. Jones had talked about. I went into the bedroom.

"Tim, wake up. I'm in labor."

He instantly got up and started getting dressed.

"I'll call Hoo."

She sounded sleepy until I told her I was in labor. Then she perked right up and said she'd be over in a moment. Next, I called Kelly. She wanted to be there.

Tim got my bag, and we drove to the hospital. As soon as I got out of the VW, my water broke. We went in, and I was taken to a labor and delivery room. Dr. Jones was not on call, his partner was.

"Oh no, can't you call Dr. Jones?"

"No, hon. But Dr. Parrates is just as qualified. Otherwise, Dr. Jones wouldn't partner with him"

I can't believe I decided to spend money we don't have so Dr. Jones could deliver my baby and now he won't.

The nurses got me settled, said I was progressing nicely, and let Tim in to visit. I held his hand tightly during the strong contractions.

"This is quite different than Kyle."

He nodded.

Suddenly, I felt an urge to push. As I did so, something moved, for what felt like a foot, in my abdomen. It was either the biggest bowel movement in history or it was the baby.

"Tim, you better go get the nurse."

Tim blanched paper white and left the room.

Soon, a nurse was at my side. She checked beneath my covers, then said, "Don't push."

"Huh?" Everything inside me was saying, "Push."

"Don't push! Pant. Like this." And she demonstrated.

I panted.

Another nurse came in, and she told her to call the doctor stat. "She's ready."

Soon, I was being wheeled down the hall to the delivery room. It was a little after midnight. As I got on the delivery room table, I started pushing as my body directed.

A very pregnant nurse, I recognized from last time, came to my head. "Do not push, pant."

"I can't…" I wailed.

"Yes, you can. Pant."

"I c-can't."

"Yes, you will. Pant. Now. Pant." She brought her face inches from mine, looked in my eyes, and panted.

Finally, I broke the push and began to pant.

"Good," she offered. "Dr. Parrates is on his way. You pant until he gets here."

I nodded. Between contractions, I motioned the pregnant nurse over. "Weren't you engaged two and half years ago to the son of the guy who owned Kyle's Clock Shop?"

"I am." She laughed. "We got married, and I'm having twins. I remember you. You had a son and named him Kyle."

"That's me. Congratulations! Twins, I thought I wanted that until I had one."

She laughed. "Yes, it will be a challenge. Now keep panting. Parrates will be here shortly."

For twenty minutes, I panted. Then a strange doctor came in, introduced himself as Dr. Parrates, sat down below my feet, and said, "Push."

I pushed.

The nurses cheered me on. "That's it, keep pushing. The baby's coming! Can you see in the mirror?"

"No, can't see," I said between gritted teeth as I continued to push.

The nurse quickly reached up and adjusted a mirror hanging over head. She did it in time for me to see a baby slide out and into Dr. Parrates's hands.

"A baby! That's my baby!" I exclaimed.

"Yes, and she's beautiful. Born at 2:32 a.m. on December 15."

"She? I had a girl baby?"

The nurse laughed. "You sure did!"

A few minutes later, she brought me a papoose-ed baby. "Here she is."

"Ohmigosh, she's beautiful. Isn't she?"

"She is. She was born quickly, so her head isn't cone-shaped. Now, I'm going to go put her in the nursery. You'll have her a little later."

Dr. Parrates came to the head of the table. "You only have a little episiotomy. It should be no problem. Why didn't you tell me you had a bleeding problem last time? Due to that, I'm going to instruct the nurses not to push on your uterus."

"Thanks." I smiled. "That's the best news I've heard all day, other than just delivering a beautiful girl baby."

He smiled.

A girl! We have a girl!

After I was settled in a regular room, Tim came to visit. He was amazed we'd had a girl. "The nurse is taking her all over the ward, showing her to people because she's so beautiful."

"Are we still going to name her Kristi Lee? Keep the alliteration going? And your middle name?"

"Yeah, I think so. She looks like a Kristi."

After Tim's visit, Kelly came in telling me how beautiful the baby was. "See, I told you you'd be having a girl."

Indeed, she had. But I would only believe it when I saw it. Tim had four boys and now, finally, a little girl.

We brought Kristi home a few days later. She weighed in at 7.4 ounces. Those missing eight ounces made a lot of difference in getting through the birth canal. Her brother was happy to see his baby but after a week wondered when she was going home. I hated the thought of going back to work, but Tim (who had graduated with his BA degree that summer) was looking for a job.

I felt completely blessed when the night before I was to return to work. I witnessed Kristi's first smile. Tim held Kristi on his knee and was playing patty-cake. He held her hands; and when he said, "Mark 'um with a *K*" and tickled her tummy, she lit up with a gummy smile. Her first, and early according to Dr. Spock, and so nice to see.

After I'd been back to work for a month, Tim had a vasectomy. The surgery was done at the hospital I worked at and only cost $25.00.

ULTIMATUM

When Kristi was about six months old, Tim had to get a laminectomy or back surgery at the hospital. It would relieve pressure on his spinal cord. It was a major medical procedure. I chose a surgeon at my hospital who was good with a scalpel but did not have a good bedside manner.

One evening, after work when I'd gotten both kids to sleep, I tried to get Tim's reel-to-reel operating. I could get the large tapes to turn but couldn't get the sound to come through the speakers. As I pushed buttons, trying to remember which ones I'd depressed before, someone knocked on the door.

Kelly's father came in as soon as I opened it, immediately putting me on alert. He reached out to pull me in for a kiss, but I stepped back.

"What are you doing? Stop."

"I'd just really like a kiss," he answered.

"Nope. Not gonna happen." I walked toward the kitchen. I didn't want to sit down.

He followed me. "Please, just one kiss. You can give me one, can't you?"

"No, Rod, I can't. I'm married. And not only am I married, I'm happily married."

"Please," he begged. "It will mean so much to me."

I maneuvered myself toward the living room, not wanting to get trapped in the kitchen. My heart was beating loudly in my ears, and my knees trembled. "No. That's not going to happen."

Rod's eyes welled up with tears. "Please," he whispered. As tears ran down his face, he reached out and grabbed my shoulder. "Please, just one little kiss. Surely you can spare one kiss."

I twisted away. "No, I can't." I eyed the telephone. *Please ring! Ring.*

Just then Kristi started crying. She had never cried after I put her to bed, not once. I ran into her room, picked her up, and returned to the living room. She continued to wail as I gently rocked her back and forth.

Rod looked from the baby to me and took a step back. "Well, I guess I should get going."

I nodded.

He turned around and went to the door. I didn't move, other than trying to console my crying baby. Finally, he closed the door, and I quickly locked it. Through the small panels of jalousie-glass I could see Rod move down the driveway toward his car. *Thank God.*

I looked down, and Kristi had quit crying. She was looking up at me with her huge blue eyes. "You did that for your mama, didn't you?" I took her back to her bedroom, lay her in her crib, started her crib mobile, and tiptoed out.

Just as I returned to the living room, I saw Rob's car reappear in our driveway. He got out and knocked on the door. I didn't unlock it but opened the jalousies.

"Yes?" I said.

"Don't tell Kelly I was here."

"I won't this time. But…"

He waited.

"See that reel-to-reel over there?" I pointed, and his eyes followed. "I put it on record as soon as I saw you drive up the first time. It recorded everything. Tim has it set up with multiple microphones." My voice shook with anger, yet my voice was low and resolute. "If you *ever* come back or try to touch me again, I'll play this tape for Kelly and your wife. Grandmother, your mother, will hear it. I'll take it to the pastor of your church! Tim's brother writes for the newspaper. I'll have an article written about this tape and the past eleven years of your unwelcomed advances. Then I'll tell some policemen I know from working at the emergency room what you've been doing and that I've got proof. I'll bring sexual harassment charges against you. Do you understand?"

"There's no need to do all that."

"Well, don't give me a reason. Because I mean what I say. Leave me alone."

He nodded. "I will." Then he returned to his car and drove off.

I still didn't feel safe, so I called Tim's brother, Tommy, and told him that if I ever called him and started calling him Fred, would he please drive over here as quickly as possible?

"Sure," he answered. "Is someone bothering you?"

"Someone has, and I think it's over. But I want insurance in case it isn't."

"Yes. Do you need me to come over now?"

"No, I'm good. Thanks." We hung up, and I turned Tim's reel-to-reel off. *Thank God, it was running.* For the first time ever, I felt good that I had handled the incident. But I didn't feel good about my anger. *I sounded just like TheLady.*

As soon as he got home from the hospital, I told Tim about Rod and all the times he had tried to touch me inappropriately. I begged him not to tell Kelly or act differently toward her family. I omitted the part about my outrage and what I'd said in anger. I concluded by saying, "I don't think Rod will bother me anymore, but I needed to tell you nonetheless."

Tim gave me a hug. "Now, I understand how tense it is when you two are around each other. I knew you didn't like him, now I know why."

THELADY MAKES HER EXIT

TheLady had an aneurysm explode in her head the previous year. That left her with the cognitive ability of an eight-month-old baby. She could recognize people from her past, and she'd get excited and smile and make sounds, but she could not talk and had no control of her bowels.

I didn't understand my father's love for TheLady, but he had loved her. For two years he cared for her at the farm. He picked her up out of the hospital bed he'd ordered, set her in a wheelchair, and hand fed her. He changed her diapers and gave her baths. She died when Kristi was two years old.

A month before she had gotten sick, TheLady and my father went to her lawyer so she could change her will. She gave everything to her son. Ned got the farm, her $30,000 savings, and everything else except for the car my father and her had been driving. He wasn't nursing her those two years because he thought he'd inherit anything; he knew exactly what he was getting. The only way someone could be that devoted was love. I admired him for that.

I wondered if all her anger and hate had contributed to her death. I hoped our relationship could improve without her presence. Within a brief time, he had moved and rented a room in another town.

TIMES THEY ARE A CHANGING

My two Judys filled in much of my alone space. I loved laughing with them. They thought the world of Tim. So I didn't inconvenience them with any problems or disputes that came up in our marriage. Likewise, I didn't confine in Kelly for the same reason. I kept it to myself and pretended we had no problems.

About three years after getting to know Hoo, she married and moved to Chicago. And her way of coping with moving (she'd moved a lot too) was to turn her back on the old and embrace the new. (Unlike me, I tried holding on to every friend I'd ever made.) Hoo didn't write. I shoved the feelings down. Her absence made me and Vee much closer.

Eventually, Tim and I moved an hour away, but Vee spent almost every weekend with us. Our kids played together, and we played canasta, listened to music, and talked. She was the stand-in me. If I couldn't go to a show because I had to be at work early the next day, I'd suggest Vee go instead. I had some close men friends and fervently believed that men and women could be friends. Tim agreed.

DISCONNECT

The first year in the new house, I began sensing a disconnect between Vee and me. I brought it up, and she said it was my imagination. I continued to have bouts of depression. Making the pretense of "perfect" hard to maintain. For example, Vee once borrowed one of my favorite nightgowns. Instead of giving it back, she bought me one. I didn't like it but didn't want to make waves and buried my feelings.

After two years in the house, Tim lost his job. We moved to Maryland for him to work at a state institution for mentally challenged adults. We had a two-bedroom apartment in an old brick building. It used to be nurses quarters when the place was a nursing school. I fell in love with the treed grounds, the mountains, and the tiny town where we went to get groceries.

It was at this apartment that Kristi went to first grade. We watched her, our timid little girl, walk toward the bus without looking back. But on the bus, Kyle said she sat on his lap. Both kids were blonde and had blue eyes. Kyle was outgoing, and Kristi was so shy she was almost backward. They couldn't have been more different, nor could they have been closer.

The next year we moved to Hagerstown, Maryland, so Tim could work at a group home for mentally challenged adults. I worked at a car dealership and went through a slew of babysitters to watch the kids after school. I felt guilty when I was at work, feeling I ought to be with my kids. When I was with my kids, I felt bad about all the work piling up. A catch 22.

That spring Tim got a job offer from NSA, which he had applied to two years previously. We talked it over. We hated for him to leave the field he had gone to college to get his degree so he could do that kind of work. But the field paid so little, and we had a growing family. After long talks, he took the job.

Before we left, Tim took the kids and drove to Florida to see his folks, mine, and Kelly. While there, he talked Vee into taking a week's vacation. She did, and she and her son drove back up with him. I was so happy to see her! I'd been best friend bereft since we'd moved. For some reason Maryland wasn't conducive to making good female friends. I did make one male friend, but there were things I could only talk to another female about. We took her to see the sites, to a Beach Boy's concert in front of the Washington monument, and we toured D. C.

Too soon, it was time for her to leave, and she boarded a bus to go home. We'd had a wonderful time together. But there was still some nebulous something in the way of what used to be our easy friendship. She was a little sharper with her words, a bit more critical, and somehow absent. I asked Tim if he noticed anything different. He didn't. But he and I saw hugely different things when we encountered people. He could tell you what they were wearing and what they drove.

I could tell you their eye color and how they were feeling, despite how they said they were.

We moved to Laurel, Maryland, and Tim began working at NSA. I went to work at a huge hospital where I was in charge of Medicaid accounts and patients. I kept urging Vee to come back for a visit, and she always said she couldn't right then. She talked about her boyfriends on most of our phone calls.

YOUR HUSBAND REALLY LOVES YOU

Two years after living in Laurel, Maryland, we were slated to go to Germany with Tim's career. NSA advised us to go home and see our parents before we left. We were told to tell them that what to do should a foreign government kidnap us. In that case, they needed to let the Department of Defense handle the press. The kids were now ten and eight and were excited to live way across the ocean.

Tim flew to Florida a few days before me. I had to work out my two weeks' notice at the hospital, so the kids and I flew down later. We all stayed at Kelly's house. As Tim and I were going to the grocery to buy food for our stay, we ran into Vee, also shopping. Again, I was thrilled to see her. We talked a while, then Tim said he'd start our grocery list. As he walked off, Vee said, "I'm so glad you're here. I've missed talking to you."

"We haven't really talked much, at least not about anything important, in the last so many years," I answered.

Vee nodded. "Yes, and I think I know why."

"Why?"

"I'll tell you when we have time to talk."

"How about tomorrow night after you work? I'll come over."

"Perfect," she said.

197

I watched her walk away and wondered why I sensed she was nervous. *There's nothing she could say to me that I would judge.* Surely, after all our years of friendship, she knew that.

Friday night I drove over to Vee's apartment. Her son had grown into a teenager. After greeting him, we went into the bedroom where she took a valium.

"Are you nervous?" I asked.

"Oh, I always take one about this time."

"Always, why?"

"In case I get nervous."

"Okay." I shrugged. It made little sense to me, but maybe it did to her.

"I've just come out of a terrible depression," she started. "It was the longest one ever, lasting about six months. I wanted to wet my pants in front of people who told me it was nothing, to shock them into hearing me."

I nodded. "I don't think I will get depressed anymore."

"Why?"

"Two reasons. I've read everything a psychologist named Albert Ellis has written. He believes depression comes from within us. After all, a big blue giant isn't standing over us, pushing 'depression' into our heads. Much of it is about our inner dialogue. And I filled mine with demeaning words aimed at myself. It took time, but I've defeated that. And…"

"Sounds good. I'll try to read his books. What else?"

"I will call a thing a thing. I've swallowed anger, hurt, and frustration all my life. No more. I'm going to say it when I feel it. I think doing those things will eliminate depression for me."

Vee nodded. "I had such an enjoyable time in Maryland. You are so lucky to have Tim."

"I think we are so lucky to have each other, equally lucky."

"Ah, part of you saying what you feel, huh?" She laughed.

"Yes."

"Well, I want to tell you how much your husband loves you…"

"O-kay."

"Remember when you lived in New Port Richey and you had two tickets to go see a Tony Orlando concert? But you had to get up early, and you suggested he take me."

"Yes, I remember." I had had trouble sleeping, and when he walked in at 3:00 a.m., I was up. He'd told me he and Vee had gone to have a few drinks after the concert and then after it closed got to talking.

"Well, we went to the concert and then a lounge."

I nodded. He had told me this.

"Then we drove out to the beach. I don't know if it was the wine, the waves, or the fact that I do have a crush on him, but we started making out." She looked at me.

I used my childhood ability not to show what I was feeling on my face. "And?"

Vee fiddled with a match case in her hand. "And I've got a spot right by my ear, and if I get hit there, I'm ready to… you know, I'm ready to go further…all the way." She looked at me again.

"Go on," I encouraged.

"And I was ready, willing, and able. But he pulled back and said, "Vee, I can't. I made a commitment.'"

"Hmm…"

"See, that's how much he loves you. So much stopped."

"Well, two things come to mind. I'd have much rather he said, 'I can't because I love my wife.'"

"Oh, that's just words! You know what he meant."

"And," I continued, "I'm glad he stopped at going all the way with you, but that's his line. Mine was way, way back there at kissing, let alone making out. He knows my line, and he didn't stop at it."

"You're missing the point." She shook her head.

"No, I hear what you are saying."

"And please, say nothing to him. I don't want it to ruin our friendships."

"I won't." *Ruin our friendships? Mine and hers or her and his? I won't say anything right now.*

It was late, and after listening to some music, I went home. I said nothing to Tim.

YOUR HUSBAND REALLY LOVES YOU II

The next evening Tim and I, plus his brother Tommy and a friend named Barb, all went to the beach. We ordered drinks and watched the sunset. Tommy was upset because he had gone to a football game with his father and one of his dad's friends, a woman, and while they were there, his father put his hand in her purse and drew out a cigarette. Tommy thought that was a little too familiar, and when he and his dad drove away, he told his dad. His father said they were just friends. "It's not like I'm sleeping with her." Still, Tommy thought they were closer than they should have been.

"So, you're thinking he's having an emotional affair?" I asked.

"Yes, something like that. He's spending energy with this woman that he could spend on his wife," Tommy countered.

"I understand. Do you think it's an affair if they haven't had sex but maybe kissed?"

"Heck, yeah. Especially if it's spending time together in secret."

I nodded. "What do you think, Tim?"

He finished his drink. "I don't know." Then he got up. "I'm going to refuel. Anybody else need anything?"

"I'll go with you," Tommy offered.

And the two brothers walked toward the concession together.

Barb looked at me. "What's going on? There's all kind of tension in the air."

"I found out last night that Tim and Vee made out a couple of years ago. She told me to assure me of how much he loves me—because she offered herself to him and he said he had a commitment."

"Oh, geez. Are you going to tell him?"

"Not right now."

"I'm sorry, Sadie. You going to be okay?"

"Not your fault. Just theirs. And yes, I'll be okay."

That night after we went back to Kelly's, I borrowed her car to drive back over to Vee's house. It surprised her to see me. We sat in the living room and began talking when she was called to the pool area where her son was swimming with a friend. A neighbor had thought he'd seen the boys with a marijuana joint and alerted Vee.

She came back in saying she was glad the neighbor had told her. But it was her son's friend's joint and not his. He didn't smoke. "I believe him. It rang true."

"Yes, unless it was a half-truth because they ring true as well."

Vee nodded, got a funny look on her face, and said, "Right. And that kissing session, I told you about last night wasn't the only one." She fumbled to get her valium bottle. "Want one?"

"No, thanks. I want you to tell me every single time something happened. How long it happened, and how far down your throat his tongue went."

She swallowed a little yellow pill. "God, Sadie." She searched my face.

My face told her nothing. "Start at the beginning," I instructed.

"Remember Hoo's naughty Christmas party and you were pregnant and didn't go?"

I nodded.

"Well, we walked out together. And…I kissed him."

"And he kissed you back." It was a statement, not a question.

She nodded, then told tell me how many times they met and made out. Sometimes it was when I'd asked her to fill in for me, and other times they met. When we moved into our house, she said, it'd happen when I went to bed early.

"What's 'it' that happened?"

"We fooled around, you know."

"No, I want it spelled out."

"We'd bring each other to climax. We never had full-out sex…He wouldn't."

"Oral sex?"

Vee looked down. "Yes."

"Go on," I said.

"Remember when he drove us up to Maryland?"

"Yes."

"Well, once the kids were all asleep in the back of the car, and I…uh…" She faltered.

"Go on, you?"

"Oral sex."

"In the car? Driving down the highway with all our kids in the back. My two and your one."

"Yes, but they were asleep."

God, I hope that's true.

"And this time? He flew down before me."

"Yeah." Vee looked away. "We got together the night before you flew in…" Then she burst into tears. "Ohmigod, I've ruined everything. He'll never talk to me again. Ohmigod."

"That's not true," I reassured her. "We'll all get through this. It'll be okay."

She shook her head and excused herself, and I heard her crying in the bathroom. She came out and went to the kitchen where she got down a bottle of whiskey. She took two glasses out, but I shook my head, and she put one back.

"Think you ought to do that? On top of valium?"

"Yes. Damn it. I've just blown up a friendship of ten years. Why not?"

"No, I told you. We're all going to stay friends. We can weather this. I'll call him and have him talk to you."

"It's after 2:00 a.m.!"

"Right, well, he'll be sure to be there."

I called Kelly's house, and Tim answered on the first ring.

"Hi, I'm at Vee's house, and well, you need to talk to her."

"No, I don't want to talk to her. I want to talk to you."

"Okay, you can talk to me later. Right now, you need to talk to Vee."

Vee was looking at me with tears streaming down her face, shaking her head.

"No. I only want to talk to you."

I glanced at Vee. "Timothy, you need to talk to Vee about your last eight years of indiscretions!"

Vee burst into tears as I heard Tim say, "No, I want to talk to you. I'll come pick you up. Ten minutes." And he hung up.

I told Vee he was coming to get me and that he and I would talk. Then she and he would talk. Then we would all talk so we would know we could look at each other and get over this.

Vee shook her head. "I'm going to bed. This will never be the same."

"*Yes*, it will!"

13 WEATHER WARNING

HUSBAND'S VERSION

TIM DROVE UP in his rental, and I got in the front passenger seat.

"You may not believe this," he said as he put the car in gear, "but I love you."

"I don't believe it."

He drove to a spot on the beach and stopped, turned to me, and said, "I'm sorry."

I looked around. I didn't know how I knew, but I knew. "Is this where you brought Vee after the Tony Orlando concert?"

"Yes." He looked down.

"Bad choice. Then and now."

"What do you want to know?"

"Everything. I want to know each and every time you met. When? Where? For how long? How far down her throat did your tongue go? And vice versa."

He nodded and started at Hoo's naughty Christmas party. She had kissed him. He told me of every time she had, and a couple more, so I knew he was being honest.

"If you love me, why?"

"I do love you. Why? Because…because I thought you'd never find out."

"You had no scruples against making out with your wife's best friend?"

"I did. But because she was your best friend, I thought she'd never tell you…"

"And what I didn't know couldn't hurt me?"

"Yes, something like that."

"The incident she told me about happened right here, after the concert."

"Yes, and I told you the same thing."

"Right, even the 'Vee, I can't. I've got a commitment' statement. I wish you had said, 'I can't. I love my wife.' Saying I have a commitment sounds like you have an albatross around your neck."

"Albatross?"

"Yeah, it's something sailors said in a poem by Coleridge. It means they have a heavy burden to carry."

"No, that's not how I felt or feel. I mean, I'd made a commitment that I would keep."

"Well, as I told her, I'm glad you stopped there that night. But my line was way, way back at kissing. All those kisses you gave her were mine. All those fingered and tongued climaxes were ours."

He flushed red.

"You stopped at intercourse. Does that mean you don't think you had an affair? Like the conversation about your father and his woman having an emotional affair."

"Yeah, that conversation made me uncomfortable."

"I meant it to do that. I already knew about your make-out session here!"

He looked at me.

"You had an affair! And if you think that didn't impact us before this, you're crazy! "I sensed something. I just didn't know what it was. I thought the dysfunction was between Vee and me. But Timothy, there were times you didn't touch me for months! You had a willing partner who loves you lying beside you in bed and…nothing…zip…nada. That was you and Vee coming between us."

"All I can say is I am terribly sorry and I love you."

I shook my head. "I don't believe you love me. Or maybe we have completely different definitions of love. As for sorry. Right now, I don't know if you are sorry—or you are sorry you got caught."

"No, I am sorry, and I love you."

I sighed. "Well, in less than a week we will be in Germany. Everything I own is on a ship on its way over there…"

"I want you to come. You are coming, aren't you?"

"Yes. But only because I don't know what else to do."

He nodded.

"And tomorrow, you will have breakfast alone with Vee. Reassure her we can all remain friends. It'll take some work, but we can."

"I don't really want to do that…"

"But you will."

He nodded. "Yes, I will."

"Then we'll all have an early dinner out together. So we'll know we can all look each other in the face after all of this."

He nodded.

"Now, take me back to get the car. I'm tired."

"I love you," he said as he put the car and drove me back to Vee's house. Everything there was dark. He waited until I got in Kelly's car and followed me back to her house. It was 4:00 a.m. The sun would be up soon. The kids would be up soon. Everything would appear just as it had the morning before. But everything in my world had shifted. The monster in my middle was back, shredding the inside of my stomach.

As we walked up the driveway, Tim walked beside me but made no move to put his arm around me. I knew my force field was vibrantly in place. My legs felt like they each weighed one thousand pounds, and my lungs couldn't get enough air. We got into our night clothes and lay in bed. I turned on my side and watched the glow under the door.

I remembered a book I had gotten for the kids and decided not to read to them. It was filled with existential dread, which is fear of the unknown. It's the fear that comes when one's existence is threatened, one's well-being, when one's understanding of love is under assault. The book had no redeeming qualities in it. The main character was neglected by his parents and sent out in the garden, where a monster ate him. *God, I don't want this monster to eat me.*

DAY AFTER VEE-DAY

I must have dosed because the long, bright fingers of the sun streaming through the windows woke me. At first, I didn't move, then I turned my head to look at Tim. He was asleep, his blond hair a golden halo around his face, even the room had a lustrous sheen. I looked up at the textured ceiling, feeling the monster in my belly clawing at my stomach lining. Well, me and the monster are awake.

How could the sun dare to shine? My world had blown up. A giant meteor had dropped into the middle of our marriage lake. And I balanced myself carefully on the first tsunami wave. I could only ride it out. I couldn't go back before detonation. Those days were gone. I didn't want to fall backwards into the black hole and follow the meteor to its deathbed. So I rode the wave, the first wave, not knowing how long it would last or how many would follow.

Tim's eyes fluttered opened as soon as I got out of bed. "It's early."

"Yes, but we've got things to do and you've got people to meet. Vee."

He sighed. "I don't want to."

"Well, she needs to know you don't hate her. Do you hate her?"

"No." He sat up on the side of the bed.

"I think we can all remain friends, and the first step is you and her talking. She thinks you hate her...for telling me. Just reassure her we can still be friends. And then we'll all meet at Vegie's for an early dinner at 4:00 p.m. Tell her to meet us there. We all need to look each other in the face."

Tim nodded, got up, and gave me a hug. "I'm sorry."

"I know. We'll get through this."

While he was gone, I puttered around Kelly's house. I told her the digest version of what Vee had told me. She encouraged me to not let this break me and Tim up. I called another friend; and she said to leave him, not go to Germany, to take the kids and run. Run where?

Tim came home looking tired. For a man who rarely dealt in emotions, he probably was exhausted.

"Is she meeting us for dinner at 4:00 p.m.?"

"Yes, we're picking her up. You want to know what we talked about?"

"No, that's between you and her. Does she feel better?"

"I think so."

"Okay." I wondered if I was reacting normally. Is this how other people react to an affair?

At three thirty we picked her up for dinner. Tim and I wore jeans and a T-shirt. I'd put on no makeup. But Vee wore short shorts, and a very low-slung blouse, and a well-made-up face. I got in the back and let her sit up front. I watched the back of their heads, my husband and my best friend. They made small talk. I dug my fingers into my thighs and clutched my middle.

We all sat in a booth at Vegies, where we ordered their deep-fried vegetables with dip. I sat across from Tim and Vee, she next to the wall, and Tim on the outside part of the booth's seat. I felt the monster in my belly mangling and raking claws into my stomach's lining. Tim's jaw was clinched tightly shut. He was uncomfortable.

"Okay," I began, "I wanted us all to get together and know we could look each other in the face."

Vee's mascaraed blue eyes looked over at Tim, who was looking at me.

"We can get through this," I urged, "but some things will have to change."

"What things?" Vee asked.

"Well, you two being alone together for one. I'll no longer go to bed early when you're visiting. And of course, no more hugs between you."

Vee's black eyebrows rose into her hairline. "Hugs! Why can't we hug? We've always hugged. They're innocent."

"They didn't stay innocent for long, did they?"

Vee frowned at me, looked down, then at Tim. "Is this okay with you?"

He turned his head toward her and said, "Yes."

Vee looked stunned. Then in a faint voice, she murmured, "I can change your mind."

Tim shook his head. "No, you can't."

"Oh yes, I can…"

Tim again said, "No. You can't."

Her whispered words echoed in my head. I felt disoriented and gripped the end of the table with my hands. Had I heard her correctly? It had a surreal quality to it. I looked at Tim. His face had turned red. He'd turned slightly away from Vee. He was angry. I reached for his hand, and he gripped mine in the middle of the table. I glanced at Vee. She looked first annoyed and then sad. Just for a minute, I felt sorry for her.

After dinner we went by a card shop, where Vee and I spun cards in one rack.

"Vee, I think I may be in shock. I will need you to write me while I'm in Germany, so we can work through all that may come. You never wrote when I was in Maryland, but I'll really need you to do so now. Okay?"

"Sure," she answered. "I think you are making too much of this."

Making too much of this? Something about her demeanor was unsettling, but I'd decipher it later. "Whatever I'm '*making of it*' in your mind, I know I'll need you to write. Will you?"

"Yes, I said I would."

That didn't sound like a solid vow. It sounded like a quick answer to get me to stop asking.

As we walked to the car, Vee said, "You know, I saved him from having a midlife crisis."

I stopped her from walking by pulling on her arm, and I walked in front of her. "Bullshit! You *are* his midlife crisis."

She looked at my hand on her arm, then glared at me. "Sadie, really, you are…"

"Stop. Don't you dare tell me I'm making too much of this. Don't tell me how to feel."

"Is this part of you saying what you mean and being who you are?"

We continued walking side by side. "Yes, it is."

"Well, you're being mean, and I'm not sure I like this *new* you."

"Good," I growled. "Because I'm not sure I like the *old* you."

We got into the car. I claimed the front seat, causing Vee a misstep because that where she thought she would sit. We drove in a silence as thick as molasses. After we dropped Vee at her house, we drove to the beach, parked, and walked out on the pier. We both watched the ocean. The waves rolled and reared, topped with white spume. They raced to shore, where they vanished or retreated.

Tim put his arm around me.

I turned to him. "I don't understand…Am I not thin enough? She's smaller than me. Am I not sexy enough? She knows how to be sensual. What?"

"No, it has nothing to do with what you are or aren't. Really, it doesn't."

"It has to! I have to lack something that she has."

"No, it's not about that. Believe me."

"I know I've loved you the best way I knew how. I don't know what I could have done differently."

The waves captured our attention again. The immense surging blue giant hypnotized us with its pulsing, swelling rush.

"Is there anything I could have done differently? And don't say 'nothing.' There is always something."

Tim cocked his head to the left. His thinking mode. "There are a thousand things I could have done in another way to be a better husband…"

I shook my head.

"No, I could have. And there must have been times I frustrated you or made you angry, but you never voiced it. I want to see, hear, and feel your emotions."

I froze for a moment. *Ohmigod, he's right.* "That's true," I sighed sadly.

"But that is not the reason Vee happened. You know, I married a quirky little girl. Where did she go?"

"She…uh…she didn't know how to be married, so she turned to other models to show her how, like TV."

"I never wanted to marry a TV wife. I wanted you. All of you, just as you are."

"Yes, I see now. I hid me."

"I've told you I want to know your feelings, be that anger, disappointment, or joy. All of it. I never wanted perfect."

"Okay, be careful what you ask for. I plan to tell you exactly how I feel from here on out. The other way didn't work well…one more thing…"

Tim nodded, his sky-blue eyes looking at me.

"I always thought if you cheated, I'd see it in your eyes. I'd know it, and I knew nothing. I feel betrayed by myself. How can I believe anything from now on?"

"You didn't know because we, Vee and I, worked so you wouldn't. It's not like it was plainly in front of your face. We concealed it."

"Okay, but I don't want to become that person who thinks everyone is hiding or cheating."

"Then don't. I think you'll have better radar after this, and if you feel something is amiss, say it. Speak it. Ask about it? Flush it out."

I remembered years ago feeling funny when he took Vee to the concert. I hadn't been able to sleep. He came home so late, but I had pushed the feeling down. "Right, I will do so from here on out. You may not like this version of me."

"I will. I'll have the full unadulterated you. It's what I've always wanted."

One day later we were in Baltimore, where I was scheduled for a lie-detector test, along with the Minnesota Multiphasic Personality Inventory test, and a psychiatrist visit—all to obtain a secret security clearance and be able to get a job on base in Germany. Would they see that I'm undone?

It was an exhausting day. That evening after dinner, Tim and I talked.

"You know, I know a lot of women would run out and have an affair because you did, but I wouldn't even know how to do that." I bit the side of my lip.

"Some would, but it wouldn't help anything."

"I know. Doing that would not only not help us, but it would injure me."

"I'm glad you know that because you are right."

"But if I did want to have an affair, I wouldn't even know how. How does one do that? I've only made love with one man, you. I don't know how to flirt. What would I do, approach a guy at a bar and say, 'I don't know how to have a one night stand, but I'd like to. Will you have sex with me?' That wouldn't work."

"Oh, it might. And I'm glad you are not doing that."

"I'm not. I saw infidelity galore growing up. I promised myself that I would not do that unless I was legally separated or divorced. None of that bed-hopping for me."

"You thought of that when you were a kid?"

"Yeah, I told you, life was serious for me."

"I don't think I ever thought deeply. Not even after one failed marriage."

"Obviously not." I looked at him. "No, sorry, that was a dig…"

"One deserved."

"No, digs are passive ways to say what you mean. What I meant by 'obviously not' was that you didn't come up like me with danger, intrigue, lies and cheating all around you. So, of course, you didn't think that way. As for not thinking so after your first marriage, well, we think differently."

Tim laughed. "Yes, I've never known anyone who thinks like you…"

"You told me that before we got married…when I was that quirky girl."

"Yes, and she's back! And I'm so glad."

Again, I said, "Be careful what you wish for…"

PAMELA K. KEYSER

FOREIGN COUNTRY WITH SEISMIC FEELINGS

Four days later, on August 4, we were in Germany—away from everything and everybody I knew. People I encountered saw me as a whole person, but I was a person in pieces. It amazed me that they didn't see it in my face or sense it. Likewise, I wondered if any of them were among the walking wounded. If they were, would I see it? I could still sense how a person felt in spite of how they said they did. But right now, I didn't have the emotional energy to reach out.

I had my thirty-seventh birthday a couple of days after landing in Germany. Tim got me a cake, and the kids sang "Happy Birthday." That evening, I took off my wedding band and put it on the counter. Tim noticed but didn't say anything, nor did he give me a disapproving look. It made me realize how much I watched his expressions. When he'd sneeze, I used to wonder if I'd created dust. No more. I could only depend on his words, not his expressions, and certainly not my interpretation of them. I told him I'd no longer try to figure out why or if he was feeling something. I'd ask. And I invited him to be precise with his words because that is what I would depend on from now on out.

Our townhouse was brand-new. It had two stories, three bedrooms, marble floors with an attic, and a basement. In the daytime, I contended with home builders, kids, lunches, and dinners. Tim went to orientation. After the kids were tucked into bed, I'd break my rule of not drinking when I had problems and I'd grab a bottle of wine and sit and sip. We had no TV, no stereo that worked on German frequency.

It was just Tim and me. I promised myself not to choke these feelings down. I gave myself permission to feel them and to speak them. Tearfully, I'd ask, "You are the one who cheated, so why do I feel humiliated?"

"I wish you didn't. You did nothing wrong."

"I falsely believed I was happily married. And I *was* wrong. Oh so wrong."

"We had happy times…"

"True, but I believed in the state of our marriage. I thought I knew, but I didn't. And I don't know if I can ever believe me again."

"You can. You will. And please quit punishing yourself for something I did."

"How am I punishing myself?"

"By letting yourself feel humiliated. You did nothing. All these feelings of hurt, resentment, and humiliation have the root cause of me. Remember that. You did nothing wrong."

By then it'd be about 1:00 or 2:00 a.m., and we'd go to bed where we'd make excellent love. It was one way to communicate that didn't need words. The next morning we'd get up, and the day would repeat. By the time the kids were in bed, I was undone again, and we'd talk until the wee hours of the night.

During those nightly talks, I told him that when I first found out about Vee, I'd felt empty, no feelings. But I recognized that as shock and it was over, and now I was experiencing an avalanche of feelings. "I can't believe you betrayed my trust, when you knew how much it cost me to give it."

"I am so sorry," Tim would say.

"Everything is messed up. Our marriage, if we have one. Friendship. Vee was my closest friend. How could she do this? My relationship to God. Vee and I bonded over our growing relationship to the Big Guy. How can I go on believing? In you, in her, in friendship, in God, in anything."

Tim said, "We have a marriage, and we can get through this."

"I don't want to just get through it. Remember when I said I wanted a great marriage? That's still what I want, but we both lost track of that."

He nodded. "You and Vee and your friendship, that's between you guys. As for me, I'll keep my distance."

"Why?" I turned to look at him. "Because you think you'd fall back into it?"

"No, definitely not. I can honestly say I feel no attraction to her now."

"Why? Why now? Why not then?"

"Now, because of how she's treating you. Why not then? I don't know for certain…this is not an excuse, but she was sensual…"

"If you want sensual, she tried to teach me how. How to flirt, how to seem sensual. To her meant letting a guy feel he could take you home that night and make mad, passionate love to you. She tried to teach me that at a bar. But I didn't want to do that. So if sensual is what you want…"

"No, it's not what I want. You couldn't do that at a bar because that's not you. The guy wouldn't be able to take you home that night, and you didn't want to pretend. Vee wasn't pretending. He could have taken her home. That's the difference."

"I was being me, and she was being her."

He nodded.

"But you chose her…"

"No, I never chose her. I played around with her because…partly she was available, but she was always a side dish. You are the real twelve-course dinner. That's what I want permanently. And I'm so sorry I betrayed you. I hate all the pain I've created in you, that along with your precious trust. I hope to earn it back."

"I hope so too. I just don't know right now. I don't even know if I want to stay married. I don't know if I can. I don't know…" I looked at Tim and saw him wince. "And I'm so sorry I keep doing this! We talk, and I'm good for like fifteen to eighteen hours, then I'm right back to square one. I'm sorry."

"No. Don't you ever apologize for how you feel. Speak it. Maybe I need to hear it."

Relief swept over me. He owned his betrayal, which somehow made it easier for me. We went upstairs arm in arm. But eighteen hours later, we sat and talked again, and I cried again.

September came, and the kids went back to school, which gave me longer to flounder in my circular thoughts, to ride the tsunamic wave, fall in the trough between waves, and crawl back on one.

I'd written Vee a letter as soon as we arrived in Germany, along with my father and Kelly. After that, I wrote no more except in my journal, putting the blood from the infidelity wound on paper. Tim was working shifts now, days, evening, and mid-nights. When he got off an evening shift, at about twelve midnight, we'd talk, and I'd cry and question until about 3:00 or 4:00 a.m. Then we'd go to bed. I'd get up with the kids, get them off to school, and go back to sleep on the couch. If he worked midnight to 7:00 a.m. (mids), we talk until about noon, then he'd trudge up to bed to rest up for another shift. I'd greet the kids home from school, fix dinner, put them to bed, and sit with my journal and a bottle of wine.

I thought I might be turning into Aunt Ruby and voiced my fear to Tim.

"No," he answered. "Your aunt drank her bottle and went to bed alone without talking to her husband. You are talking to me. If wine helps that, then for now, it's okay."

"Will we know when it's not okay?"

"Yes. We will. I will."

"And you'll tell me?"

"Yes."

I forgot friends' birthdays and anniversaries. I forgot to remind Tim of his oldest son's birthday, Mike. I had made myself responsible for reminding him. And now I'd forgotten one of Mike's most important birthdays—his eighteenth. And Tim didn't remember because I had made him dependent on me to remind him. I loved those boys, and I'd failed them. I failed many outward things during that time period because I was in crisis mode. I was a raw nerve ending exposed to the elements. Every evening through August and half of September, I confronted Tim with my doubt, fear, pain, and perception. In mid-September, I could go every other day, until my anxiety built back up. Then Tim would patiently sit, hold my hand, and answer my every question.

OCTOBER AFTER THE METEOR CRASH

Our sponsor in Germany was a divorced man about our age. A sponsor would meet us at the airport and answer questions. His name was Richard; and he was tall, athletically built, and helpful. He showed us around Bad Aibling, the town and the base. Richard and his girlfriend took us, along with another couple, to a German discotheque with a DJ. I learned my first German phrase, "Michael Jackson, beat it, bitte."

Dancing had always been a space of freedom for me, and now was no different. When I was on the dance floor, I wasn't the walking wounded. I was just part of the music. It told me what to do. In the past, I'd have danced exclusively with Tim. Not now. I asked our neighbor and Richard to dance, and if nobody felt like it, I got out and danced by myself. In the past, Tim usually grudgingly danced after a few beers. Although, this time he began right away.

On the way off the dance floor while the DJ took a break, I asked, "How come it's not taking two beers before you dance?"

"Because I know how much you love it."

"I've always loved it. But pre-Vee you still nursed a couple of drinks before getting up."

"Yes, but I'm doing differently now. Choosing differently."

"Wonderful, don't revert to form down the line. I like this." He smiled.

Earlier in the month, there was a picnic on the base. We brought some food, sat with friends, drank wine, danced, and watched our kids play. There was an extremely attractive Navy guy who captivated most of the women's attention. He sat beside me, and we joked back and forth. I could sense Tim not liking our banter. In the past, I would not have wanted him to feel that way and quit talking to Sean. Now, I continued. I was doing nothing wrong. If Tim was uncomfortable, it was his own inside-out feeling.

Sean spilled his beer on his lap, and I rounded up all the napkins I could and laid them on the puddle near his crotch.

Tim's eyebrow rose. "I'm working a mid," he said. "I'm ready to go home."

I looked at him. "I'm not. You go on. I'll get a ride home later."

I sensed he'd rather go home, but he stayed. This is the post-Vee me.

As we forged a new marriage, I still became consumed by the pain every couple of days. But instead of needing to talk it out every night, now it happened about twice a week. I saw that as an improvement.

Tim owned what he'd done, and that made it easier for me to allow myself to feel, speak, and cry. I told him I didn't know who he was anymore. Because who I had thought he was, he wasn't. "I once told Vee that you had such integrity that a woman could undress before you and you'd tell her to get dressed." She must have laughed inside.

"She told me you said that. She felt guilt. I did too. I never felt comfortable with your lofty compliments about me."

"You don't like compliments?" I asked.

"No, compliments are okay, but being placed on a pedestal is uncomfortable."

I was quiet.

"Your turn," Tim prompted.

"I did place you on a pedestal. But your feeling uncomfortable has only to do with yourself. And you never talked to me about putting you on a pedestal."

"True. I held back too."

"So, in our new marriage, if we have one, we will promise to love each other enough to tell the truth—even if it's not pretty. Okay?"

"Yes. Truth first and always."

"Okay, I'm not only figuring out who you really are. I'm doing it at the precise time you are also evolving because of Vee. I am grieving our first marriage, or my idea of it."

"I hope we'll have a better, great second marriage."

I nodded. "We'll never get our first marriage back. That girl will never return. And yes, she did a lot of pretending, but she did other stuff that you may miss."

"I'll get over it."

"Thanks for giving me time to grieve that marriage. It helps."

"I'll do whatever it takes."

As soon as I found out about Tim and Vee, I had wanted to cut myself. Get the pain on the outside. I'd gone into Kelly's bathroom and grabbed a safety razor out of her medicine cabinet. I took off my watch and looked at the faint line where I'd cut before. I heard the kids laughing in the living room, and I looked at myself in the mirror. I saw someone in pain but a survivor. I saw strength even though I felt I was put together with spit and bubblegum.

"I'm not fifteen anymore." I put my watch back on my wrist. "I'll speak my pain. Yell it, if I have to scream it. Beat pillows. But this time I will not cut myself." I nodded to the woman in the mirror with the sad green eyes. I put the razor back in the medicine cabinet, and as the girl in the mirror reappeared, I whispered, "I promise."

NOVEMBER AFTER THE TSUNAMI

The first week in November, I told Tim I'd like just us to go to Berchtesgaden. I would tell him there what I'd decided about our marriage. He made all the arrangements, getting off work and having a babysitter for the kids. I also prepared. Friday night we relaxed. The next day we took a boat out on the Konigssee, an alpine lake. The freshwater was magical. Hitler had his Eagle's Nest in Berchtesgaden, so the area was not bombed. The water was clear, and mist swirled around the edges.

We had dinner at a German restaurant and retired to our hotel room. I asked Tim to sit down, and I took out a couple of pieces of paper. "I will read them to you."

Tim nodded.

***

Hello Love,

It's been a long time since I've "written" you. Remember all those long and short, silly, and sweet letters? I used to prefer writing to talking—but now I prefer the latter. However, right now I have a lot to say and I'm hoping the pen and paper will help structure my words.

First, I want to say the words, "I forgive you." But let me explain. Forgiveness is something taught to us when we are little boys and girls. Sometimes it is imparted to us by force. We're told to kiss our big brother after he's been forced to say he's sorry. It makes forgiveness seem easily dismissed and obtained with a kiss. From my experience, forgiveness is a multifaceted and hard worked at process.

In order for me to say these words, there had to be some violating deed done to me. Correct? Yes, but both parties have to agree to that fact. And I think we have. I thank you for saying, "What I did wasn't right, and you have every justification to be angry and hurt." Thanks for that—because it gave me permission to go through the pain of healing. If you had said instead, "I'm so sorry *you* are hurt." You would have been consigning the responsibility of both the pain and forgiveness to me. So I bled and cried and raged…and slowly began healing. I know it wasn't easy for you either, to watch.

In order to say the above words, I had to decide if the violation, all by itself, without my personal connection to it, was forgivable. There are some things that might be so repugnant to my internal code of ethics that forgiveness would be unattainable. I discovered that the affair with Vee is forgivable, *this time*. I don't mean this as a threat, although that is how it might sound. What I mean is that if anything like this happens again, I wouldn't be able to sustain it. It would breach my sense of personal identity so acutely and so much that I could not forgive you and remain true to me. I won't ask pardon for this or try to offer moral vindications for this attitude. I don't think it's right—I only know and am stating my limits.

Next, I had to decide if I was forgiving from a posture of strength or weakness. Forgiveness from weakness comes from fear. Fear of not being able to live without you. And it is contrastingly different from forgiving that comes from love. A loving essence, full of vigor and strength to overcome emotional pain. I am glad you are in my life, but I could live without you. I choose to be here. I choose at times to depend on you. I choose at times to need you. But I am complete within myself and could live without you.

For a long while, I wondered if you were sorry you and Vee had an affair or if you were sorry, you'd been caught. I played this question over and over in my mind. Then, lately, I decided it doesn't matter. A man who doesn't care about his wife also wouldn't care if he got caught.

What happened between you and Vee hurt a lot, for many reasons. The lies it implied, the uncaringness about my feelings. The fact that you are my husband and I love you and she is my best friend and I love her, the eight years it went on. Finding out made me feel stupid. I should have "felt" it, sensed it, or seen someone else in your eyes—and I didn't. It made me feel betrayed on two fronts. I questioned your values; I questioned mine. I questioned the concept of love, marriage, and friendship.

Oh Lord, the stages I went through. Starting with numbness to sadness to anger, with tears and rage throughout. I especially mourned the loss or "rape" of my innocence and trust. This I gave to you as a gift. I was like a loving child who jumps into their parent's arms from the top of a slide, knowing they'd catch me. Well, now I give you that same trust. But now I give it to you as an adult, knowing you can drop me and hurt me. But possibly, just maybe that makes it a better gift, a better trust. My innocence cannot be restored. But I refuse to let it turn me into a suspicious, jealous person. I still believe that affairs do not "happen." I believe that choices are made. I won't watch your every move or monitor your friendships. Not even with Vee. So the choice is yours. And this time we both know the cost.

Since learning of you and Vee, I've gone through stages. Worked out complicated emotions, and this thing has changed me. In some ways, it's evident. In other ways, not so apparent. And still in other ways, I'm still evolving. I've never experienced such a surge of personal growth as I have in these last few months...Roses from ashes.

So I am ready to begin again, but I have no idea of the ending, and that scares me.

I love you, but my love is different. I don't know if it's better or worse, and that scares me.

I feel something is missing. I've tried and tried to identify what "it" is. What "it" could be. But I don't know—and that scares me because I am usually so good at figuring out these things. I'm afraid it might mean a defection in me.

But knowing all this, and knowing you know, and knowing we both don't know the outcome, I am still ready to begin.

But putting my ring back on a second time is a lot harder that it was the first time (I was scared then too). But I am ready to try. To start. To begin.

With this ring, "I thee wed." Let's go. Let's begin again.

Love,
Sadie

***

Tim wiped a tear from his eye. "Thank you," he softly said. "I want you to know how much I appreciate you. Also, in the future, I will be 100 percent transparent. Where I say I am is where I'll be. You can check."

"I told you, I will not become that suspicious person."

"Right, but just know that if you need to get ahold of me, it won't be hard. I'll be where I said I would be."

I nodded and placed three wedding bands on the bed. He looked at them, and then up at me. "I'll put our ten-year-old band on." I handed him a second thin white gold band. "You can put this on me, and it signifies our second marriage." I put my hand out.

He took the small thin band and slipped it on my finger next to the other ring.

I then took the larger white gold band in my hand. "I would like you to wear this to signify our new and improved marriage. Okay?"

He nodded, and I slipped it on his finger next to the one he'd put on ten years earlier and never taken off. He leaned over and kissed me. "Shall I get the cheese and wine?"

"Yes." I smiled. "Wine, without me whining! Will wonders never cease?"

"Hey, be nice when you are talking about my wife." He wagged his finger at me, and we laughed.

That night we slept with our feet entwined like old times. I'd ridden the tsunami wave and survived. We'd survived. Little did I know that that was only the first wave and that many would follow. I wanted it to be over, but the ripples from the original impact were on their way.

RETROSPECT

First, thank God this happened! It knocked me out of my pretend bubble, my shaping myself to be what I perceived my man wanted. I wouldn't wish this on anyone else because it was acutely painful. And if I said this to Vee, she'd have answered, "See what I did for you?" But what she and Tim did was destructive. It is to our credit (Tim and I) that we arose from the ashes better and stronger. She didn't do that, we did. It could just have easily been the end of us.

I had been heading toward this position before Vee. Like deciding I would not be depressed anymore. That was before the explosion. And the accelerated evolution of myself didn't stop when Tim and I put on our second wedding bands. My eyes had been opened, and I was hungry for more self-knowledge. Tim once asked me what I wanted out of our marriage. I said I wanted to peel off the layers, like you peel an onion. I wanted to get down to the shiny, vulnerable, center and share that with his heart.

I had no idea other waves were coming. I'm glad I didn't. I don't know that I'd have thought I could endure them. But when you are riding a tsunami wave, you try to balance and keep your head above water. You don't worry about the next wave because this one has all of your concentration.

I never went back to pretending. I became fully myself, but not always my best self.

FATHER'S DEATH

Bad Aibling, Germany, was a fascinating tiny village; and all of us loved exploring it. Every morning we would see eight-ish German women on bicycles, riding to town to get the food they would cook that day. Because they shopped and cooked daily, they didn't have huge refrigerators. Americans, by contrast, drove everywhere even if it were within walking distance. We had huge refrigerators to hold weeks of food. And by age eighty, we would walk with difficulty, not riding bikes up and down hills to town.

My father died in May, and I flew back home. It was a ten-hour flight, and I had plenty of time to think. After

TheLady had died, my father said he'd met a wonderful woman by the name of Hazel. I was happy for him. That Thanksgiving, he called me, and we awkwardly tried to talk. He asked how I was, how was Tim, Kyle, and Kelly. I asked about him. During this call, Tim walked by, and I put my hand over the receiver and said, "It's my father, and I don't know what he wants." After we hung up, I told Tim that that was the strangest phone call I'd ever gotten. It was almost like he only wanted to wish me a happy holiday.

A year later, he married Hazel, who I called Mom. She told me they had been sitting at her dining room table with the phone placed on it. She called her son, Rick (who was my age), to wish him a happy Thanksgiving. After they hung up, she handed the phone to my father, and he hung it up. She retrieved the receiver and handed it to him again. And he hung it up. After the third time, he asked why she kept handing him the phone.

"To call Sadie."

"Why would I call Sadie?" he asked.

Handing him back the receiver, she said, "To wish her a happy Thanksgiving."

She had initiated that strange phone call. She didn't know it was the first time since I'd left home at age sixteen that he'd called me at all, let alone to wish me a happy holiday.

Now he was dead. He'd died of a myocardial infarction at seventy-two. They had been planning a trip to come see us that October. I hoped Hazel would still come. Rick picked me up from the airport, along with Aunt Ruby, who'd flown in on another airline. He drove us to Key Largo, where my father and Hazel had bought a house.

Hazel was crying as she greeted me. "I don't know how I'll live without him." She was gutted. They'd been married seven years by then. We drove eight hours up to Jacksonville,

Florida, to bury him. I don't think Hazel ever quit crying. I didn't cry.

I was grateful we'd had the last seven years on acceptable terms. In his mind, I had become a respectable wife and mother. He loved his grandkids, especially my daughter. She could wrap him around her little finger.

After the funeral, I went to the bank and helped Mom change her joint accounts to single ones. The clerk handed her a paper to sign, and Mom burst into tears.

"How am I going to sign my name? I'm not Mrs. Jett Brooker anymore."

"No, but you're still Hazel Brooker," I urged. I vowed to sign all my papers, cards, and correspondence, "Ms. Sadie Keyser."

Mom explained that she and Jett had agreed that the house they lived in would go to Rick and me. They had each put $2,500 toward the down payment of their modular home. It was between the canal and the Atlantic Ocean. Then she'd always say, "I feel sad when you and Rick have to clean out of all my stuff."

"Mom, you're gonna live to be one hundred!"

Rick asked if I wanted him to buy me out. But I didn't. If Mom and my father had wanted us both to have it, that was okay with me.

My father's death didn't impact me much. He'd hardly ever lived around me for most of my life, and now it felt like he was just away again. I'd never asked him any of the tough questions I had. I didn't want to destroy the pleasant relationship we'd had since he married Hazel.

While in the States, I went to see Tim's parents and Kelly. Kelly's dad came over a couple of times while I was there, but he steered clear of me. I couldn't wait to get back to Germany, to my kids and to Tim.

14

CHAPTER

AFTERMATH OF TSUNAMI

RIPPLES IN SECOND MARRIAGE

I MADE MANY friends in Germany. One was Richard, who'd been our sponsor. In the beginning of November, he asked if I'd go shopping with him to get his girlfriend a robe. He drove us to Rosenheim, which was a bigger city than Bad Aibling. We wandered stores, and finally he picked out a tie rope with pockets.

He asked if I wanted to go to his apartment and listen to music, and I did. We talked. He told me about his divorce, his two little kids, and how he still missed being married. We agreed that Germany was magnificent. I borrowed his phone to call Tim at work on the day shift. I told him I was at Richards and he'd drop me off on post by the bookstore. The kids were staying on base after school and meeting us there as well. We planned to go to Munich.

Richard dropped me off and waved as he drove off in the snow that was now coming down. We all piled into the car when Tim drove up, and immediately the inside windows fogged up. This called for heavy duty defrost, and it was hard to hear each other talk. As we drove out of base, Tim asked if I'd had an enjoyable day.

"Yes! We shopped in Rosenheim, then went to Richard's apartment and listened to some music and talked. He decorated it really well for a bachelor.

"Went to his apartment!" Tim hissed as we went out the gate.

"Yes."

His face turned red. "I really dislike you going to his place! That's reckless and doesn't look good."

"Look good?"

"Yes, if people see you hanging around with a guy, they'll start talking."

"Let them talk. I don't care."

"Listen, I care. And I don't want you to do that anymore!"

"Do what? Be friends with Richard? Or go to his place?"

"Both!"

I shut down. I turned and looked out the passenger window as the big flakes of snow bombarded the landscape. The car skidded on a turn, and we decided it was too dangerous to go to Munich.

The radio was on, and the kids were singing to the songs in the back seat.

Up front, the quiet was oppressive.

"I'm sorry," Tim said. "I shouldn't have talked to you that way."

I turned to him. "Right. You shouldn't have. And you being uncomfortable with me being friends with Richard, shopping with him and going to his apartment is all about you. It reflects how you've acted in the past. I have never given you any indication that I would do something like that."

He nodded. "You haven't. But it still makes me uncomfortable."

"Then you'd better work on that because I will be friends with whoever I please. Male or female. And your discomfort is yours, and yours to work on."

He sighed as we drove into our garage. "You have changed."

"Yes. I have. Before I'd have quit a good friendship because of your insecurities and I'd have resented it. Now, I say what I think. That's what you wanted."

"I did. Sometimes it doesn't happen like I thought it would."

ANOTHER RIPPLE

Things were not happening like either of us had thought. After we'd put on our second marriage bands, Tim went back to his old way of being. Working shift, sleeping long hours, and playing every sport he could in between: bowling, volleyball, and softball. We had our second marriage bands on, but we were operating like we had before.

In mid-November, after I put the kids to bed and Tim was upstairs, I looked out our back window. In back of our yard, there was a row of townhouses, mainly filled with Americans. I couldn't be sure, but I thought I saw a kitten. I decided to investigate.

I quietly let myself out the front door and walked around back. I got about halfway down the sidewalk before I saw a tiny form. I walked a few more steps, knelt, and called the kitten. "Here kitty, kitty, kitty…" The little furry ball took one look at me and took off down the walk and over a fence.

I walked back to our front door to find Tim standing in it in his robe. "Why are you going to see Darren?"

"Darren?" He was our neighbor on the backside, and our next-door neighbor was having an affair with him.

"Yes! Darren. I saw you walking toward his house!"

"Oh, did you now?" I asked as I pushed past him into the living room.

"Yes, damn it. I did!"

"Did you also see me kneel halfway down the walk?"

"Kneel? No, I got so mad I had to close the curtain. It really disgusts me."

"Well, you should have kept watching because I went back there because I thought I saw a kitten! Yes, a cat. And I saw the baby about halfway down the walk. I knelt down to coach it to me, but it ran away. I wasn't going to Darren's damn house! And I'm angry you would think so."

"What am I supposed to think when I look out the window and see you headed that way?"

"Oh, I don't know. That I'm visiting any of the other five Americans who live there? But no, your mind goes to Darren!"

"Yes, everyone knows he's a man who will bed any woman. That you would go there makes me sick."

"Not this woman. Again, this is because *you* were unfaithful. And now you are insecure and pointing fingers. I've never been two-timing. I've never wanted to be and would never be. Yet you don't know that. That's what's sick." I slouched down in a chair opposite the couch.

After a couple of minutes, Tim said, "I'm sorry I jumped to conclusions."

"Me too."

"I'm really sorry. I'll work on that, okay?"

I didn't answer.

"Come on, it's late. Let's go to bed."

"You go. I'm too keyed up to sleep. I'll be down here and not anywhere else, promise!" I said sarcastically.

"I didn't mean to upset you."

"Really? It seems like you did. Just go. Leave me alone, please."

He stood, went upstairs, and I heard the bed creak as he got into it.

I sat and wondered how we'd gotten here. My second marriage could be a lot shorter than my first one. Because I wasn't willing to pretend everything was okay when it wasn't.

EXPENSIVE CALL

At Thanksgiving, just a year into our second marriage, I told him I was thinking of going to the States for a while, a long while, and leaving the kids with him in school. He said okay and didn't try to talk me out of it. I made an airplane reservation for the day after Christmas.

The end of the first week in December, I received a telephone call. The kids were playing next door, and Tim was sleeping because he worked the midnight shift. I answered the ring quickly.

"Sadie! It's Vee?"

"Vee? Wow! How are you?"

"I'm good. Now you know how much I love you because I'm calling you long distance from Florida!"

"Right."

"I've met a guy…" And she told me all about him. I listened. I asked few questions. I knew she noticed my silence. She trailed off by telling me again how much spending the money on the phone call proved she cared about me.

We said our good-byes.

HELLO/GOODBYE

That night after Vee's call, I was in the kitchen making dinner when the bells in the church started ringing. The kids and Tim all came to see what was happening, and we saw a bride and groom come out of the big double doors.

"Are they getting married?" my daughter asked.

"I believe they are," I answered.

Soon the kids lost interest and went back into the living room.

I stirred a pot. "Poor girl," I said.

"Why poor?" Tim asked.

"Because it's her wedding day, and she thinks everything will be grand. But it isn't. And she won't know that until he breaks her heart."

"Is that how you think of marriage?"

The spoon froze in my hand. "Ah…sadly, I think it is…"

"Sadie, I'm so sorry. I don't want you to feel this way."

"That makes two of us."

"It occurred to me that if I want you to stay, I will have to fight for you to stay."

I thought about it. "Yes, or at least use your words and say that."

"I want you to stay."

"I don't like how we are right now."

"Me either. We'll change it."

I shook my head. "Can we?"

"I think we can. I know we can. Please think about it. Let's not give up on us. Let's improve and raise our kids together."

"Let me think about it."

He looked at me a long time. "Okay. But not too long. Your plane leaves in a week. And I'd really like you to cancel and not be on it."

"I'll think about it while you work tonight. Promise."

SICK THOUGHTS

After Tim went to work at midnight, I got out some writing paper and a bottle of wine. I wrote Vee and told her I knew my silence had hurt her. But I was in pain! My emotional intestines were exposed, and I was bleeding out, and she'd never even asked how I was!

"You think you proved how much you care for me by calling after over a year? All I ever asked for was the cost of a stamp. But you couldn't do that."

I went on, "I told you I would need you to write! To help me understand stuff. Like were you ever my friend or did you just remain friends with me so you could play around with Tim?"

On and on I wrote. Finally, I finished the letter, signed it, sealed it, and put her address on the front along with a stamp.

I took out some library books on divorce, thumbed through them, and shoved them back under the couch. That morning, I'd read a story about a mother in Washington D. C., who shot and killed her only daughter. She attempted to kill herself but only blew her arm off. She called an ambulance. There were letters to the editor about how evil she was.

My daughter was the age I was when my parents divorced—and my world changed. I knew divorce changed kids' lives. My kids came to me when they wanted to talk about a problem or work through some complicated thoughts. I was their emotional center. Tim was more reserved and distant, a good father but not warm and fuzzy with emotions.

But Tim could provide for them. He made a good living. If I left and took the kids, I would have to work two or three jobs to support them. What kind of emotional support would that be if I was never with them? But the thought of leaving my kids doubled me over. How could I do that? They'd feel abandoned.

For that night, I understood how a mother could kill her children and then herself. She felt there was no other way out. She felt death was preferable to abandonment. I wrote in my journal how I understood how a woman could do that. Not because she wanted to hurt them, but because she wanted to spare them. And if they were gone, and she'd facilitated their deaths, why would she want to stay alive.

I wondered how her husband felt. I knew his child's death had been a massive blow to his being. But did he miss his wife? Or had all that love turned to hate. Could he, in the wee hours of the morning, understand why she might have done that? Would he be okay going forward? Would work, sports, and other family help fill the gap? It would never heal the wound, but would he be able to live a life afterward?

I thought of my two beautiful babies upstairs asleep, safe and sound. If I divorced Tim and took them, they would be unhappy because neither of us would really be there for them. If I divorced Tim and left the kids, they would feel abandoned by their mother. A big emotional gash that would change who they were. Could I divorce Tim and live by them? I'd still have to work two jobs just to pay rent. When would I see them? Would they understand that although I didn't physically have custody of them, I loved them?

Oh! And what if Tim remarried? Another woman raising my children. I hadn't thought of that. What if I stayed married? I could. Even though right now in our second marriage, I was miserable. Shit! They'd feel our disconnect. Kid's always do. So how could I be doing them a favor by doing that?

I wrote in my journal again, how I understood why a woman might kill herself and her kids. I wrote that one sentence on a page by itself and circled and circled it with the pen. After a full bottle of wine, I fell asleep. The kids woke me up. They were late for school. So I dropped everything and called Tim, asking him to get off early and come get them.

He came home and took the kids. While everyone was out of the house, I picked up Vee's letter and my journal. It was open to the page where I'd written how I understood a woman killing her kids and herself.

I stared at my writing. I remembered understanding last night, although I didn't understand this morning. No, this morning I was filled with guilt and horrified by what I'd understood the night before. God, I'm terrible! Oh no, no, I will not go back to calling myself names. No. What would I tell a friend? My litmus test.

I'd listen to them and tell them they were in pain. They needed help. I'd tell them to find a psychologist. I knew the base had one. I would make an appointment today. I couldn't handle this alone.

Tim came home. He'd brought me coffee, and he asked me if I'd thought about staying.

"Yes, I almost stayed up all night."

"And?"

"And I need to see a psychologist. I'm messed up still."

"Okay."

"And you have to stop being paranoid, jealous, and seeing me as unfaithful. I won't live that way."

"I agree. You were right. It's my own insecurities. I promise never to do that again."

"How can you promise?"

"Because I'm in charge of me. If I start feeling that way, I'll get help. I won't visit it on you."

"Okay. And I will continue to have male friends. I will continue to go to dances when you work and dance with other guys. I will continue to be me."

He smiled. "That's what I want."

"Not while it's happening. Sometimes you don't. But I still believe that men and women can be friends! I believe being unfaithful or faithful is a choice. Your penis doesn't run turbocharged ahead with you holding on to the base, trying to brake, yelling, 'But I don't want to.' Infidelity is making a choice. It may be a hundred little choices before the big one, but still those are choices."

"I agree." He shook his head. "That's quite a visual."

"Yes, it is. But next time you get all wrongly paranoid, remember that I was cheated on and I don't follow you around, spy on you, or check to see who you are talking with at any time."

"I know. You are amazing."

"Well, it helps that you are being so transparent. Thanks for that."

He smiled. "Staying?"

"Yup, one more question. Why do you want me to stay?"

"Because I love you, and selfishly, I'm a better person being married to you than if I wasn't."

"Okay, I will."

He got up, picked up the envelop, and said, "A letter for Vee?"

I told him it was and about her phone call. I told him the contents of the letter. "You think I'm being mean?"

"No, I think you are being truthful."

"Okay, you go on up to sleep, and I'll make a psychologist appointment."

"Oh, you look tired too. Make the appointment later. Let's go to bed together."

"Is that an indecent proposition?"

"It sure is."

PSYCHOLOGY AFTER TSUNAMI

That afternoon, I made an appointment with Mr. Stiles, the base psychologist. It was one week away.

The psychologist was a man with combed-back brown hair, blue eyes, and around my age. I told him about Vee.

"I don't know if I reacted like most people."

"Well, there are no rules for how to react." He shrugged. "But I do have a question."

I nodded.

"Was there any time during your formative years where you felt like you were the fixer, the glue? The person who kept things together?"

I thought a minute or two. "Yeah, growing up, my parents used to wake me up when they were arguing and sit me between them. When I cried, the fighting stopped."

Stiles nodded. "Do you see any correlation to that and how you reacted to the affair?"

Again, I sat in silence for a while. "Yes. I wanted everybody to stay together, and by sitting in the middle of a fight, I was doing that. The same with the affair. I was in the middle and wanted everyone to stay together."

"Yes. Now read me your letter to Vee again."

I did.

"That's quite normal. You weren't being mean. Like your husband said, you were being truthful."

"And about my understanding why a woman could kill her kids and then herself?"

He smiled. "It was a wine-infused understanding. And you didn't *do* anything, you just thought."

"But it scared me."

"That's good."

I sighed. "I guess it is because it brought me here. But I still don't know. Do I leave, or do I stay?"

Stiles looked at his office clock, then turned the pages in his calendar. "Hmm, didn't you say you cancelled your flight?"

"Yes, so I could talk to you. But I still don't know what to do."

"And you have to decide right now, immediately, why?"

I shook my head. "Because I hate limbo."

He nodded. "Are there other alternatives besides limbo?"

I stuck my tongue out at him and laughed. "Yes, damn it. I could use the limbo to open myself up to my husband, again."

"Yes, that wouldn't be limbo."

"Right, but I'm afraid of getting hurt again."

"From what you told me, no matter if you stayed or went, you were in for a world of hurt."

I sighed. "True. I hadn't thought of it like that. I will. I'll give it another full-on, open as I can be, try…again."

"I'd like you to keep seeing me for a while," Stiles said.

"Oh yeah, that's a given. I don't want to navigate this alone anymore."

In another of our sessions, I brought up words.

"Words?" He gave me what was becoming a familiar look, like, *Oh no, what now?*

"Yes, the corpuscles of our communication. Yet few give them much thought."

Stile's laughed. "But I bet you have."

"A word conveys memories, belief, imagination. They are fabulous points of construction toward understanding. You can dress written words up, like calligraphy. Or print them in straight letters, and they mean the same thing.

"Okay…"

"So we ought to pay more attention to them. Like the word or concept of cheating. What does that mean to you?"

Stile's laughed. "More important, what does it mean to you. I'll bet you've given that a lot of thought."

"I have. It isn't the act of cheating that is so bad, it is the aftereffects of it, the broken trust. The act was being intimate with someone other than your partner, keeping secrets from them, and often lying—all of which breeds distrust."

"Yes. I can agree to that definition. Your trust was broken."

"Yes."

"Has it been repaired?"

"Hmm…" I twisted a strand of my hair. "In the process of…"

"I'll ask again, has the trust between you and your husband been repaired? Restored."

"Partly." I looked at him. "Which means no. Not yet. A work in progress. He's done many things right to help me down that road. Taking responsibility for his actions and never pointing at me. He didn't put a time limit on when I would heal. I think I'm more impatient with myself than he is."

"Why is that?"

"Because I want it over. I want…it done."

"Then accept what is. It is not over, but it is better. Quit looking at the end prize and appreciate the steps you've accomplished. Which are huge."

"Yes, I need to do that. I'll work on it. And he's transparent and meticulously honest."

"What's meticulous honesty? Is it different from the honesty between you before?"

"Yes, well, he wasn't honest before. He lied by omission, by not telling me about Vee. And in his actions when she was around, keeping it from me."

"And now?"

"He is actively honest. If I ask questions about him and Vee, he answers in total. He never tells part of the truth, and I think he did in our first marriage. And I let him because I questioned nothing. Now, maybe because he knows I ask questions, he tells the complete truth."

"Is it okay with you if it's because he knows you'll ask?"

"Heck, yeah, it has the same result. And the more he sees me handle the truth well, the more at ease he'll have saying it. I can't ask a question and then get angry at the answer, or at least, I choose not to do so.

"He never minimizes. Vee did. She's a master at that. But Tim, again, took total responsibility. And he was patient. Before I put my wedding band back on, he never pushed. He was willing to wait as long as it took."

Stile's smiled. "Kind of like now, healing will take as long as it takes."

"Yes, exactly…but…"

"But what?"

"I want more. Twice, I've almost bailed on our marriage, our second one. And whatever got me there, he was willing to change. But…"

"But?"

"Twice, we, us, as partners and as parents, went back to acting like we had before."

"How was that?"

"It felt like 'okay crisis averted, now back to normal.' And I don't want it back to normal or like it was. Eventually, he goes to work, school, sports, or whatever and the kids and I fade into the background again. That was the norm in our first marriage, not in this one. When he's home, I want him present and engaged."

"Have you told him?"

I gave Stiles a look! "Of course, I have."

"Then give him a chance to do it."

LOOKING AT THE UGLY

I talked with Stiles for six months. During which I started working thirty-two hours a week and taking college classes. For the abnormal psychology class, I brought out all the poems I'd written as a kid and I'd stuffed in the lining of my suitcase. I separated them into piles according to the age I was when they were penned.

I could read just the first few lines and remember when it was written. I had all my ages from eight to twenty-three lined up neatly in rows. But I had a stray pile to my right and a little behind me. I knew what they were. I knew what they were about.

That group of writings was about being kidnapped and raped by my mother's boyfriend. I sighed. I didn't want to go there. But a voice in my head told me that now was the time. I was strong enough. So, one by one, I opened the scribblings and read them. Some days I only read one. But I read them.

I told Tim something bad had happened to me when I was nine, that my mother's boyfriend took me and held me captive. He grabbed my hand and told me he was so sorry that had happened to me and I could talk to him anytime about it.

But I hadn't wanted to talk about it yet. I had to sit with it a while. Plus, I wanted his attention and concern every day and not just in times of crisis. I didn't include the rape in my school project. But I began reading more of my poems from back then and writing in my journal.

15 CHAPTER DEALING WITH MULTIPLE AFTERMATHS

SOMETHING BAD HAPPENED PART 1 (EXPLICIT SEXUAL CONTENT)

IT TOOK TEN years for me to tell Tim what happened in part. I told him about the first of the three nights Dale, my mother's boyfriend, kidnapped me. Dale had fooled me by saying my mother was sick at his apartment. I had already become her caretaker, and immediately I wanted to go to her. I'd been to his studio-type apartment before, so I led the way up the stairs to his door.

Once he let me in, I saw my mother wasn't there. After he locked the door, I thought I might be in trouble. After he tied my hands behind my back, I knew I was. That night, he first assaulted me in his filthy bathroom. I put up a good fight, kicking and screaming through my gag as he carried me into the room. The room had one bright light bulb hanging from the white peeling paint and a filthy tile surround. The sink was stained with rust, green, and brown layers of toxic grime.

After I quit kicking, he sat me on the side of the bathtub, also dirty with yellow and black stains. The room stank of vomit, urine, and cigarettes.

Quickly, he pulled me up and my pants down to my ankles and deposited me on the toilet. The seat wobbled and my feet didn't reach the floor.

He lit a cigarette and ordered me to pee.

I couldn't urge a drop out of me. And he got more impatient as he waited. Finally, he threw his Winston cigarette between my legs and into the toilet where it hissed to death. But his eyes were now stuck on the place between my legs.

Dale then unzipped his pants and forced me to perform oral sex. I tried to keep my head away from him, but he was in control.

Then he sat on top of my legs, facing me backward on the toilet. His weight bore down on my thighs and I thought they might break. I tried to wiggle out from under him, but that increased the pain. He held the small of my back and tried to insert himself. I screamed, "Noooooooo" under the handkerchief, and that earned me a slap upside my head.

Nearly every time he tried to push himself in. It smushed out sideways, but he kept trying, getting increasingly angry at me. He'd cuff me upside my head every time it did not work, which made me sick to my stomach. Then he stood and invaded me with his hand. I screamed for my mommy! At some point, I went from looking at the peeling paint on the ceiling to floating above myself near it. I kept chanting one of my mother's favorite saying, "*This too shall pass.*"

Then he tired of the game, pulled me to my feet, restored my panties and slacks, and ordered me to follow him. He pushed me down on the mattress in the living room. I tried to turn on my side so I wouldn't hear my heartbeat. I was afraid I'd hear it stop.

Dale drank until he passed out. Then he pulled me to him and spooned me. I lay awake, looking at the long, spiky, black hair on his arm. A magazine had fallen from his bedside table to a picture of elephants. Males marched ahead, and females wrapped their trunks lovingly around their babies. I made myself disappear into the picture.

RETROSPECTIVE AFTER RAPE I

When I told my husband what happened, he did the best thing in the world he could have done afterwards. He held me and told me he was sorry and didn't ask for any more information. As a young person, I had told a few select people about one of the most benign abuses in my life. And their reaction would shut me down. Most folks would get a horrified look on their face and say with high emotion, "Ohmigod! You poor dear." I had stuffed my own feelings down within my depths. I hadn't processed it. And I couldn't handle theirs. Another way that stopped me was when they said, "Ohmigod, you are so strong." When they said that I then wanted to continue to appear strong. I then portrayed strength, even though I felt like I was put together with spit and bubblegum.

But I'd only spoken aloud about the first evening at Dale's. It took me a long time to unpack the subsequent nights and the violence and abuse. Then too, Tim, although uncomfortable hearing it, didn't push or prod me. I could sense his unease, but that's how I felt too. And I decided I never want anyone to be comfortable when abuse is being spoken about. It should disturb us.

STRIKE THREE

I didn't have a typewriter at home. So one night when Tim was bowling, I got a babysitter for the kids and went back to the office to type my report. My fingers kept messing up. The parts of my childhood that bothered me caused my fingers to spasm. For example, "black" would come out "blaake." I'd erase it, start again, and come up with another misspelling of "black." To get through the poem, I'd have to relax and breathe deeply. I'd thank myself for letting me know. Then I could get the verses typed.

In the middle of this, my office phone rang. Who would be calling me there at night? The babysitter? I grabbed the receiver. "Hello,"

I heard a lot of noise on the other end. Then Tim said, "Hi, I'm calling from the bowling alley. You'll never guess what just happened?"

"What?"

"I bent down to throw my first ball and my slacks ripped all the way up my backside."

"Well, that could be embarrassing."

"Yeah, it was. Could you run home and bring me another pair of pants?"

I sat stunned at the other end of the phone. *Go get your pants?*

After a minute or two of silence, he said, "Hello? Are you there?"

"Yes, I'm here." Then I was quiet again.

"Hello? Why aren't you saying anything?"

"Because I'm typing a paper for my class, which is due tomorrow. I'm not doing something fun. I'm not relaxing at home with the kids. I'm busy!"

"Oh."

I remained silent.

"Okay, guess I shouldn't have asked that, maybe. Don't worry. I'll get my own pants."

I hung up. I wasn't worried. I was angry. Yet, again, our life had gone back to me and the kids on the peripheral while Tim worked and played sports.

That night, he again said he probably shouldn't have asked me to fetch him some slacks.

"You think? Probably? Hell, no, you should not have. We've talked about this and talked about it. You are not plugged into us, we the kids and me. We get things straight between us, and then you revert to who you were in the past."

"I think you might be overreacting."

I stood up on the couch and began jumping up and down, up and down.

Tim's face turned white. He put his hands out as if to stop me. "What are you doing?"

On each up bounce, I loudly said, "This…is…overreacting! This…is…what…overreacting…looks like!"

"Okay, okay, I get your point. Get down, you'll wake the kids up. Please."

I stopped my demonstration and sat in the couch's corner. "No, you don't get my point. I want more than just someone who puts in the motions. That was first marriage style. I want emotional honesty and connection all the time."

"I'm not sure I can do that."

"Then I can't stay. As soon as the kids are out of school, in three months, we are leaving. You can be a working, sporting, and home-absent husband to someone else."

"Don't say that."

"I just did. Look, I love you, but maybe love isn't enough. I'll let you know the date of our exit. I'll probably live in Florida because I have friends there, and Mom's there. Good night."

Here we go again. I walked slowly up the marble stairs to the second floor and looked in on my sleeping children. Kyle was now thirteen, and Kristi was eleven. I'd have to make sure they were okay. And as hard as it would be for me, if they preferred living with their dad, they could.

THIRD TIMES THE CHARM

I amended the "We are leaving" statement to "We will have a legal separation for one year. Then regroup and see where we are." Tim agreed. I continued to go to school. I wouldn't tell the kids until I had to do so. We were due to take home leave anyway in June. After three years at Bad Aibling, Germany, we had paid leave to go back to the USA.

The first month I moped around, read all the books on separation I could find, and wrote in my journal. Then it dawned on me. That I could view this as one door closing (our marriage) or focus on the door that was opening (the rest of my life). With my new attitude, I started sending boxes to Kelly's, things I wanted to keep that might be too bulky for a suitcase. I also went to a JAG (Judge Advocate General) on base. As a lawyer, he drew up a separation plan for Tim and me for one year.

We were in the car driving to Munich when I told him about the separation papers.

His blue eyes widened. "Why would you do that? That's serious."

"Yes, because it *is* serious."

"You know I will treat you right, don't you?"

"Of course, you'll treat me right and that's why you won't mind signing the papers."

That night after the kids were in bed, we divided our property in case we didn't reconcile after one year. That went smoothly until it came to the hand-cut wood in-laid, picture of the Konigssee. I wanted it, and he wanted it. We argued. For the first time ever, we got loud. I gave him the finger. He looked hurt. He yelled that the picture was his. Period.

The next day Tim and I talked about our reactions the evening before. I was sorry; he was sorry. We never wanted to do that again whether or not we were married. We agreed to never raise our voices (and me, my finger) to each other again.

I also realized I could buy another one. The base still had them, made by the same artist. Maybe I would do that. Tim and I were friendly and still making love. Once again, that was one area we could express how much we loved each other. Words only got in the way. Since I was looking toward the open door, I felt lighter.

About six weeks before the kids and I were slated to leave, I realized I'd left a gigantic hole in our separation agreement. Sex. When he came home, I said, "We have to talk."

He nodded and helped me get the kids to bed. "What's wrong?"

"Nothing. It just struck me we need to talk about sex."

"Huh?" He put his beer down. I had his full attention now.

"Listen, we'll be separated for a year. I don't know what you will do sexually while I'm gone…" Tim shook his head. "No, wait, hear me out. I don't know what you will do. You may think nothing, but something might come up. If you become intimate with someone, I just don't want to hear about it when I get back."

"I'm not even thinking about that…"

"Well, I am. It will be easier for me to ensure that you know nothing, should I have sex with someone else. It'll be harder for you in this small-town environment."

"What do you mean, you having sex with someone else?"

"I'm not planning on it. I can't imagine even how I would do that. But I'm not opposed to it either, should all conditions be right and all my systems say go…"

He looked at me like I'd grown another head.

"I'm not saying this to hurt you or threaten you. I just wanted the discussion out in the open. I'm kind of a virgin, in a weird way, because I've only ever made love to one man. And I love you. But we are separating. And I will be trying out the terrain to see if I can navigate on my own. Neither of us would be unfaithful, in my mind, because we would be legally separated, pending a reunification or divorce."

Tim still looked like someone had hit him over the head with a heavy weight.

"Hon, it'll probably never happen. But I wanted to speak this. If you want to, it's okay, we'd be separated. Only again, please don't let me hear about it when I get back."

"You think in ways I never would. You think in ways I don't think anyone would…"

"I know. I've heard that before. It's just the way I think. Seeing all angles keeps me safe, or it used to. We'll see… Okay, I've got to study. End-of-term tests are coming up. You know how I like to over prepare."

"I will have another beer on our balcony," he said as he left the room.

I heard the refrigerator door open and close, then listened to his footsteps up the stairs and the bedroom door to the balcony open and close. I wished I'd given him a hug. But maybe after announcing we are both free to have sex, as long as it's quiet, isn't the best time to do that. I wasn't sure.

Two weeks before we were to leave, I came home from the end-of-term test and crawled into bed with Tim. I heard his warm sleepy voice say, "I don't want a separation."

Don't want a separation! Huh? "Okay, tell me about it in the morning."

"Let's go to breakfast."

"Deal," I said as I closed my eyes. I'd over-studied, as was my habit, but it paid off because I got an A in the class, which was a grand feeling.

In the morning, we went to the base club and ordered breakfast. When our coffee came, I said, "It's your dime."

Tim nodded. "I don't want to get separated. Let's not do that."

"Why?"

"Because I don't think you work on a marriage by being apart."

"Okay, but I've stayed two times before, and overall, nothing changed. So why would I want to stay this time?"

We were quiet while they set our bacon and eggs before us. "What can I do to make you believe it will?"

I thought as I mixed my eggs and grits together. "Hang your jockstrap up for a year. No sports. Concentrate on me and the kids."

He hung his head.

I waited. I knew this was a big "ask." He loved sports and was part of a team, or two, every season. This year he'd been on two bowling leagues, baseball, volleyball, and basketball teams.

Finally, he looked up. "Okay."

I almost choked on my coffee. "You'll do it?"

"Yes." He nodded.

"For a year?"

"Yes."

"Hang your jockstrap up. That means no sports for a year. Nada. Zip. Zilch. None."

"I know, and yes."

I sat back in my seat. I couldn't believe he'd said yes. "Really? Any conditions."

"One," he said. "We destroy that separation agreement because we are no longer in agreement with it."

"Uh, okay. But we are scheduled to fly to Mom's house in a week, well, two."

"That's fine. You go early. See your mom. See Kelly. Have fun, but not too much fun." He laughed. "I'll come in

August as we planned, and we'll all, *all*, fly back the end of the month."

"You've totally surprised me, Timothy."

"Good."

"Oh, one more thing," I stated.

His eyebrows rose, and a weary look came over his face.

"I got a letter from Vee. Almost a year after I wrote her that letter. She replied. It was all about her new boyfriend. Maybe to make you jealous. I don't know. At any rate, I'm… uh…I've decided not to write back. She is the first friend I will walk away from…but I'm done."

Tim looked at me and slowly smiled.

"What?" I asked. "What?"

"I think that's a really healthy choice."

"That means I won't call her or see her when I get back."

He nodded. "Well, you'll be joining me because I wasn't going to either, and it made me uncomfortable to think you would."

"Why?"

"Why? Because she's never been nice to you. Or concerned about you. Or supportive of you. I hated the time and energy you wasted on someone who only thought of themselves."

"I know. But I love her. I will miss her, no, I'll miss the fantasy of what I thought our friendship had been. But it really wasn't…"

"Now, you'll have room in your life for a *genuine* friend."

"Maybe."

"Definitely." He reached over and squeezed my hand.

AUTOPSY

After home leave, Tim and I sat in our living room talking quietly. I told him I had not realized that there would be more waves. I thought once we got over the first big one, it was one and done. He said he had expected other ripples.

"And there may be more to come."

"Ugh," I said.

"But if we keep the fact that we love each other in the forefront and commit that we will work through the waves and troughs and never utter the word divorce again, we'll make it."

"Ugh! That sounds hard."

"It could be. But living the way we were before Vee wasn't easy either. It was hard in a different way."

"True. You know, I think so many things contributed to that happening. This is a reason, not an excuse, but I'm not sure, despite everything you said back then, that you were ready to be married."

"Thanks for that," Tim said.

"And when I look back at how I was. I didn't command respect. I didn't respect myself. I choked down some very legitimate concerns and annoyances. I didn't trust me. I didn't respect myself enough to speak how I felt. So it's not all that surprising that you didn't respect me either."

Tim rolled his shoulders. "I hate to think I didn't respect you because I do so much now. But by my behavior, I must not have. That's difficult to admit."

"I know. But it's critical to the autopsy of our first marriage."

"Autopsy?"

"Well, after someone dies, they do an autopsy to find out the cause, means, and manner of death. We're just slicing into the concept of our first ten years together. Finding out why and how the first marriage died, so we can avoid it now."

"Okay, cut away."

"Again, these are reasons, not an excuse for an affair, but I didn't respect myself. I tried to take up as little space and air as possible. I was vibrantly me when we married. Then I escaped and fell back on old defense mechanisms."

"Don't be so hard on yourself. I didn't talk to you to ask where that girl had gone. I didn't demand her return. I… found something to distract me."

"Vee. Did you ever love her?"

Tim's eyes opened wide in surprise. "No, never. She was your great friend and a good diversion for me, I guess. But love her? Never."

"If we had broken up right after it happened. Do you think you would have turned to her?"

Tim was already shaking his head before I finished the question. "No, no, and no. You say I didn't respect you because you didn't respect yourself and that may be partly true. Because I had a huge admiration for you. You came through tough times, which would have killed the love in most people, and developed into a woman with a huge heart. I have always valued your opinions and beliefs. You think deeply. No, I'd have never chosen Vee."

"Why not?"

"Well, because she could cheat on her best friend. I did too, and that you are opening your trust and heart to me again is amazing. I'm not sure I could do that. And I would not want to be with a woman who could victimize her best friend."

"I thought you liked her sensual ways."

"I responded to them. I wouldn't have liked them on a long-term basis. For that, I want openness with no game playing. She was good at games."

"And I'm not."

"Thank God you're not. I like that about you."

"I think you are right. There may be more waves, but we know we love each other, so we'll decide we are in it for the long haul."

Tim took my hand. "Yes. We'll weather whatever may come. Together."

"Remind me that when I want to run."

"I will. And you remind me should I fall back into lazy husbanding."

"Husbanding? Is that a word?"

Tim smiled. "It is in our own personal marriage dictionary."

RETROSPECT

We made the right choice in deciding to stay together through thick and thin. Because eventually, after a trauma, you have to let it go. But not until you've done all the work, together, of trying to figure out what happened. Not in a "I blame you" kind of way, but in a "how could we avoid it now" way. Also, I think if we'd divorced, I'd have become bitter. Maybe I could have overcome this, I don't know. I'm glad I didn't have to do so.

Staying atop my own tsunami wave was all-consuming. I never looked around to see if Tim, Kyle, and Kristi had climbed up on their own swells. All of us had been impacted by the meteor's crash. Tim was as devastated by his betrayal as I was. And he had to watch me choke, drown, and pull myself back up above the waterline again and again. He had damaged his own soul; he was also bleeding.

Tim, likewise, had to examine his values, his identity, and what he was capable of doing. No matter what had happened to our marriage and our family, he would know he was the cause. The meteor that blew us up. If the impact had been the family's demise …well, wherever he went, there he'd be.

When I examined the tsunami wave Tim had ridden, I saw shame. I'd felt shame in the past, and it is a dark hole with no acquittal or grace. Some people may think he deserved this feeling. But I loved this man and did not want him to suture a scarlet letter to his heart. He had made an enormous mistake, a series of them, but he was still a good man. I knew he wasn't merely sorry he'd been caught because I daily saw his deep remorse. I'd also seen other people struggle through infidelity. I've seen the betrayed berate the betrayer repeatedly. I knew the betrayer felt they had no right to talk about their pain and their hurt, about how the damaging expletives and profanities slung at them lacerated them. I never wanted to be that person. In the middle of my pain, I *wanted* to see his injuries and administer to them, as he was to me. How could our marriage be restored if I constantly threw stones?

And the kids, they didn't know that a meteor had dropped into the center of our lives. But they knew things had changed. Some adjustments were good, some bad. Now that the wave wasn't as high, the revisions were still in effect. I was no longer the quiet little TV wife. I voiced my opinion, and this sometimes created discussions. This might have been scary for Kyle and Kristi because it hadn't happened before. I stepped into my quirky self and thus became a quirky mother. I think this was especially hard for my extremely shy daughter. I now wore funkier clothes, less makeup, and often had my hair in pigtails, quite different from a TV mother.

Now, I realized that the separate tsunami waves we were all balancing on had swept us to separate islands. And from those atolls we had, at first, attempted to come back together as a family. We tried to get back to business as usual or back to normal, and it hadn't worked.

But from the time Tim retired his jockstrap for a year, we began growing a new family dynamic. We went on trips together. We watched the kid's school programs and sports. We played board games and talked. Tim got to know his children better; and they, their dad. And I got to appreciate him in a new light. We might all still be riding the residual waves of the tsunami, but we were all balancing on the same wave now, and that made all the difference.

MOVING ON

Smaller waves and ripples impacted our marriage for the next two years. But before we'd discuss it, we'd remind each other we were in for the long haul and there would be no running away. I had always been the one wanting to run; Tim was steadfast. But with our agreement in place, it took divorce off the table. We would work things out.

During the next six years I needed him to interpret what constituted "normal" teenage behavior. I had never had a teenage life and really didn't know. When my teenagers wanted to trick or treat on Halloween, I thought they were too old. When I asked Tim, he told me that older kids go out as well. When I heard about the pranks that accompanied Halloween again, Tim informed me it was normal.

My children's teen years were also hard on me because I had taught them to question authority. And now they were questioning mine. I was still the emotional center, but Tim was much more involved. I was also the disciplinarian. Once, our son was grounded for the weekend for something. I came home from work to find the second car gone, and Tim in the house.

"Where's the car?" I asked.

"Kyle, took it to the movie."

"What? He's grounded for the weekend you know that. Why's he at the movie?"

"Oh?" He studied the pot he was stirring. "I thought the weekend started on Saturday."

I laughed. "Give me a break. No, you didn't."

Tim kept stirring.

"Here's what I think happened. Kyle came to you with a story about going to this great movie. Before restriction, he had promised to take four of his best friends, and if he did not take them, nobody would go."

Tim looked at me. "Something like that."

"Geez, Timothy, am I going to have to ground you too?" He just didn't like confrontation or saying no over and over. They could wear him down.

"No, just give me a warning this time."

"Consider yourself warned. Next time tell him to call me or wait until I get home, if you don't want to say no."

"Well, in essence that will be a no." He smiled.

"Right, it will be. And we'll be a united front. Okay?"

"Yup, I can do that…er…have him call you, I mean."

16 CONFRONTA-TION OF PAST

CHAPTER

RAISING KIDS TO BE ADULTS

WHEN KYLE GRADUATED high school, Mom Hazel came up. I couldn't believe we had a kid who is eighteen years old. We sat out on the deck the evening after graduation. Tim said it had gone by too fast. There were things he'd wished he'd done.

I felt like I'd done my best and didn't have any regrets. I'd raised them to be smart, independent adults. Kyle was ready for the world. In fact, he took a job in London, England, at a hotel. Just two months later, Tim put in his papers for us to go to England with the Department of Defense. We talked to Kristi, who was in her junior year of high school, and she was all for moving. Kyle quit his job, came home, and moved in with us. By going to the UK with us, it was legal for him to stay the three years, where his visa was temporary.

We moved to England in November, and we loved it. We rented a house off base on Rook Tree Lane. It had two large bedrooms and a small one upstairs, a kitchen, living room, dining room, and half bath downstairs, along with a laundry room. I loved being in a foreign country that spoke my language, or at least a close facsimile.

Kyle worked for a year in London at the hotel, then went back to the States to go to college. But he often came to visit. During one visit, while Tim was getting eye surgery in

261

the States, Kyle asked me to sit down. He was nineteen now, and if he wanted me to sit, it had to be something important. I sat. Then he said, "I'm gay." After a while, he asked, "Did you hear me?"

"Yes, I heard you. It makes no difference to me."

"And don't feel guilty because you let me wear a dress once when I was four years old."

I laughed. "Yeah, that crossed my mind. Do you have a boyfriend?"

"No, but I've always been attracted to guys. Will you please tell Dad and Kristi, but after I'm gone?"

"Sure, but why don't you?"

"I'd just feel better if you did."

"Right. I will. No problem."

My feelings the next week after he told me surprised me. I'd had dreams in place for him I hadn't even realized. Marriage. Children. I always knew that I would love any girl he brought home to be his wife because I always loved all his friends. So I had to tweak these dreams. Marriage? I still hoped he'd have a long-term partner someday, marriage or not. Children? Not required. I'd never been that person who couldn't wait for grandchildren. If that happened, wonderful. But my identity didn't depend upon it. Now, I knew that I would also love any guy he brought home (that he loved) because I always loved who he loved.

I told Kristi, and she cried, which surprised me. "Oh, honey, why are you crying?"

"Because he was teased so much in high school!"

"He was?"

"Yes, a lot."

"Why didn't you guys tell me?"

She looked at me like I was crazy and sniffed. "Tell you? Because you'd have driven up to that school and waited for those guys and gotten in their face and told them what-for."

"I probably would have. You guys didn't want me to do that?"

"No, he wanted to handle it on his own. You were a good mama lion, but sometimes we have to do the biting."

"Yes, you do." I could see how they'd want to handle it themselves. I wish they had told me when it was going on. But I couldn't have guaranteed that I'd have let them handle it alone. So perhaps I had taught them that by my overgrown protectiveness.

"You gonna tell Dad?" Kristi asked.

"Yes, he asked me to…"

"What will Dad say, do you think?"

"He'll be okay. We love you guys as is. We love the you of you."

She nodded. And I reached over and gave my seventeen-year-old daughter a hug, and she let me. A treat that had not happened a lot since she had become a teenager.

When Tim got home from his trip, I told him. He nodded. I asked how he felt about it. "Doesn't change anything…I'll write him."

In his letter to Kyle, he told him he was still young, only nineteen, and not to paint himself into a corner. That even though he may not have liked sports or felt he was good at them, it did not mean he was homosexual.

"You may be gay. You may be bisexual. Keep your options open. And if you are gay, it doesn't change the fact that you are my son and I love you."

Kristi graduated high school at seventeen; she wouldn't be eighteen until six months later. Mom Hazel came for the graduation. My kids adored her. And she had helped fill the motherless ache in me. I had to work, but Tim took her on a trip to Scotland. She'd look around our house and say, "When something happens to me, you and Rick will have a terrible time getting rid of stuff." I didn't think she had that much "stuff," but she did.

In December, Kristi went to live with a high school friend in San Antonio, Texas. We took her to the airport. And just like when she got on a school bus for the first time at five and a half years old, she didn't look back as she boarded the plane. I didn't think she was ready to meet the world, but she was of legal age and I couldn't stop her. She was still so shy she was almost backward. She had trouble saying what she thought and felt and avoided all conflict. I remembered ten years earlier in Germany when I realized I only had eight years to get her ready for adulthood.

I took the kids to a local German grocery store. I gave them some money and told them they could get whatever they wanted. Both came back to show me what they'd chosen. Kristi tried to hand her choices to me. I told her she would have to take them through the checkout line.

"No, no, I can't. Mom, please, you do it."

I again told her no, and she put all her treats back on the shelf rather than go through the register line.

I did this every two weeks, and it took her three months to be ready to walk up to the register.

"But you'll come with me?"

"I will, but you must put the items on the conveyor belt and hand the clerk the money."

She put her items back.

After another three months, she was ready to go to the register, put her items down, and pay the clerk. So long as I was right beside her.

After a couple of months of doing this, I told her I would wait for her at the end of line where the bags were. "No, stay with me in line. Please?"

"Hon, I'll be less than a yard away. You can do this."

She put her items back.

After months, she let me wait at the end by the bags. Then by the wall. Next by the door. Finally, she was okay with me on outside where she could see me. After almost two years, I could wait at the end of the block for her. Many of the people I knew thought I was mean. Some in the stores even offered to do it for her. Yet I felt it was vital for her to learn to operate on her own.

However, she was still painfully shy, and I worried about her out in the world. She had much to learn. She wasn't street smart at all. Yet I wouldn't have wanted her to go through what I had to get street smart. I knew she was vulnerable, and yet I was three thousand miles away in another country. And she learned some hard lessons, and all I could do was encourage her to stand up for herself and keep trying. If I'd been there, I would have been that mother lion running down her enemies whether she wanted me to or not. So, in that way, maybe it was good I was three thousand miles away

JUST THE TWO OF US (AGAIN)

After the kids left, Tim and I moved to another location in England. It was near the Scottish border. We rented a beautiful stone house on Hookstone Garth, in a quaint little village. We were empty nesters now, and it was fun getting reacquainted without kids. At this base, Tim worked a grueling twelve-hour shift of two midnight shifts, two evenings, and two days. It screwed with his sleep schedule, and he began looking tired.

One evening when he was working a midnight shift, our telephone downstairs rang and rang. Once it punched through my dream sleep, I ran down the stairs to answer.

Kyle said, "Hey, Mom, sorry to wake you but I've got a question."

"Is everything all right? Are you okay? What's wrong?"

"Nothing. Nothing's wrong. Sorry to be calling so late, but I wanted to ask you something."

My heartbeat had finally slowed down now that I knew he was okay. "Sure, what?"

"You know the guy I like? Mitch. He's in Venice, Italy, with his art class. And I found a roundtrip flight for $500, and I wondered...if...if...you'd pay for me to go there?"

"Me? Pay for your trip to Italy to see your boyfriend?"

"Yeah, I know it sounds crazy. But I'd like to show him around, and he'd be really surprised at me showing up there. And I don't have the money. So maybe you could put it on one of your credit cards?"

"To go to Venice to see your boyfriend?"

"Yes, I know it sounds crazy..."

"Kyle, I don't even handle the credit cards, don't know our balances or payments. I don't use them. Call your dad at work and see what he says. At least he's already awake enough to make an informed decision."

"Okay. Sorry, I woke you. I'll call Dad."

"Great. Love you. Bye."

I trudged back up the stairs, nestled into the covers of our bed, and immediately went back to sleep. Only to be awakened again by the phone ringing.

I raced back down the stairs, grabbed the receiver, and said, "Hello?"

"It's me, Kyle. I called Dad, and he said it was up to you to decide."

"He said *what?*"

"He said you could decide, Mom. Please, I know it's totally crazy, but $500 round trip is a good price. But I'd have to book it soon..."

Tim said I should decide? At 2:00 a.m.? I know he doesn't like to make decisions or say no, but this should have been easy...

"Mom? Mom, are you there?" Kyle's voice brought me out of my head.

"I'm here. Sure. Go ahead."

"*What?* For real? You're gonna pay for my flight?"

"Yes, for real." *Really, Timothy! You told him to call me because you didn't want to say no.* "Absolutely for real. Have fun. Call me when you get home." I gave him our credit card number and information.

"Wow, Mom, you're the best. Not every parent would pay for their gay son's trip overseas to meet his boyfriend. You guys rock."

"That we do! Now, I'm going back to bed. Talk to you next week. Call, okay?"

"I will. Thank you. I love you."

I said nothing to Tim until he got the credit card statement. He rushed out of his office with it in hand and said, "You said okay to Kyle's $500 airplane trip on our credit card?"

"I sure did."

"I thought you'd say no. Why didn't you?"

"Why? Because you should have. You told him to call me again at 4:00 a.m. and wake me up so I could tell him what you couldn't?"

Tim was nodding.

"Well, anytime you do that, shirk responsibility and hand it to me, I'll give an opposite answer to what you'll think."

He was shaking his head. "Five hindered dollars!"

"Yup, next week, he might want to take Mitch to South Africa. I hear it's nice this time of year."

"Oh no, not on our credit card."

"Well, hopefully that's what you'll tell him."

"Oh, no worries, that's exactly what I'll tell him."

He never passed a decision like that onto me again.

THE REST OF THE BAD—RAPE II
(EXPLICIT SEXUAL CONTENT)

Our empty nest allowed us to focus entirely on each other. One evening, I told him about the other two nights and three days at Dale's apartment. I knew telling him about the first evening had partly freed me. By speaking my experience aloud, I had brought the ugliness out into the daylight. And any residual self-blame and shame were burned away. The truth can set me free; I believed that. Again, he sat near me but not anxiously holding on to me. He believed that if I were going to tell him about it that I could handle it. Yet, if I needed encouragement, he would reach over and give me a hug. He was supportive but not smothering.

I took a breath and told him about what had happened after the first numbing and painful experience in the bathroom with Dale. I had shutdown. I'd seen folks engaged in oral sex as they slept in our living room, with me behind the couch. But I never watched it in full. I always lay on my bundle of blankets in the crook of the sectional, put my fingers in my ears, and sang softly to myself. I hated the sound people having sex made. They sounded like hurt or dying animals and looked like a pair of Siamese fighting fish I'd seen in a pet store. I could not figure out why they did it.

Therefore, when Dale had me perform oral sex on him, it wasn't completely foreign. But it was smelly, awful, and scary. He'd hold my head against him, and if I tried to turn it, he'd hit me, hard, on the side of my head. My mind would scream for my mommy, and tears would roll down my face and onto him. When he hit me, it made my ears ring, and sometimes for hours afterwards I wouldn't be able to hear well, which was okay with me. But that made him angry too.

The first night he tried making me swallow! *Ohmigosh, he's peeing in my mouth!* I had shared the janitor's lunch at school that day, and I promptly vomited all over him and the bed. He jumped up, kicked me aside, and cursed as he tore the top sheet off his mattress. Then he got a towel and rubbed my smelly stomach contents off himself. He also used the same towel to get it off the bottom sheet, but it just smeared into the threads. Next, he grabbed himself a drink and said, "Girl, you are as worthless as your mother." I was glad the janitor had shared her lunch with me in the bathroom; otherwise, I'd have had nothing to barf. He made me perform the act again and again. But after that he always shoved me away before the swallowing part happened.

The next day he told me to stick my tongue out and lick his butt. He'd hold it apart and shove my face in there. I got cuffed upside the head for not understanding what to do. So he illustrated what he wanted on me. Bucking earned me a kick with his foot to my chest. It took my breath away.

He became enraged that I was defective. He said my tongue was too short, but he could remedy that. He grabbed a blackened rag from under his sink and pulled me off his bed. "Stick your tongue out." Then he balled up his fist and hit me in the ribs because I was slow in doing so. I cried. And he grabbed my tongue with the rag and pulled me around the room three feet or so. With me kicking and trying to scream until he lost his grip. Pain overran my brain; and I became one gushing, surging, heaving pain receptor. I could taste and feel blood. "Open your mouth," he ordered, and he'd hit me in the chest, on top of the purple bruises, until I did. Then he again wrapped the rag around my tongue and dragged me a few more feet across the floor.

The first time he did this, I was dehydrated and he gained a firm grip. But within seconds of the first tug, my saliva glands went into overtime. So his subsequent attempts did not take me that far across the flooring. Plus, by then I'd learned to quit kicking. I'd dig my bare heels into the floor, pushing myself in the direction he was pulling. After three or four times, he quit and threw me back on his mattress, plopped down on it, and started snoring.

My mouth bled, and I was afraid to get it on him or his sheet, so I swallowed it. Sharp pains emanated from my mouth. I had difficulty swallowing saliva and felt my tongue swelling, taking up more room in my mouth. Can you break or sprain a tongue? "Mommy, mommy, mommy!" I whispered, careful not to wake him. But the words came out distorted, like, "Ma-ee." I didn't know if he'd actually made it longer, but I tried extremely hard to make him think it was…

During the quiet periods, he slept, always with his legs lying over me. And I'd grope around for my slacks and pull them on. Then I'd conjure up my mother in my mind. I could see her asleep in her bed, and I'd will her to wake up. *Mommy! Mommy, please come get me. Help.* I couldn't wake her. I finally got away from what was happening. I became the large beast in the yellow magazine that fell off his table and onto the floor beside me.

I knew he was angry at my mother and wanted to get back with her. I couldn't understand how what he was doing to me would help him accomplish that. I wanted my mother so bad; I ached for her. I usually had a gag in my mouth, so I could only make whimpering sounds when I cried. Eventually, my tears dried up and I became automated, robotically doing what he ordered.

His hand, fist, or feet would snap me out of my reverie; and I would know I'd done something wrong. And I would shake my head to get rid of the cobwebs in my brain and pay attention, so I wouldn't get hit again. He continually bit circles around my nipples. He said it'd make them swell, and I'd be more like a woman. That area swelled and turned purple.

It was painful to lie on them, but I preferred being face down because it was harder for him to get to me.

He drank out of a bottle constantly, the honey-colored drink he called whisky. I hated the smell of it. He tried to get me to drink some, but I turned my head and it spilled. He picked me up and threw me against the wall. After I landed in a heap, he hopped around, saying, "Oh no. Oh God." He grabbed my head and felt it all over. I thought he was sorry he'd done it. I winced as he touched the goose-egg swelling on the back of my head, where it had contacted the wall. He said, "Oh, thank God. I was afraid it'd show." He never tried to get me to drink whisky again.

He masturbated on the bed beside me, then told me to do as he'd done. But I didn't do it correctly. I never got the rhythm right. So he would plant his huge hand over mine, and force me to do the motion he wanted. Eventually, I let my arm go slack as he forced my hand up and down. My dark at the end of the tunnel was the knowledge that he'd fall asleep afterward for an hour or so.

He continually tried to thrust himself into me. But inevitably, it wouldn't work, or it wouldn't work well. I'd seen erections in my living room, so I knew what his was. But nearly every poke would end up with him only going part way. Enough to hurt, enough to make me bleed, but then his erection would wither. I thought I'd broken it. Now, I know that because of drinking, he couldn't maintain an erection. But at the time, he blamed me and I blamed myself. When that happened, he would jerk me up, turn me over, and beat his fist against my butt and back. All the time, screaming, "There's something wrong with you! You're deformed! Ugly! You're not made right." Although I didn't believe much of what he said, I believed that.

He tried his best to figure out what was wrong with me by probing my every orifice with his fingers and tongue.

He paid special attention to the part of me between my legs. He said I was made wrong. He probed with his screwdriver, ruler, and other objects, trying to figure it out. By then I'd quit paying attention and disappeared into the body of an enormous beast. One nobody would ever challenge. I could feel the hard earth between my feet and the sun beating down on my back. And I wasn't alone, I was with my family, safe and protected.

He must have fed me or given me some water, but I don't remember that. After the third night of him demonstrating on me what he wanted me to do to him, I pooped and peed in my slacks while he was still sleeping. When he awoke, he noticed my mess, swore, grabbed me by the arm, and jerked me toward the bathroom. I hated that bathroom! And again, I became a wild child, kicking and screaming into my gag. He threw me on the floor, took the toilet paper off the roll, and told me to clean up. He untied my hands. I pulled my slacks down, and the smell permeated the room, and Dale left. I scooped what I could of the liquid yellowish mess and deposited it in the toilet.

Then I stopped in mid-action. It had bothered him. *Good.* So instead of cleaning what remained, I smeared it all over me.

"You done yet?" His angry voice exploded into the room.

"Mm, mmm," I mumbled through the gag. So he came in holding his nose and lowered it from my mouth and walked back out.

After a while, he called out. "Are you done?"

"Almost," I answered.

The second time, he asked, I pulled up my slacks and said, "Yes."

He came in, pulled them down, and said, "Jesus, what's wrong with you? Clean up!"

"I can't. It's dried," I said. He said nothing as he angrily tied the gag back in place and retied my hands behind me. Then he jerked me into the living room and threw me in the corner, away from his mattress. I scooted under the dining table.

He drank more whiskey and muttered to himself and fell asleep. I got up and went to the door, but it was locked. I didn't know where he'd put the key, and I couldn't reach the handle with my hands tied behind my back. I went to the window in the dining room and looked down. I saw the heads of people passing by. No one looked up. I rested my forehead against the cool glass. I wondered how badly I'd be hurt if I broke it with my head. Would it help? Would anyone look up and see me? Would anyone help? I didn't want to chance it. So I crawled back under the table.

I sat up when Dale awoke. He took a swig of whisky, then came over and lowered my gag. "I think it's time you go home, don't you?"

I nodded vigorously.

"Okay, I'm going to untie you and give you bus fare to go home. But don't be tellin' your mom about what happened here. Cause nothing happened, you understand me?"

Again, I nodded.

"Nothin' could happen 'cause you are ugly and deformed."

I nodded.

He untied my hands. "Get up."

I did.

He took the key down from the top of the doorway and unlocked it. "You keep your damned mouth shut, or I'll come find you. I know where you live. And I'll do worse to you and your mother. You understand?"

I nodded, not trusting my voice.

He handed me a quarter, pushed me out the door, and slammed it.

I ran. I sprinted down the stairs and exited the door. I jogged down to the bus stop. Fearfully, I watched for him to change his mind and come after me. So I scurried two bus stops down. I didn't think he'd be able to walk that far. If he didn't see me at the first bus stop, maybe he'd think I'd already gotten on a bus.

People stood away from me. I knew I smelled and there was a stain all over my pants. I didn't care. I was free. I was going home to my mommy. She'd make everything all right. *Mommy. Mommy,* I chanted.

Finally, the bus came, I deposited my quarter, got on, and sat upfront behind the driver. I flew out of the bus as soon as it came to my stop. I ran the blocks to where my house was, where my mommy was. I opened the front door and vaulted up the stairs and down the hall to her bedroom. I felt like I'd fought a war to get to her. I opened her bedroom door; and she rose up on an elbow with an uneasy, pained, raw expression on her face. She looked like she was about to cry, and she asked, "You okay? He didn't hurt you, did he?"

"No, I'm fine." I answered, and she dissolved back into her bed.

I backed out the door, closed it, leaned against it. Something heavy lodged itself in my stomach and chest. *Mommy*, I whispered to the door. *Mommy.* I felt anger surge through my chest. *She can't help it! She can't,* I whimpered, and I hit myself in the face. *She can't help it!* I slid down her door and sat on the floor. To distract myself, I dug my filthy fingernails into my forearms and raked them upward over and over, drawing blood. Slowly, I got up and gingerly walked to the bathroom to draw myself some bathwater. It would be stained red from many sources, like my life.

Tim pulled me to his chest. "You didn't tell your mother?"

I shook my head. "No, I couldn't."

He held me tightly. "Well, you told me. And you did nothing wrong. I love you."

That sounded wonderful.

RETROSPECT

I'd run home to my mother before five, but I'd run into the mother who *needed me*. She needed me to stay alive. She needed me to take care of her. She relied on me to shoot her up. The mantra in my head kept saying, "*I'm alone.*"

With my mother's reaction, I tossed the rape incident behind the curtain in my mind. I wasn't aware there was a curtain and didn't realize it until I was much older. I didn't forget it; I never brought it forward into the conscious thinking part of my mind. If at this point, I'd have had therapy, I'd have had a lot to unpack. But I didn't, nor did I have anyone to confine in or anyone to comfort me.

AFTERMATH OF RAPE

I knew as soon as Dale locked the door that this was bad. For years, decades really, I blamed my nine-year-old self for going with him. I should have screamed as soon as the lock clicked. I ought to have gotten out of there sooner. I told myself I was a worldly child, older than my years, and I should have known better.

I told few people about this incident. I told Diana, my best friend, when I was almost fifteen years old, so she'd know why I was so weird around guys. I told a psychologist a few months later when I was back in New York with my aunt. He had an office with its own entrance in my aunt's house in New York. After I told him, I got scared and refused to go back.

A year later, I was living on my own. But I pretended I lived with my father and stepmother so I could finish high school. It was Thanksgiving, and TheLady picked me up so I could pretend to be part of the holiday. Before I got in the back seat, the lady grabbed the front of my dress and shoved me against the car door. "Your aunt in New York said you were raped when you were a kid. But that's *not* true, is it?"

"N-no," I stammered, shocked that she knew, that my New York aunt knew, that the psychologist had told them. Faced with her anger and the wine on her breath, I gave her the answer she wanted. The minute the word "No" stumbled out of my mouth, I felt the animal in my gut rise and claw at my stomach lining. I was so angry at myself! What a coward I was, a loser, someone who couldn't stand up for themselves as I'd demonstrated to myself over and over.

I slumped into the back seat, wishing I were dead. Angry that I'd made an agreement with God not to try suicide again until age twenty-five and only then if I had not learned how to be happy. I heard and felt TheLady get behind the steering wheel. "I knew you were lying," she hissed. "And I won't have Jett feeling bad about something that didn't happen."

Ah, so that's why she asked, to spare my father the hurt. And a very faint, small voice inside my head asked, "But what about *my* feelings?" I shoved the thought away.

CONFRONTING RAPE

I was thirty-six years old before I confronted my rape and abduction, before I could utter the word "rape." My daughter turned eight years old that year. The age I was when my parents divorced. As I held her on my lap one night, hugging her, I knew that there was no way I'd ever blame her if something like that happened to her.

She was just a kid, and even though I had told her not to get in the car with anyone unless they told her our secret word, I wouldn't blame her if she did and something bad happened. She was innocent. She could never imagine the depravity adults can visit on kids. She would not have the experience to see it. And neither was I.

No matter how mature the surrounding adults thought I was, I was just an innocent kid, also not equipped to know the depth of evil. Despite what I had known and seen, there was nothing that could have prepared me for kidnapping and rape. Holding my daughter and rocking her gently, I imagined I was also holding my little nine-year-old self. I told myself, "It's okay. It wasn't your fault. You couldn't have known."

ACKNOWLEDGING MORE SEXUAL ABUSE

Dale wasn't the first person to target me sexually, and it wasn't the end of me being sexually molested. Just like getting hit became a familiar violence, so did sexual assaults. The earliest encounter happened between my half brother and me when I was six years old. My sixteen-year-old brother was lying on his bed dangling me above him in the air. He directed me to sit on what he called a piece of wood sticking out of his pants. I knew it wasn't wood; and I'd twist, turn, and tell him no. It bewildered me. My parents had already shown me glossy five-by-seven-inch pictures when they told me about sex, so I knew that was his penis. Why was he lying to me?

My brother and I had a playful and contentious relationship. Sometimes he tried to boss me around, and I didn't take that well. I forgot about this incident until about a week later. I was in the kitchen with my mother and her mother, Grammy. They were washing, drying, and putting dishes away when I told them about the incident. They froze and looked over at each other. A large tell that something important was happening. In just a minute they unfroze, and my mother casually told me not to tell my father. That's when it became my fault. I'd done something so bad that I couldn't tell my father.

The next sexual molestation happened during my two stays at the juvenile home. One matron singled me out for special washings in the shower. Then Dale kidnapped me. Some of my mother's other boyfriends liked to bounce me on their knee, and I somehow knew this wasn't right. But I didn't know how it was wrong, and they always gave me a quarter afterward.

It happened three or four times during my teen years. I told my father as he was driving me to town about the first time with my grandparents' good friend. He told me I could ruin a man's reputation by telling tales like that, so I didn't bother to tell him about any others. Sometimes, it was just a man grabbing my breast when everyone had left the room or grabbing me for a kiss. Or like the old man at the house where I rented a room during my senior year. I came out of the shower to find him naked as he wrapped his arms around me in a hug. It may not sound like terrible abuse. But I was so scared and scarred by Dale's rape that any unasked-for touch by a man put me in a deep state of fright.

I was set up to be molested. I was easy pickings by sexual predators. My brother had touched me, my mother's boyfriends had, and Dale had raped me repeatedly. I walked with my head down, eyes downcast, and with my shoulders slumped to hide my breasts. And I moved guardedly and behind people (because I could see where they were). I was unhappy, quiet, and had no supporting adults beside me. I radiated self-consciousness, vulnerability, and passiveness. In the encounter with the old guy at the house where I rented a room, I had wondered if I had a "molest me" sign on my back. In retrospect, I did. Molestation happened way beyond my teens with Kelly's father. But I no longer blamed myself. I was setting myself free.

17 GROWING INTO ME

THE NORTH OF LONDON

The countryside in the north of London differed completely from the south. In the south, hedgerows divided properties. Brits have used hedges in this part of the UK since Roman times. As populations grew, they cleared more land for crops and animals. Ownership needed to be delineated. The British have a fancy term that historians used to characterize how rich landowners enclosed fields for their own use: *the Enclosure Movement.*

In the north, the divider between fields, property, and corrals for animals were dry stonewalls. Thus, one industry died (hawthorn plant nurseries) and another was born. This method of enclosure goes back to the Iron Age. We found it amusing when our neighbor pointed out a sheep-creep. It's a square opening in the stone's lower wall and filled in on top. This allows sheep to pass from one field to another. Farmers remove some upper stones to make a bigger opening for cattle, which, of course, is called a cow-creep.

Tim and I got to know each other again as individuals. We could go out in the evening without worrying about the kids. And we took advantage of it. For example, it privileged us to see a live play of Sir Arthur Conan Doyle's *The Hound of Baskervilles* in the outside setting of Brimham Rocks. A 320-million-year-old rock formation. It is a National Trust site filled with natural enormous stone formations, carved by wind and ice, aided by continental shifts. I gripped Tim's arm throughout the performance. Either because of the chill in the air or the mystery of Sherlock Holmes's words, I'm not sure which.

We toured York Minster, or the Cathedral and Metropolitical Church of Saint Peter, in York. Worshippers built it in 637, but it burned down in 741 and rebuilt in more splendor. It saw damage during William the Conqueror's campaign to overpower northern England. The Danes destroyed it in 1080, but it was again built back up, this time in the Norman style. The inhabitants added through the years, like the Gothic north and south transepts. Not all insults to the cathedral happened only in the past. In 1984 there was another fire in the south transept. Over 114 firefighters worked to save it. They extinguish the fire by pouring thousands of gallons of water on it, thus collapsing it. And although the beautiful glass window was shattered, the leaded iron held together. It was taken down and restored. It was an eerie place. I sensed many spectral beings, all benevolent but unnerving.

"You feel that?" I asked Tim as we stood in the cathedral's entrance.

"No, what?"

"I feel beings all around us, and it felt like one walked right through me."

"No, I felt nothing. They trying to scare you?"

I shook my head. "No, I feel they are having fun at my expense."

Tim didn't see things that weren't there, but he believed I did.

MOM HAZEL DIES

In August, we went back to the USA for home leave. We flew into Miami and stayed with Mom Hazel for a week or so. Then we drove near Baltimore and saw Tim's brother, sister-in-law, and Mom (his father died a year after we moved to England). On the way up, we stopped to see Kristi, who had joined the army and had a baby, Tyrell. We also saw Kyle, who lived in Baltimore proper. Then we went to the Smokey Mountains and stayed with Kelly, where both Kyle and Kristi and Tyrell came to visit.

Since of kids were both living on the East Coast, we decided to buy a house for the future. Tim planned to retire in three more years. Tim thought he'd like to build a house, and so in the summer's heat, we marched up hills with a realtor to look at land. On the way back to Kelly's, I spied a "For Sale" sign pointing up the hill just feet from her driveway.

It was a gray two-storied house with high ceilings and big rooms. We bought it and would rent it until Tim was ready to retire. Negotiations took a couple of months. By then we were back in England, but we'd given Kelly power of attorney. In October, it was ours. We called our realtor to inquire about getting it rented. But when Tim came home that evening, he looked defeated and sick.

"What's wrong?" I asked.

"This shift work is killing me. Nothing is fun anymore."

I studied him. "Aren't they offering early retirement? Let's retire early."

He shook his head. "No, if I can hold on three more years, we'll have more retirement money."

"True, and you could fall over dead the day after you retire. Whatever your retirement income is, we'll be fine. Retire."

"I don't know…"

"I do. I want you healthy and happy, a few more dollars won't guarantee that. Really, retire early. We even have a house to live in!"

Slowly, he looked at me. "Yeah, we do. Don't we?"

"Yes, let's go now. Put in your papers tomorrow."

He did, and DOD scheduled us to move back to the United States on November 4. Excitedly, I called Mom Hazel and told her.

"I expect you to come visit and help me plant flowers." She knew the name of every plant on the planet.

"Well, I'll be eighty-three years old in a few weeks, and I don't think I can do the bending down and getting up anymore. And soon I'll be giving up my driver's license and moving in with Rick."

"No, problem. All I want you to do is to sit in a lawn chair and point where I should plant what."

"Point with my cane?" She laughed.

"Mom, you don't use a cane."

"Yet."

"You are a young eighty-three-year-old! You will live to be one hundred!"

I didn't notice what she wasn't saying right then. I realized it later. We hung up, and I made lists of the many things we had to do before moving. We had to prepack, get some pictures framed, the house cleaned, and Tim's car sold. I jumped into high gear.

But on November 3, we, and our two cats, took a taxi to Manchester airport, over fifty miles away. We sorted our cats into freight and ourselves into an airline seat. And flew the twelve-hour flight to Atlanta, Georgia. When we landed on November 4 in the evening, Kelly was there to pick us up. After giving her an enormous hug, we found our cats and loaded them and our luggage in her van. We'd only driven a mile or so away from the airport when Kelly said she wanted to get an iced tea.

All I wanted to do was sleep. I wanted nothing, and she and Tim got out at a diner. After a few minutes, the front doors opened, and Kelly looked in and said, "Sadie, I have some sad news."

"What?" I mumbled, hardly straightening up.

"Hazel died this morning."

My mind stalled. Hazel? Or did she say another name? Tim's mom? EJ? No, I think she said…I sat up. "You mean Mom Hazel?"

"Yes, Rick had a tough time finding my phone number, but he finally did. She died of a heart attack. I'm so sorry."

My mind was still scrambling about trying to make it *not* be Mom. *Not Mom Hazel.* It'd been twelve years since my father had died, and she and I only grew closer. She couldn't be…

"Hon, we have to decide if will drive straight to the funeral. It will be in Jacksonville, Florida. Or go back to Kelly's tonight and leave in the morning."

Mom Hazel is dead? Then I thought about her telling me she would soon give up her driver's license and moving into Rick's house. She had lived independently all her life. I had hated the thought of her losing privileges. In my mind, I visualized her jumping into my father's arms.

"Sadie, what do you want to do? Go or stay?"

"Umm, let me call Rick in Florida." I pointed at a pay phone outside the diner.

Tim and Kelly nodded. I called Rick's house and talked to his daughter. She was extremely upset at losing her grandmother.

I said, "Well, she was just going to get more and more limited, not being able to drive, go here and see there. I'm not sure I'd wish her back just for me."

Her daughter told me she *would* wish her back, and then she sobbed.

"I'm so sorry. Listen. Tell your dad and mom we will leave tomorrow for Jacksonville. Tell them I love them, and I'll be there as soon as possible."

I told Tim and Kelly that I didn't want to make the cats endure a lengthy car ride after a twelve-hour airplane flight. "Plus, that way I can get a good night's sleep before starting out."

We decided. We drove into the North Carolina Smokey mountains. Kelly's roommate said she would feed our cats over at our house.

The next day we picked up Kristi and Tyrell, who was ten months old, at Ft. Stewart, in Hinesville, Georgia, and we drove to Jacksonville.

Mom's funeral was a blur. There was an open casket, but it wasn't my mom Hazel in it. The essence of her was dancing on a cloud with my father. This was just the husk. And while I had loved the covering that held her spirit, it was the spark of her being that I missed. I already missed it.

BACK TO BEING REDHEADED STEPCHILD

We didn't stay long after the funeral because we had to get back to the cats. As we drove away, Kelly asked, "Didn't your dad leave the house to you and Rick?"

I hadn't even thought of her estate. "Yes. Rick offered to buy me out once, but I didn't want to. I guess I wanted to hold on to the place where my father was genuinely loved. A place where we all visited."

Lynn was driving, and she looked at me in the rearview window. "Well, Rick was talking about what he was going to do to the house like he owned it."

"Oh? I'll e-mail him tomorrow. I'm sure he was just talking about repairs."

"No, sounded like decorating…for him and JoJo."

"I'll e-mail him this week."

In a couple of days, I wrote Rick and JoJo and asked.

JoJo answered, sounding terribly upset that I would ask about inheritance so soon after the funeral. "She left the house to Rick. But she left you $2,500.00 and the ring your father gave her. We'll get that to you as soon as possible."

"No hurry. I just wanted to know. Thanks."

I sat at the keyboard, stunned. My feelings tumbled out on top of each other. My father and her had left the house to both of us. She had said numerous times that she pitied Rick and I cleaning out her stuff. When had she quit saying that? Why didn't she tell me she'd changed the agreement? Why did she change it and let me find out at her funeral?

I loved this woman. She had done a lot toward healing the motherless child in me. She said she had lost a baby girl a few years before Rick was born so I was healing her as well. I had cried at her funeral, not at my father's. I thought she had loved me. Was I wrong?

Mom? Mom, did I make you mad?

Tim found me staring into space at Kelly's computer. "What's wrong?"

There were times I wished he hadn't learned to read me so well. "Umm, I just got an e-mail from JoJo. Mom left the house to Rick."

He pulled up a chair and patted my shoulder. "I'm sorry."

My voice cracked. "I don't know what I did to make her angry."

Kelly walked up, and Tim told her what I'd found out.

"You did nothing wrong. Don't assume that."

"Yeah, but…"

"You don't know her reasons. Don't assume you do," Tim said, and Kelly agreed.

I sighed. "I know exactly why she's leaving me $2,500. They each paid $2,500 as a down payment on the house. So she's paying me back, but it feels like she's paying me off."

"Sadie, she loved you. You know that…"

I nodded as I rose from the computer. *Do I? Know that?* I felt like Mom had taken a baseball bat to my head, and I'd rebounded across the room and ricocheted against the wall. *Mom?* The monster in my belly clawed at my stomach's lining. I was shattered, gutted, and I couldn't breathe.

I told Tim and Kelly I was going to bed. I looked at the ceiling and prayed to the Big Guy. *What happened? Did Mom love me?* I tried to stop the swirling kinetic over analyzing thoughts in my mind. I found no answers. It was easier in the daytime when I could keep busy and keep the questions at bay. But at night, they consumed me.

In the darkness, my feelings of grief, betrayal, and abandonment overflowed like a torrent of hot lava. The blazing pain came from the bottom of my core, spewing through the emotional gash of betrayal and abandonment. I slept little. I'd grab the front of my nightshirt and try to tamp down my terror and panic. *Mom?*

I'd depended upon Mom Hazel for needs I hadn't even realized. For my sense of belonging, security, and relationship. Not only was she physically gone from this earth, the grief of which was overwhelming; but now our love, our relationship, was in question.

Toward the end of that first year after her death, I realized my feelings of abandonment had more to do with just Mom Hazel dying. Attached to Hazel's rejection was my biological mother, who I'd never mourned. I mourned her now. It was connected to my father's neglect and how I never mattered to him. I agonized, thinking I hadn't mattered to Mom Hazel. Oh, I knew I had to a degree, but not enough. *Maybe not enough.* Mixed in this torment stew was my half brother, Dan's recent disdain of me. We'd had a good relationship as long as I depended upon him to help me order my thoughts. As soon as I became an adult with my own opinions, he would deride my viewpoints. I asked him once why he was so mean to me. I loved him. He wrote back, "Because I can." *What?* I realized that my love for him was allowing me to let him belittle me. I told Tim about it. Then I told him I would get under my bedcovers and grieve my relationship with my brother. I was going to tell him that, no, he could not do that to me, that I would block him if he tried. He didn't talk to me for a couple of years, then started again, like nothing happened. But something had, and I no longer trusted him. I loved him, but I was leery. Our relationship was never the same. I anguished about him now also.

I didn't mind Rick having the house. She could have left everything she owned to the Humane Society. It was hers to do with as she wished. But she'd *let* me continue to believe that she was abiding by the agreement she'd made with my father. That was the betrayal and the origin of the hurt, which called our entire relationship into question. *Mom?*

I'd had people who had said they'd loved me as I was growing up, and they did right up until it came to possessions, money, sex, and trust. *Mom? You didn't trust me enough to tell me.* God, that hurt! Every night for a year, I agonized, wondering if I'd fantasized her feelings for me. Had I made them up? She had said she loved me. But that was just words. In action she had acted like it. But had she? I felt like that redheaded stepchild who was only nominally accepted.

A little over a year of turning myself into a pretzel, asking the unanswerable question of had she loved me, I *chose* to believe she had. I wanted to feel that she had loved me. I don't know what happened at the end. I don't understand why she didn't trust me enough to tell me she'd given Rick the house. All I'd have said was, "It's your house, Mom. Do whatever you want with it." But I guess she didn't know that. I so wish she had known it so we could have loved ourselves past that…But "if wishes were horses, beggars would ride."

The second year after her death, I told Mom Hazel it was okay. I didn't understand, but I loved her anyway. I designed a five-piece bedroom set with the $2,500 she left me. The headboard was in the shape of an angel with outspread wings. She protected and encompassed the sleepers. Mom Hazel had been an angel to me, one who restored mother love. And my heart was still intact and stronger than ever.

Later, JoJo told me that Rick had asked her for the house. That was fine with me. I had made peace with it. Mom had loved me, and whatever she did with the house was her prerogative.

Future betrayals or abandonments would hurt but would not have the power that they once had over me. That was because I recognized that much of my hurt from the past, and I didn't need to include them in my present.

LOVING THE JOURNEY

Our three years in England near the border of Scotland were good for us. We reconnected as individuals, without children. Yet our shared parenthood remained in the background. I no longer had *any* secrets. He knew everything in my past, from the good to the ugly. And I also freely shared my thoughts and feelings in real time as they happened. The secrets had kept me sick. Now, I chose now not to have any.

We peeled ourselves until we were down to our shiny, vulnerable center. In revealing my layers to him, I also revealed them to myself, which led to self-love. I love myself, warts and all. I can honestly say *I love me*. I love us both as imperfect human beings trying our best to be true to our authentic selves. I no longer thought Tim was omniscient and knew my inner being. That's what communication is all about.

Oh, but communicating can be difficult. Our words often meant different things to us, resulting in misunderstandings. That meant we had to communicate *more*. We had to muddle through. There were times I got so frustrated, I'd storm off and refuse to say more. Tim would come in and coach me toward speaking. And when I did, we eventually reached an understanding. Sometimes Tim would be the one who got frustrated. I knew that this meant he needed time. So we'd agree that we would revisit the conversation in twenty-four hours. I am quick with words; he is not. And we must honor both of our communication styles.

By the time Tim took an early retirement from the Department of Defense and we moved to the Smokey Mountains of North Carolina, we knew how to talk to each other. We listened, and that strengthened our bond. We respected each other. We wanted the best for each other. If Tim said he wanted to go to the West Coast to take a class, I'd encourage him to do it. Would I miss him? Yes! But I wanted what made him happy, and he felt the same.

We had discussions, but fair ones. We never used "You" statements, like "You make me so angry." We used "I" statements, as in "I get so angry when you..." It sounds like an insignificant thing, but language and words are important. Saying "I" instead of "you" puts the responsibility for the feeling where it ought to be. We sometimes agree to disagree with no hard feelings.

We trust each other; we rebuilt it after Vee. We rebuilt it from the ground up. Even though he no longer has to be transparent to me, he is. I trust him to be where he said he would be without it, but he chooses to continue it. He follows through on what he says he'll do, and so do I. Or we honestly say we are not sure we can do that right now. I remember Dr. Tnuh once said that I wouldn't have to always use my litmus test once I trusted myself as much as I did my friends. And to a great extent that is true. I trust me. I can handle whatever comes. And I can especially deal with the truth. I'd much rather an ugly truth than a pretty lie.

And Tim wants me to be me. He doesn't just put up with my quirkiness; he encourages it. He encourages all the newest things I get interested in trying. He entertains my one thousand questions, many of which cannot be answered. He's happy that I make friends of both men and women because he trusts me. We describe ourselves as, I'm the electricity and he's the ground. He flies a little higher because of me, and I don't float away into the void because of him.

AUTHENTIC

One morning, I arose early to meet a friend for breakfast. I dressed hurriedly. As I went to step into my shoes, I saw two identical pairs, except one was blue and the other one pink. I placed the pink one on my left foot and the blue one on my right. It felt right.

I gave Tim a so-long kiss in the family room. He looked me over. "You look nice, hon."

"Thanks," I answered and hurried off.

As I took off my shoes that night, I laughed with delight. I have worn different shoes every day since.

END NOTES

I have traveled through abuse to fear to love, then back to fear, and finally back to love. If I'm afraid to take a step forward, today I take it because it means I will grow by doing so. I went from abuse victim to survivor, from a thriver to joyousness. Oh, now and then I'll have a sad day, but I still feel the joy underneath and know it will soon bubble to the surface. I am not broken or defective. I am whole, rich with love, and I cannot explain it, but I am joy!

I believe you can be joy too!

BOOK CLUB DISCUSSION: POINTS TO PONDER

THESE ARE SUGGESTED questions. You can follow all, pick and choose, or make up your own.

Chapter 1:

- What did Sadie's childhood horse herd do for her? How did your imagination help during your childhood?
- When Sadie has the run-in with her mother with a knife, she begins to not trust them. Do you think this is the lone incident that created this? Or do you think there were others before that helped breed this? What was your first big realization about your parents?
- She was given decision power early. Why did she decide to go back a grade and which parent to live with? What kind of decisions were you able or not allowed to make as a child?

Chapter 2:

- Sadie agrees to inject her mother with heroin. How does she feel about doing it? When have you been conflicted about doing something you agreed to do?
- Fear became Sadie's childhood copilot. What feeling permeates your childhood? How do you think you'd react if it were fear?
- Sadie is ecstatic to be reunited with her father. What changed her enthusiasm? Why did she never call him Daddy again? Did you have a big divide between yourself and anyone else during your childhood (mom, dad, aunt, uncle, cousin)?

Chapter 3:

- Had Sadie been influenced by how her mother felt about her aunt Essie? How have your guardians colored people in your life?
- Why does Sadie question what love is? What is yeast-less love? Did you have questions like this as a child? Young person? Adult?
- Sadie believes TheLady doesn't even like her, let alone love her. Who does she choose to love her? What do you think this does for her?

Chapter 4:

- Did TheLady set up and sabotage Sadie's school dance? Why? Have you ever been set up?
- How did Kelly overcome Sadie's reluctance to become friends? In doing so, did she give up one of her childhood defense mechanisms? How about you?

- Why didn't she tell Kelly that her father kept trying to touch her? When have you kept quiet?
- What were Sadie's views of trust? What are yours? Who do you trust? Sadie wanted to work past her fears and trust again? How about you?
- Why didn't Sadie tell Dr. Tnuh about wetting the bed at the farm? Sadie carried this shame for a long time. What do you carry?
- Sadie says that being hit became a familiar violence. Do you think that's true? Can violence just become usual part of your life? How does feeling that way color your world?

Chapter 5:

- Sadie wakes up happy one day. Even if nothing ever changes, she believes she would be happy. Do you feel that way? Have you ever?
- Why is she drawn to Tim? Was it because he waited three weeks to kiss her?
- Why was Sadie embarrassed to meet his parents since she knew they'd done nothing wrong?
- Sadie's sexuality is awakened. Is this good? When did you first feel sexual attraction?
- Sadie describes herself as Tim's fill-in girlfriend. Is she? If so, why would she consent to that?

Chapter 6:

- Sadie wonders if teenage foreplay was normal and beneficial. What do you think?
- Dr. Tnuh asks if Tim fits a pattern. Sadie answers yes, but… How is Tim different? What man-pattern do you see in your life?

- Sadie says emotional abuse was just the environment she grew up in so it was hard to see. How about you?
- Sadie agrees not to ride off into the sunset and over the rainbow. Why? Have you ever decided to see how things play out when it was scary to do so?
- Sadie tells Tim how she's unhappy with him not giving her notice of a date. Why is she able to do this? What happened? Do you withhold annoyances instead of speaking them? And how does that make you feel?
- Sadie is amazed that Tim wants the best for his ex-wife. Why?

Chapter 7:

- Sadie decides to make love for the first time. How did she feel safe enough to do so? She stayed true to her vow to not do so until all systems said go. How do you think this made her feel? Why did you make your first decision to make love?
- Sadie is responsible enough to get birth control pills, but not to ask questions? Why? Is it an old defense mechanism? What resulted from this? How responsible or not responsible were you?
- Sadie almost wears two different shoes. Why doesn't she?
- Sadie asks what time Tim will drive out of town so she can run to a gas station and wave at him as he drives by. What does Tim say? Why did Sadie not even consider that he'd do that?
- What is Sadie's life litmus test? How does it help her? What do you have in your life to help you sep-

CRACKS IN THE RED GLASS

arate fear from courage or past defense mechanisms against stepping into the new?

- Tim hands Sadie a song called "Too Late to Turn Back Now," and she listens over and over. Then she decides to view it as just a song and not read too much into it, so she won't lead herself on. How have you ever led yourself on or fooled yourself?

Chapter 8:

- Tim tells Kristi he loves her. What is her reaction? What does she do? How have you reacted? What would you have done? What did you do?
- Sadie doesn't believe she's pregnant at first. Why? She says she's in uncharted water. What does she mean? When have you felt that way?
- Sadie's math teacher judges her as sleeping around. How might this make Sadie feel? Have you ever been judged harshly? The college dean suggests Sadie place her baby for adoption. Why? What does Sadie think? How does it make her feel? Have you ever been in a circumstance where many adults weighed in on what you ought to do?
- Sadie thinks of having an abortion, but decides she'll run away afterward and forget her old life. Why did she want to do this? Is running away an old defense mechanism for her?
- Sadie is afraid of marriage. Why? How do you or did you feel about it?
- Sadie's father doesn't come to the wedding or ask who she is marrying. What does this say about her relationship? Yet she always includes him. Should she? What would you have done?

- Sadie admits she doesn't know how to be a wife or a mother, so she pretends. Is this one of her childhood defense mechanisms that she carried into her adulthood? How have you done similar?
- Sadie says she doesn't think she's in labor because she's not screaming like they do on TV. Is this where Sadie is getting her wife and mothering directions? What did you rely on when you became a mother?

Chapter 9:

- What is Sadie's reaction to getting married? Why did she react that way? How did you react?
- Tim says because Sadie could think of one good marriage is good enough odds for him and agrees they'll have a great marriage. Do you think those were good enough odds? What odds did you think your marriage has or had? Did you think of it before marriage?
- Sadie almost runs away again, but she has nowhere to go. Is this a pattern for her?
- Tim and Sadie have the option of her going to California. Why doesn't she? Have you ever had what Sadie thinks of as fate or the Big Guy intercede in your life?
- Sadie says Tim becomes her Dr. Tnuh. Why? Who encourages you in your life?
- After going to the hospital for birth of her first baby, Sadie shuts her mouth and doesn't speak. Why? Did this help or hinder her? How do you react when faced with completely new situations?
- Sadie had a hard birth. Could she have made it easier? What are your feelings on childbirth?

Chapter 10:

- Tim was Sadie's go-to guy for baby advice (and the Dr. Spock book). Yet she still didn't say some things, like telling Dr. Jones her feeling about drinking a beer and breastfeeding. Was she letting her past interfere in her present? If she'd talked about it, could she have overcome the feeling? What did you never ask or say?

- Sadie introduces Kyle to her mom, and she tells her she's angry at her. Why? Did Sadie need a mom or a mom substitute? Are you close to your mother? If not, have you found another female mentor?

- TheLady says tells Sadie she knew she'd get pregnant out of wedlock and it was lucky Tim married her. Sadie realizes TheLady wasn't being mean; it was just who she was. How do you think it made Sadie feel? Have you ever suddenly seen who someone clearly was in your life?

- TheLady wanted to trade recipes, and Sadie wonders if she is now a part of some "married ladies club." Why do you think TheLady said this? Tim says, "Quit trying to figure it out. She can't bother you now unless you let her." Good advice?

- Sadie thinks she should be completely recovered after six weeks of Kyle's birth. What gives her this idea? Do most women think this? What do you think?

- Why did Sadie judge herself? She grew up being insulted. Why would she do that to herself? Do you talk yourself down in your head?

- Sadie says if she'd married before the age of twenty-three, she'd have married someone who would have abused her. Do you think that's true? Did she have to recognize the abuse so she wouldn't repeat it? When you married, were you ready to be married?

Chapter 11:

- Sadie said she made it a point never to sound like a wife. Why did she do this? How did it make her feel? Were there times or are their times you have tried to pretend your feelings away? How did it make you feel?

- Why didn't Sadie demand to go with Tim to Wisconsin for college? It was a big decision. Have you ever withheld your feelings about a big decision, one that could have been detrimental to your way of life?

- Sadie dreads telling Tim she is pregnant. Why? What do you think she expected him to say or do? Have you ever been anxious to tell someone something, only to have it turn out to be okay? Was Sadie's past experiences informing her present ones? How about you?

- Sadie endured three doctor examinations while trying to change doctors. Why didn't she yell at them? Why didn't she tell Tim she wanted to go back to her old doctor? Her nonassertiveness was causing her pain and anxiety, yet she continued. Why? Have you ever not acted in your own best interest?

- Sadie again fight's Kelly's father at the Thanksgiving table. Should she have said something? Why do you think she didn't? Had sexual advances also become a familiar violence? Have you kept things quiet that you wished you'd spoken aloud?

Chapter 12:

- Sadie finally gives Rod an ultimatum. Why do you think she was able to do so? What gave you the courage to erect a firm boundary with someone? How'd you feel?

- Sadie's father loved TheLady even knowing she was going to leave him nothing. Does this at all echo Sadie being willing to love someone and never make demands? Did she learn this from his example? What were you willing to forego for what you believed was love? Did you learn this?

- Sadie says she felt a disconnection between her and Vee. Could that also have reflected a disconnection with herself? How did she disconnect with herself? How have you?

- Why does Sadie say she doesn't think she'll be depressed anymore? What are you doing that might help create your depression or sadness?

- Sadie agrees to not tell Tim about their conversation the first night Vee reveals her interactions with Tim. Why do you think she did this? What would you have done?

- Do you think by not overreacting the first night, Vee told her more about what went on between her and Sadie's husband? Is there a time to be quiet and a time to act? How have you reacted to big betrayals?

- Sadie assures Vee that they will all remain friends. Do you think this is possible? Why did Sadie want that? Do you think trying to keep them all friends was a healthy reaction?

Chapter 13:

- Tim says he did what he did because he thought she'd never find out. How good of an excuse is that? When have you been given weak excuses and accepted them? Why?
- Sadie says perhaps she and Tim have different definitions of love. Is this something she should have found out before marrying him? When in your life have your personal definitions been different from someone important in your life?
- Sadie says that she's going to go to Germany with him only because she doesn't know what else to do. Has Sadie made decision like this before (like when she left before they married)? When have you made decisions because you believed you didn't know what else to do? Could Sadie have made a different decision? Could you have?
- Sadie says she doesn't want this monster (the betrayal) to eat her. She was aware it could turn out negatively. When have you been aware something could greatly alter your life in the negative?
- Vee says she can change Tim's mind. How did Tim react to that? How did Sadie? Did it make them draw together? How would you have reacted?
- Sadie says how she really feels to Vee, telling her not to say she's making too much of it. What's Vee's reaction? What's Sadie's? Sadie spoke her truth. When have you spoken yours after much silence? How did it make you feel?
- Tim says, "I married a quirky little girl. Where did she go?" And Sadie realizes he's right, after which they talk honestly. Was this a turning point for

Sadie? How? What has been a huge turning point in your life?

- Sadie gives herself permission to feel and speak of them. And she does so repeatedly. Was this good for her? Have you given yourself permission of feel and speak? Give an example.

- Tim tells Sadie to quit punishing herself by feeling humiliated, hurt, and resentful because she did nothing wrong. It was something he did. How did Tim owning what he'd done help Sadie? Could they have gone on healthily and happily without his attitude? When has or hasn't someone owned what they did wrong in your life? How did it turn out?

- Tim and Sadie talk about their first marriage and how much of that will never return. Tim says that's okay, that he'll do whatever it takes to save their marriage. How does this aid them going forward? Are they starting out on better footing? When you've had to start again, did you begin by acting differently? How or how not?

- Sadie decides to stay, to have a second marriage, and she writes him a letter. What do you think of the letter? Is she setting different boundaries? What would you have done? Is there anything else you would have said?

- Sadie says she loves him but could live without him. She chooses to be with him. Why did she make this distinction? If you can't live without someone, is it choice or need? How does this show up in your life?

- Sadie says the trust she gives him now is a better trust. And she refuses to let it turn her into a suspicious, jealous person. She won't watch his every move, but if it should happen again, she'd be gone.

Is this a healthy boundary? How have you reacted after betrayal?

- Sadie thinks there will be no more waves after they both commit to a second marriage. Should she have anticipated more?
- Sadie's father dies. And while she's sad, she isn't greatly impacted. Why? Have you ever encountered this? A loss that wasn't as big as most people expected it to be. Why do you think that was the case?

Chapter 14:

- Sadie makes friends with Richard and goes to his house, which upsets Tim. And she tells Tim how she feels. How different is this action than what she'd have done in their first marriage? After a hurt or betrayal, have you ever reacted differently than you would have before? Tell us what happened and what the difference was.
- Tim sees Sadie walked behind their house at night and instantly thinks she's going to visit a guy. Sadie says this is his own insecurities and refuses to make them hers. Is she right? Are these things Tim's to wrestle with? How would it have different if Sadie had made herself the one who did wrong? Have you stood up for yourself in similar situations? How?
- Vee's call upset Sadie, and later in the kitchen, they hear wedding bells, and Sadie feels sorry for the bride. Why would she feel this way?
- For one night Sadie understands how a mother could kill herself and then her kids. Why did she understand this? What in her background helped her feel this way? Have you ever felt dark thoughts

that scared you in the morning? What were they? What happened?

- Tim asks her to stay, and she does, but does she decide to stay with him or to see a psychologist?
- Sadie again goes back to therapy. How did that help her? Was it a healthy reaction rather than dealing with it on her own? How about you were their times you went or wished you'd gone to a psychologist? What might have happened if you'd seen one have done? What might you have learned?
- Sadie comes across a pile of poems about her rape when she was nine years old, and she decides to slowly read them. What did this do for Sadie? Are their parts of your past you've never confronted?

Chapter 15:

- One of Sadie's escaping mechanisms is to become part of an elephant herd from the cover of a magazine. What escaping mechanisms do you have or have had? Explain.
- Tim doesn't push her for information, and Sadie said this was helpful. Why?
- Sadie is not willing to be in the peripheral in Tim's life. Earlier, she was willing. What changed? Are you the peripheral in someone's life? Why? Or if not, how did you change that?
- From the Sadie who never spoke what she thought to the one who talked to him about what would happen if they had sex with someone else during their separation is quite a distance. Do you think it needed to be talked about? Would you or have you done so about some big uncomfortable issue between you and someone else?

- Sadie asks him to give up sports for one year. She knows it's a big ask, but she asks it. Do you think that was fair? If he'd said no, what do you think might have happened? Have you spoken any big "asks" of someone you love? What happened?
- Sadie decides to walk away from Vee, and Tim thinks it's healthy. What do you think? With her abandonment issues, this was a huge step toward making boundaries.

Chapter 16:

- Sadie says she had no regrets raising her son. If you have children, do you feel that way? Why or why not?
- Her son tells her he's gay, and her feelings surprised her. Why? How would you react if your son or daughter were gay? Have you ever encountered this issue?
- Sadie tells about a year and half period when she gets her shy daughter to buy what she wants at a grocery store. Do you think she was mean? Why did she do that? How have you prepared or not prepared your kids for adulthood?
- Tim tries to make Sadie decide about something he is capable of doing, and it has expensive results. What do you think of her doing that? What would you have done? Did it work?
- Sadie tells Tim the rest of her rape experience at nine years old and that all she wanted was her mommy. When she gets home, how does her mother react? How does Sadie distract herself from her pain? Did you ever reveal a big truth to someone and not

receive the reaction you expected? What did you do to elevate the pain?

- TheLady told Sadie the rape wasn't true, and she agreed. Why did she do that? How did she feel afterward? Have you ever been bullied into saying something wasn't true that you knew was? How did you feel?
- While holding her daughter, Sadie realizes she was just a kid when she was raped. And she forgave herself. Have you forgiven yourself for stuff that happened when you were a kid? If so, how? If not, why?
- Sadie lists being sexually targeted at an early age. Had this also become familiar violence? Was she set up to be molested? How does our early life influence these things? Did it happening so young contribute to her being unable to talk about it? What else might have stopped her? What could or would stop you? If your child said she was molested, what would you do?

Chapter 17:

- Sadie's stepmom dies. How does this differ from when her father died? Have you had significant losses that impacted you differently? Tell.
- Although Sadie loved her stepmom, she says she wouldn't wish her back. Why? What is your attitude toward death?
- Sadie felt like the money her stepmom left her was a payoff. Why did she feel that way? How would you have felt? Have you ever been left something that made you feel funny? Or have you ever been left out? What were your feelings? Then and now?

- Why did her stepmom not telling her she'd left the house to Rick impact Sadie so greatly? Later, she reflects on why. What was it? Have you been hurt by someone promising you something then taking it away but not telling you directly?
- Sadie people profess love right up until it came to possessions, money, sex, and trust. Do you think that's true? Was Sadie treated differently because of any of those? Have you ever been?
- Sadie said she "*chose*" to believe her stepmom loved her, because she could never now get an answer from Mom Hazel. What did that do for her? What would have happened if she'd continued in limbo or decided she hadn't loved her. Have you ever decided anything that you were not sure of but you chose to believe? Tell.
- Sadie said she no longer had any secrets from Tim. He knew it all. And that secrets are what kept her sick. Do you think she was set free by giving up her secrets? Have you felt the freedom of giving up secrets? Do you still hold some? What does that do for you?
- Sadie says communicating is difficult and that means you need to communicate more. Do you think this is true? How good at communicating are you with your significant other, with friend and family?
- Tim and Sadie agreed never to make "you" statements, only "I" statements. What is the difference? Which do you employ?
- Sadie says she and Tim rebuilt their relationship from the ground up. How did they do that? What did Sadie do? What did Tim do? Together what did

they do? Have you ever rebuilt a friendship or love after a big incident? How?

- Sadie says she trusts herself to handle whatever comes. Is that why she doesn't go through his phone and track him? Because she can handle whatever happens? Do you have this kind of self-trust? What would it take to have it? What might it do for you?
- Tim wants Sadie to be completely herself, and she feels the same about him. What does that do for them? Does it increase or decrease conflict? Are you encouraged and celebrated to be yourself? If so, tell us how. If not, why not?
- Sadie ended the book with her wearing two different shoes as a pair. Why did she wear them? How'd Tim feel about it? And how did it make Sadie feel? How do you express who you are? How does it make you feel? If you don't express it, why not? How does it make you feel?
- At the end Sadie says she is joy. She believes you can be joy too. Do you believe it? Are you joy? If not, what blocks your joy? How can you become joy?

ABOUT THE AUTHOR

PAMELA K. KEYSER is more than an adult survivor of childhood abuse. She has a loving long-term marriage, two productive children, supportive friends, and lives a life of joy every day. She has broken many harmful generational cycles: verbal, emotional, physical, sexual abuse, as well as drug and alcohol addiction. She does inspirational speaking about how she got out of the abuse cycle. Her first book, *The Red Glass* (theredglass.com), told of the abuse from *A* to *Z*. In *Cracks in the Red Glass: Evolving Away from Abuse*, she writes not only of more instances of abuse but also about how she journeyed from fear to fearlessly living. Today she lives in the Smoky Mountains of North Carolina with her husband. She is always writing.

CPSIA information can be obtained
at www.ICGtesting.com
Printed in the USA
LVHW021034231221
706788LV00001B/3